THE SHOSHONI FRONTIER

VOLUME 1 IN THE UTAH CENTENNIAL SERIES

THE SHOSHONI FRONTIER

AND THE BEAR RIVER MASSACRE

by

Brigham D. Madsen

With a Foreword by

Charles S. Peterson

University of Utah Press
Salt Lake City
1985

VOLUME 1
IN THE UTAH CENTENNIAL SERIES
CHARLES S. PETERSON, SERIES EDITOR

Copyright © 1985, University of Utah Press
Salt Lake City, Utah 84112
All rights reserved.
Printed in the United States of America.
First paperback edition 1995

Library of Congress Cataloging-in-Publication Data

Madsen, Brigham D.
    The Shoshoni frontier and the Bear River massacre.

    (Utah centennial series; v. 1)
    Bibliography: p.
    Includes index.
    1. Bear River Massacre, Utah, 1863.   2. Shoshoni
Indians—Wars.   3. Indians of North America—Utah—
Wars.   4. Indians of North America—Great Basin—Wars.
5. Utah—History.   I. Title.   II. Series.
E83.863.M32   1985   973.7   85–13389
ISBN 0-87480-494-9

STERLING M. MCMURRIN
Friend and Colleague

Contents

Illustrations

Maps

Foreword

In important respects the Shoshoni people of the Great Basin and central Rockies have received short shrift in American history. Notwithstanding the large area they occupied and their close contact with whites during the period of westward expansion, they attracted relatively little attention either in that era or since.

This is ironic in view of the important role they played. Sacajawea, a Shoshoni woman, guided Lewis and Clark in the first American reach across the continent. The first great fur-trading region of the Mountain West was among the Shoshoni. The most important of the overland trails and the first transcontinental railroad ran nearly a thousand miles through their homelands. Mormons, early miners and freighters, mail contractors, and stage operators became their neighbors.

Yet the Shoshoni were much less drawn into the myth and popular culture of the nation than some native American groups. Vast and desert in character, their homelands were neither hospitable nor easily romanticized. Mountains, sagebrush plateaus, camas flats, volcanic plains, canyon gorges, salt wastes, and occasional rivers that became highroads to the West were its marking characteristics. The survival of native peoples in such a land was based on fragile balances between man and resources. With the advent of whites, buffalo and other big game were quickly killed off or driven out. Competition for limited resources was elemental. During the period treated by this book (1840 to 1865) the main line of settlement still lay far behind Shoshoni country or beyond it to the West Coast, and despite its fierceness, Shoshoni resistance did not attract the same attention as Indian wars in Minnesota and elsewhere on more favored frontiers. In addition, the building of Zion, the Gold Rush, territorial development, and the Civil War each attracted attention in ways that did not focus upon native Americans. In contrast to the post-Civil War decades, few reputation-happy generals working for advancement and reknown were involved, although to their sorrow, the Shoshoni did not entirely escape white men of this genre. In addition, journalists and historians paid the Shoshoni relatively little attention, then or later. As a result, the story of their resistance has more often been seen as an aside to other stories than as a cause in its own right.

Yet their story has had its narrators. Among these Brigham D. Madsen has been foremost. For more than thirty years he has focused his attention on Shoshoni history, resulting in *The Bannock of Idaho*, *The Lemhi: Sacajawea's People*, and *The Northern Shoshoni*, books remarkable for their insight and accuracy. In addition, he has written a large number of well-received articles. He has likewise served as consultant for the tribe, as an informed witness in court cases, and as a source of information for students of Indian history. When not actually concerned directly with the Shoshoni and related Indians, he has turned his attention to the history of exploration, transportation, and development in the region of which they are part.

In this volume, Madsen lays before us one of America's least known and longest Indian wars. It was the war of a great road, far flung, fragmented and scattered by tribal distinctions as well as by white men's political jurisdictions and by the environment. It was a confrontation that extended upwards of a thousand miles—from the Continental Divide to Fort Hall and then on into Oregon and Washington on the one hand and eastern California on the other. Discord began with the advent of the mountain men in the mid-1820s, became an embittered conflict as the westward movement advanced after 1840, where Madsen takes up the story, and lasted until January 1863. Their lifestyles disrupted and resources destroyed by the passing trail and settlements, Indians fought back by attacking emigrants and harassing settlers. Indian commissioners, governors in Washington and Oregon, military outposts in Wyoming and Nevada, and Mormons were all taxed to their limits by the friction that ensued.

Driven to desperation, the Shoshoni stepped up their trail-raiding resistance in the late 1850s and early 1860s. During January 1863, in one of the bloodiest massacres of Indians in the entire history of the

Far West, Colonel Patrick Edward Connor and his California Volunteers killed some 250 Northwestern Shoshoni Indians including many women and children at the Bear River near what is now Preston, Idaho. Its carnage eclipsed by Civil War battles, the Bear River bloodletting silenced Indian resistance along the Oregon Trail and won Connor an advance in rank but otherwise passed largely unnoticed. Only now is it placed in full perspective.

It is appropriate that Madsen's work on the Shoshoni wars and the Bear River Massacre appears as the first volume in the University of Utah Press's Centennial Series which will be published over the next decade in connection with the forthcoming centennial of Utah statehood in 1996. The Utah Centennial Series will not be restrictive in its attention to Utah themes but will seek to elicit a broader statement about the human relations of American federalism and how they evolved in the vast interior region of the United States to which Utah is central. The history of territories and states cannot be divorced from the history of the nation, nor the development of states from what happens in the regions of which they are part. With an interest in the nation as well as the arid interior West, the Centennial Series will concern itself with how Utah fits in larger contexts. This will be so not only in the political or administrative sense, but in terms of responses to American themes such as individualism, violence, promotion and urban growth, resource utilization, and, in the case of Brigham Madsen's book, in relation to how Indians and Whites met.

The applicability of the Utah Centennial Series' larger focus is clear in this study of conflict along the overland trails. Because of Mormon separatism during the mid-nineteenth-century decades and the southward thrust of Mormon colonization, Utah historians have tended to stress the locally dominated Indian relations in southern Utah at the expense of interterritorial, trail-related events farther north. This, together with the fact that boundaries were subsequently redrawn to place the great overland trails beyond Utah's northern border, has led historians approaching Indian relations from the standpoint of territorial subdivisions to pay the Shoshoni confrontations scant heed. In Madsen's skilled hands, one of the greatest Indian wars of its time and an important course of events in the history of western government take on new meaning as a dozen or more Indian groups, the federal government, the army, white travelers and settlers, and five territories interact. It is clear that even along the

trails of the most distant West, complexity as well as tension and conflict prevailed. Thus the editors and the University of Utah Press are
pleased to offer a book with significance for the broader West as well
as for Utah.

> Charles S. Peterson
> Utah State University
> June 19, 1985

Preface

After almost four decades of research and writing about the Northern Shoshoni and Bannock Indians, it seems worthwhile to tackle the subject of the conflicts between these western tribes and white emigrants and settlers during the twenty-five-year period from 1840 to 1864. The ever-increasing hostility finally led to a climactic massacre of 250 Northwestern Shoshoni by some glory-seeking California Volunteers on January 29, 1963, at Bear River in Washington Territory. It is first necessary to identify the various bands of Shoshoni, define the original boundaries of their country, and briefly describe their lifestyle and culture. Their homeland formerly extended from South Pass on the east to the Boise area and Carson Valley on the west. Within this vast region of the Great Basin and the Snake River plains lived seven major Shoshoni groups: the Eastern Shoshoni under Chief Washakie; the Fort Hall Shoshoni and their close neighbors, the Bannock; the Lemhi Shoshoni; the Boise and Bruneau Shoshoni bands; the Northwestern Shoshoni; the Gosiute Shoshoni; and, finally, the Western Shoshoni of Nevada. Some minor attention is paid to the Northern Paiute of western Nevada as well.

In researching documents relating to the hostilities that developed between the Indians and white travelers and settlers during this period, some new material has been uncovered that, it is hoped, will add significance and interest to the subject. Distinguishing between myths and facts about Indian and white massacres is one of the objectives of this study. I have adopted a chronological approach, examining the events of each year and generally following the pattern of first discussing Boise and Bruneau Shoshoni interaction with whites in the western Idaho section of the Oregon Trail and then to the Fort Hall

Shoshoni and Bannock and the Eastern Shoshoni of the Fort Bridger areas. This approach from west to east might appear, at first glance, to be contrary to the accepted view of following the emigrants from South Pass to Oregon and California, but as the story unfolds it will become evident that the officials of Oregon Territory looked at Indian affairs in present-day Idaho from the perspective of their headquarters in the Willamette Valley. I next look at Western Shoshoni activities along the California Trail on the Humboldt River, thence to the Gosiute bands, and finally to a closer examination of events related to the Northwestern Shoshoni of northern Utah, the chief concern of this work. An evaluation of the important Indian massacres and troop killings of Shoshoni along the Oregon and California trails and the Overland Mail Line has led to an attempt to distinguish between myth and reality as reported by Baron Munchausen, frontier newspaper editors or correspondents and observers who sometimes exaggerated the truth. Obvious fictions, like that of the Almo Massacre, a spurious calamity that supposedly took place near the Utah-Idaho border in the summer of 1860, were rather easy to uncover; other incidents were more difficult.

As the attacks and counterattacks mounted during the 1840s, and particularly during the late 1850s and between 1860 to 1862, it seemed inevitable that a climax would be reached and a major engagement between United States troops and an Indian group would occur. On January 29, 1863, Colonel Patrick Edward Connor's California Volunteers attacked a large village of Northwestern Shoshoni at Bear River in Washington Territory. This tragedy was the culmination of a quarter of a century of hostilities between Indians driven to desperation by the loss of their traditional food supplies as a result of white destruction of grass seeds, roots, and game, and adventurous volunteers from California seeking glory on the battlefield. The Mormon settlers played an important role as they swung from their policy of feeding rather than fighting the native inhabitants to exasperation and anger as the starving Indians raided their herds and killed their people. A year of treaty-making after the Bear River Massacre eventually brought some quiet and peace to Shoshoni country.

Researching such a complex subject required visits to a number of libraries and historical centers whose staffs were very helpful in locating pertinent materials. I am especially indebted to the following individuals for their assistance: Robert B. Matchette of the Military

Archives Division of the U.S. National Archives; Gary Domitz of the Idaho State University Library; Merle W. Wells and Larry Jones of the Idaho State Historical Society; Phillip I. Earl of the Nevada State Historical Society; Guy Louis Rocha of the Nevada State Archives; James L. Kimball of the Church of Jesus Christ of Latter-Day Saints Department of History Library; A. J. Simmonds of Utah State University Library; the University of Nevada Library; and the staffs of the Bancroft Library, the Utah State Historical Society, and the Marriott Library of the University of Utah. To all of these librarians and historians, my special thanks. Finally, I appreciate the assistance of the staff of the University of Utah Press in the editing and production of the book.

To those who have read the manuscript and offered invaluable suggestions for improvement, I express my appreciation. I am particularly indebted to Dr. Charles S. Peterson of Utah State University for his perceptive comments and expert knowledge of Utah history. He should not be held responsible for my interpretations of the facts but certainly deserves much credit for the wisdom and guidance he gave me. Also, I need to recognize that much of the chapter concerned with the events of the engagement at Bear River was delivered as the second Dello G. Dayton Memorial Lecture on May 11, 1983, at Weber State College under the title, "Encounter with the Northwestern Shoshoni at Bear River in 1863: Battle or Massacre?" Any errors in judgment and fact that inevitably seem to find their way into a book of this complexity, regardless of effort and attention, are my responsibility.

Brigham D. Madsen
1985

List of Important Events in Shoshoni History, 1840–64

July 24, 1847	Mormon pioneers enter Salt Lake Valley
March 3, 1849	Oregon Territory established
1849–50	Some 70,000 gold-seekers pass through Shoshoni country
September 9, 1850	Utah becomes a territory
February 1850	Mormon militia and troops from Captain Howard Stansbury's command kill twenty-seven Indians in battle at Utah Lake
September 17, 1850	Northwestern Shoshoni Chief Terrikee killed by Urban Stewart near Ogden, Utah
February 3, 1851	Brigham Young becomes governor and superintendent of Indian affairs for Utah Territory
September 1, 1851	Treaty of peace at Fort Laramie for adjoining tribes
November 10, 1851	Agent Jacob H. Holeman reports on treaty negotiations at Fort Laramie
May 1853	Joel Palmer assumes duties as Oregon superintendent of Indian affairs
May 2, 1853	Washington Territory organized
August 19–20, 1854	Ward Massacre near Fort Boise
February 5, 1855	Dr. Garland Hurt arrives in Utah Territory as Indian agent under Brigham Young
June 15, 1855	Mormon mission founded at Fort Lemhi on Salmon River
August 1856	First Mormon settlers found Wellsville in Cache Valley

March 1857   Cache Valley settlers abandon homes and move south

July 24, 1857   Mormons learn of approach of Utah Expedition accompanied by new Governor Alfred Cumming

August 27, 1857   Jacob Forney nominated to be superintendent of Indian affairs in Utah to replace Brigham Young

February 25–   Fort Lemhi mission abandoned
   April 1, 1857

September 7–11, 1857   Mountain Meadows Massacre

March 12, 1858   Colonel Thomas L. Kane meets with Governor Alfred Cumming at Camp Scott

June 26, 1858   Johnston's Army marches through Salt Lake City, and Camp Floyd is established in Cedar Valley

April 23, 1859   Mormon settlers return to Cache Valley

July 27, 1859   Shepherd's Massacre on Sublette's Cutoff

August 14, 1859   Lieutenant Ebenezer Gay's fight with Shoshoni in Sardine Canyon

August 20, 1859   Carpenter Massacre on Kinney's Cutoff in Marsh Valley

August 31, 1859   Miltimore Massacre twenty-five miles west of Fort Hall

April 3, 1860   Pony Express begins operation

May 12, 1860   Pyramid Lake War with Northern Paiute

June 2, 1860   Troops engage Northern Paiute in battle near mouth of Truckee River in retaliation for May 12 attack

July 23, 1860   One Indian and two settlers killed in encounter at Smithfield, Cache County

August 21–24, 1860   Fictional Almo Massacre

September 7–9, 1860   Attack on Hagerty emigrant train near City of Rocks at Raft River

September 9, 1860   Otter Massacre on Oregon Trail just west of Salmon Falls

March 2, 1861   Nevada Territory established

March 1861   Daily overland mail service established between Fort Bridger, Salt Lake City, and Carson Valley

April 26, 1861	Robert Burton company of militia sent to Fort Bridger
May 1861	Snake River Indians placed under Washington superintendent of Indian affairs
May 1, 1861	Lot Smith company of militia sent to Fort Bridger area
July 1861	Last troops leave Fort Crittenden for the East
July 24, 1861	California Volunteers established by order of secretary of war to guard mail line between Fort Bridger, Salt Lake City, and Carson Valley
October 24, 1861	Western Union telegraph lines joined at Salt Lake City
December 1861	James Duane Doty assumes duties as Utah superintendent of Indian affairs
July 12, 1862	Colonel Connor and the California Volunteers depart from Stockton, California, for Salt Lake City
July 28, 1862	Gold is discovered at Grasshopper Creek in western Montana, and Montana Trail to Salt Lake City becomes busy thoroughfare
August 6, 1862	Connor takes command of Military District of Utah
August 9–10, 1862	Indians attack emigrant parties at Massacre Rocks below American Falls on Snake River
September 10, 1862	Colonel Connor visits Salt Lake City from his camp in Ruby Valley
September 12, 1862	Indian attack on McBride-Andrews party on Snake River
September 19, 1862	Proclamation by commissioner of Indian affairs warning travelers of attacks along Oregon Trail
October 5, 1862	Major Edward McGarry kills twenty-five Indians in series of attacks on Humboldt River
October 20, 1862	California Volunteers arrive in Salt Lake City and found Camp Douglas
November 23, 1862	Major McGarry attacks Bear Hunter's band at Providence, Cache Valley

December 6, 1862	Major McGarry executes four Indian hostages at Bear River Ferry
January 6, 1863	John Henry Smith killed at Bear River near Richmond, Cache Valley
January 14, 1863	Report that George Clayton and Henry Bean are killed in Marsh Valley
January 22, 1863	Captain Samuel W. Hoyt and infantry leave Camp Douglas for north
January 24, 1863	Cavalry units leave Camp Douglas for north
January 28, 1863	Combined California Volunteer units reach Franklin, Washington Territory
January 29, 1863	Bear River Massacre
February 4, 1863	Connor's troops arrive back at Camp Douglas
March 3, 1863	Idaho Territory established
April 4–5, 1863	Captain George F. Price battles with Utes in Spanish Fork Canyon
April 12, 1863	Lieutenant Francis Honeyman fights with Utes at Pleasant Grove
April 15, 1863	Lieutenant Colonel George S. Evans kills thirty Utes with loss of one officer in battle in Spanish Fork Canyon
May 1, 1863	Northwestern Shoshoni attack two Mormon woodhaulers in Cub River Canyon near Franklin, Idaho
Early May 1863	Captain S. P. Smith kills fifty-three Gosiute Indians
May 9, 1863	Northwestern Shoshoni kill William Thorp in Box Elder Canyon
May 23, 1863	Camp Connor established near Soda Springs, Idaho
July 2, 1863	Doty treaty with Eastern Shoshoni
July 30, 1863	Treaty at Box Elder with Northwestern Shoshoni
October 1, 1863	Treaty at Fort Ruby with Western Shoshoni
October 12, 1863	Treaty at Tooele Valley with Gosiute
October 14, 1863	Treaty of Soda Springs with Fort Hall Shoshoni and Bannock

March 7, 1864   All five Doty treaties ratified by United
                       States Senate

"Col. Connor and the Volunteers who went north last week to look after the Indians on Bear River have, in a very short space of time, done a larger amount of Indian killing than ever fell to the lot of any single expedition of which we have any knowledge."

Deseret News, February 4, 1863

THE SHOSHONI FRONTIER

ONE

Introduction

When the American people began to look beyond the Mississippi to the open plains, mountain ranges, and deserts of the West, their initial desire was to reach the well-watered regions of western Oregon Territory and the sunny and warm coastal areas of fabulous Spanish California. Early government exploring parties and adventurous fur traders publicized the possibilities of adding this vast domain to the United States, and the spirit of Manifest Destiny soon impelled wave after wave of pioneers to hazard the dangerous continental crossing to the shores of the Pacific. As early traces became well-rutted roads, and as emigrants stirred the dust with their wagon trains, appropriated springs and water holes, and stripped the grasses alongside western thoroughfares, native inhabitants grew increasingly restive.

The Great Basin and Snake River country was homeland to the Shoshoni peoples who lived adjacent to the main paths of travel. Although smaller in area than the Great Plains, the Shoshoni lands encompassed a huge expanse of territory within the western region. It was a diverse environment, ranging from extreme desert conditions to well-watered oases along mountain fringes and main rivers; this led tribes to show considerable variations in lifestyles and food habits despite their common language and basic culture. Indeed, it could be argued that the horse-and-buffalo culture of the plains Indians gave them more in common than the Shoshoni "Diggers" had with their cousins, the buffalo-hunting Eastern Shoshoni.

Ironically, the process of white appropriation of Indian lands reached crisis proportions in the Far West, the central Rockies, and the Great Basin before it did on the Great Plains. The balance of human existence was always fragile in the desert environment of

Utah, Idaho, and Nevada, and the varied Shoshoni bands were much more precariously situated. Wildlife and native plants were quickly depleted under pressure from advancing white populations and the impact of white exploitation of the environment. White settlers and farmers occupied the Great Basin and Snake River region long before the Great Plains—the Mormons were in Salt Lake Valley in 1847 and at Carson Valley in 1857; there were miners in Boise Valley in 1862.

The Shoshoni people initially were friendly and accommodating to the passing tourists of the 1840s, but by the next decade they began to resent the indiscriminate killing of tribal members and the loss of their food stocks to emigrant horses and cattle. Soon western trails resounded to the cries of Indian raiding parties as they sought revenge and food stuffs from the westering travelers. White bandits made travel on the Oregon and California trails even more dangerous. The event that closed most of the Indian hostility in this far-flung region was the massacre of a village of Northwestern Shoshoni in Utah's northern Cache Valley in 1863—the culmination of almost two decades of Indian-white friction in the Great Basin and along the Snake River. But to understand the roots of Indian and white motivations, it is necessary to look first at the specific tribes involved and their lifeways at the time whites penetrated their homeland.

The Oregon and California trails coursed through Shoshoni country from South Pass on the east to Fort Boise and present Winnemucca, Nevada on the west. Beyond 117° 30' west longitude near Winnemucca, Northern Paiute controlled the region west to Walker and Pyramid lakes.[1] By the early 1840s, with the press of emigrant travel along the western routes, the Shoshoni and Paiute were already unwilling participants in the drama of America moving west, a movement that was to change the history of the United States and to have far-reaching consequences for these mostly Great Basin tribes.

From South Pass to Fort Bridger and the Bear Lake area of the Wasatch Mountains, the Eastern Shoshoni under their famous chief, Washakie, were the first of their tribe to meet the emigrants. Numbering about 2,000 by the time of white penetration, they were a horse people with a plains culture dominated by pursuit of the buffalo but also with much reliance on roots and berries and small game found in their beloved Wind River Mountains, where their descendants live today.

With a homeland lying astride the Mormon and Oregon trails, the Eastern Shoshoni might have been expected to be troublesome to passing emigrant parties whose cattle and horses devoured Indian grasses and whose white teamsters might irresponsibly shoot at unsuspecting tribal members. But their chief, Washakie, in firm control of his people, was determined to remain at peace with the strangers passing through his land. The main contact with white travelers and the later Mormon settlers was at Fort Bridger, where some trading took place, but these meetings were usually of only a few weeks' duration. The remainder of each year was spent in hunting buffalo on the central Wyoming plains, visiting with Northwestern Shoshoni in the Bear Lake region where fish could be taken, or wintering in the Wind River area where deer and other small game provided additional food supplies. Sometimes the Bannock and a few Shoshoni from neighboring Fort Hall to the west joined in the annual forays after buffalo. These audacious and resolute Bannock warriors were especially welcome during times of war with other plains tribes to the east.[2]

At Fort Hall, where the Portneuf and Blackfoot rivers meet the Snake River, about 1,000 Fort Hall Shoshoni formed their winter camps along with approximately 800 of their Bannock neighbors, a Northern Paiute-speaking band who hunted and intermarried with the Shoshoni but who kept their language and distinct tribal entity. Through an accident of geography, these two groups lived where the later California Trail diverged from the Oregon Trail, and this brought thousands of white wagon trains across their homeland. The Fort Hall Shoshoni and Bannock were, like their eastern cousins, mostly a people dependent on horses for mobility and buffalo hunting, but their food-gathering habits also included annual forays down the Snake River to Shoshone Falls for salmon and to Camas Prairie in central idaho for supplies of the famous camas root.

Unlike the Eastern Shoshoni, the Fort Hall people had no safe retreat like the Wind River Mountains. The Snake River bottoms near Fort Hall provided luxuriant forage for Indian horse herds and heavy stands of willows for shelter from icy storms but also offered the emigrants a way station and rest area before tackling the desert regions to the west. Some adventurous Fort Hall Shoshoni and Bannock sought food supplies as far north as Jackson Hole and the Yellowstone Park area, as far north and east as the buffalo plains of

Montana and Wyoming, and as far west as central Idaho. But their homeland at Fort Hall, crossroads of the West, doomed them to interaction with white travelers whether they wished it or not. Bannock warriors especially were willing to attack small and isolated emigrant trains. The Indians of Fort Hall, without the strong hand of a peaceful Washakie, would bear watching in the years after 1840.[3]

North of Fort Hall, in the Salmon River Mountains, the Lemhi Shoshoni, Sacajawea's people, who numbered about 1,800, ranged from their camps along the tributaries of the Salmon River into the Beaverhead country of western Montana. They also hunted buffalo but depended a great deal on salmon, camas roots, and small game, such as mountain sheep. Like the Eastern Shoshoni, they had a powerful chieftain, Tendoy, who throughout a long life maintained friendly relations with white neighbors. The Lemhi were fortunate in being located north of the Oregon Trail and only occasionally came into contact with white emigrants when the Indians made their annual visits to the famous Camas Prairie just north of the Oregon Trail. Infrequent parties of young warriors may have drifted south to the trail at times looking for booty, but mostly the Lemhi were peaceful and removed from the hostilities that affected their Shoshoni brethren to the south. For many years they attempted to retain their homeland in the Salmon River area on a tiny reservation, but it could not provide them a living. After thirty years of ceaseless efforts on the part of the Office of Indian Affairs, and after the death of Chief Tendoy, the Lemhi finally capitulated to demands that they move to the Fort Hall Reservation. They left the Lemhi River in 1907 and their descendants today comprise part of the Shoshone-Bannock tribes at Fort Hall.[4]

The Northwestern Shoshoni, who became the principals in the battle at Bear River, occupied the valleys of present-day northern Utah: Great Salt Lake along its eastern shores and at Promontory; and Weber, Ogden, Cache, Bear Lake, and Malad valleys. They numbered about 1,500 at the signing of the Treaty of Box Elder in 1863, which was negotiated by Utah Superintendent of Indian Affairs James Duane Doty following the Bear River Massacre. At that time, their ten bands were headed by Chiefs Pocatello, Toomontso, Sanpitch, Tosowitz, Yahnoway, Weerahsoop, Pahragoosahd, Tahkuetoonah, Omrshee, and Sagwitch. The Northwestern groups partook of both plains traits and the food-gathering habits of other Great

Basin people. Their horse herds were not as large as their eastern and northern neighbors, and although they traveled to Wyoming in search of buffalo, they spent part of each year gathering seeds, digging roots, fishing the streams, and hunting small game. The basins of the Wasatch Mountains provided a good summer living, and the banks of the rivers flowing into the Great Sale Lake afforded winter shelter and good forage for their horses.

While their Shoshoni and Bannock neighbors north of Fort Hall suffered exploitation at the hands of seasonal emigrants, the Northwestern Shoshoni were soon to become worse off as indefatigable Mormon farmers took over their homeland, denuding the lush valleys of their grasses and killing off the plentiful game of the Wasatch and Bear River mountains. Soon there was no place to go—Mormon settlements appropriated Indian lands between the Wasatch range and Great Salt Lake, along lower Bear River where winter camps had formerly provided sustenance, and in the delightful and well-watered Cache Valley. The Northwestern bands constantly interacted with the ever-present Mormon settlers, alternating between accepting wheat and beef from the Saints (as enjoined by Brigham Young's dictum that it was easier to feed than fight the natives) and raiding Mormon cattle herds when the gifts were not generous. It is easy to understand why the Northwestern Shoshoni, from among all the far-flung Shoshoni tribes of the Great Basin and Snake River plains, became the focus of the final attack from federal troops. Living within the confines of the only major settlement in the northern Rocky Mountain region, they were an easy target, and Mormon dissatisfaction with Northwestern Shoshoni hostility and the drain on the Saints' wheat crops and cattle herds led to insistent appeals for relief.[5]

Although they were divided into several bands, the Northwestern Shoshoni had a powerful leader in Chief Bear Hunter, who constantly attempted to negotiate between his increasingly angry tribesmen and encroaching Mormon farmers. But Bear Hunter's career was cut short when he died leading his people against Colonel Connor's California Volunteers at the Battle of Bear River, and he has not received the historical recognition he deserves. Bear Hunter was an older contemporary of Chief Pocatello and leader of the Shoshoni who lived along Logan River and Bear River in Cache Valley. His Indian name was Wirasuap or "Bear Spirit," although the Indian agents usually called him Bear Hunter. He and his tribe occasionally met with Washakie and the Eastern Shoshoni in Round Valley just southwest of Bear Lake, and during these encampments Bear Hunter was equal in power to Washakie. Peter Maughan, a leader of the Saints in Cache Valley, paid tribute to his prominence by referring to him as the War Chief of the Northwestern Shoshoni, a title he enshrined with his blood while directing his warriors at Bear River.[6]

After the 1863 engagement with Colonel Patrick E. Connor's troops, the Northwestern bands continued their precarious and occasionally hostile existence with the Mormon settlers of northern Utah until the establishment of the Fort Hall Reservation in 1869. From that time and throughout the 1870s, the agents at Fort Hall, under the insistence from the Office of Indian Affairs in Washington, D.C., exerted constant pressure on the Northwestern group to move to the reservation, and by the end of the decade nearly all had settled at Fort Hall and have since been lost to history. Of the fairly recent and detailed general histories of Utah, Richard Poll, ed., *Utah's History* (1978), devotes a single line to the Battle of Bear River and describes the "Western Shoshone" as being signatories to the 1863 Treaty of Box Elder. Helen Z. Papanikolas, ed., *The Peoples of Utah* (1976), omits any mention of the Northwestern Shoshoni, while Andrew Love Neff's earlier work, *History of Utah, 1847 to 1869* (1940), assigns a two-sentence coverage in a footnote to the engagement at Bear River. Even Joel E. Ricks, ed., *The History of a Valley: Cache Valley, Utah-Idaho* (1956), devotes only two sentences to the battle with no apparent understanding of the Northwestern bands who inhabited the valley. One must go back to the 1890 *History of Utah* by Hubert Howe Bancroft to get a fairly detailed and reasonably accurate description of the Bear River Massacre, evidently the largest Indian massacre in the history of the Far West. The Northwestern Shoshoni, though involved in numerous scrapes with early Mormon settlers, have become Utah's "Lost Tribe," even though the history of their hostile actions in northern Utah is as dramatic as the Walker or Black Hawk wars so prominently portrayed for central and southern Utah. Perhaps the fact that the Battle of Bear River took place in Idaho just a few miles north of the Utah line (although until an official boundary survey was completed in 1872, most people thought the battle was in Utah) has also led Utah historians to ignore the event and any description of one of Utah's most powerful Indian tribes—the Northwestern Shoshoni.[7]

West of Salmon Falls on the Snake River extending to Fort Boise were the Boise and Bruneau Shoshoni, named for the rivers they lived along. By the late 1850s the two tribes numbered about 300 each. They were more sedentary, owning fewer horses and relying chiefly on salmon as their principal food, with annual forays to camas prairies. The Oregon Trail went right through Boise Shoshoni territory, and both they and their friends, the Bruneau people, soon became enmeshed in troubles with passing emigrant parties. But with the opening of mines in the Boise Basin, hostility in the area escalated by the mid-1860s.

The Boise and Bruneau Shoshoni were probably the perpetrators of such widely reported attacks on emigrant parties as the 1854 Ward Massacre and the Otter Massacre of 1860. Murders of defenseless Indians by emigrants and the destruction of native subsistence supplies led to retaliation on unsuspecting wagon trains by the Shoshoni of western Idaho. Regular army troops were mustered and later civilian militia units in eastern Oregon were called to suppress Indian hostility in the Boise region. In 1863 the military post at Fort Boise was founded, bringing troops closer to the scene of action, and from this time until their removal to Fort Hall Reservation in 1869, the Boise and Bruneau bands lived a perilous existence caught between avaricious miners and settlers and military forces from Fort Boise.[8]

The Gosiute, a Shoshoni-speaking people with about 900 members, lived in the area southwest of the Great Salt Lake extending from Tooele Valley to the Deep Creek Mountains and into what is now eastern Nevada. They lived in a desolate, salt-desert region interrupted with small oases and moisture-catching mountains. Forced into an organization of small, nomadic family groups by the paucity of food, they nevertheless lived reasonably well until white occupation of their springs and other habitable areas transformed them into the "Digger Indians" of western travel accounts. Their food did not meet the standard of white palates, but they "had few rituals concerning food gathering and few food taboos; they simply could not afford them."[9]

By the 1860s, the Gosiute too found their homeland traversed, first by the Pony Express and then by the Overland Mail route. They had already suffered the loss of much of their homeland to Mormon settlers who had taken over Tooele, and Rush and Skull valleys southwest of Great Salt Lake. The Mormons proceeded to strip these grassy basins by overgrazing large herds of livestock. The starving natives periodically fought back by killing some of the Mormon cattle only to suffer death or imprisonment at the hands of enraged white farmers—despite Brigham Young's oft-repeated advice to love and cherish the red brethren. The establishment of Overland Mail stations in Gosiute territory added to the loss of grasslands and game in areas farther west toward the Deep Creek Mountains and invited Indian attacks on the relatively undefended and inviting mail stops. After fifteen years of close association with white civilization, these "Digger Indians" found very little to dig in the wreck of their formerly livable environment.

From Gosiute territory past the Ruby Mountains and along the Humboldt River to the Winnemucca region, numerous bands of Western Shoshoni scrabbled for a living, some faring better than others in the more propitious spots of the Nevada desert. Indian agent Levi A. Gheen, in 1873, enumerated eleven Western Shoshoni bands with a total population of 8,145. He listed Kiavitch's band of 1,725, located at the Big Mountains, Belmont, Duck Water Valley, and White Pine Mountains; Pohagant's band of 780, in White Pine County and Hamilton; Antelope Jack's band of 850, at Schell Creek, Spring Valley, Snake Valley, and Deep Creek; Te-mok's band of 1,125, at Ruby Valley and in Elko County; the To-so-wean-tsogo band of 430, at Ruby, Huntington, and Newark valleys; Captain George's band of 360, near the Utah-Nevada line; To-toy's band of 480 at Reese River Valley, Austin, and Lander County; Captain Charlie's band of 850 at Austin, Grass Valley, Mineral Hill, and Butte Mountain of Lander County; Captain Sam's band of 630 at Elko and along the railroad; band of Gosiutes, chief unknown, of 600 near the Utah-Nevada line; and bands of Gosiutes and Shoshones of 315 people with no known chiefs, in White Pine and Lincoln counties.[10] Many of the Western Shoshoni lived along the California Trail or the Overland Mail route and became involved with emigrant parties and later military expeditions.

The fragmentation of the Western Shoshoni, as indicated by Gheen in 1873, has continued down to the present. Although some of them finally agreed to settle on the Duck Valley Reservation along the Nevada-Idaho border, a great many still cling to their ancient locations in small colonies outside the northern Nevada towns and are presently fighting a rearguard action with the federal government to regain control of as much of their aboriginal homeland as possible. Prior to signing of the Treaty at Ruby Valley on October 1, 1863, which remains the basis for their suit against the government, the Western Shoshoni suffered the fate of all the other Shoshoni groups as the California Trail and the Overland Mail route brought in the stage companies and ranchers whose herds destroyed the fields of grass that had always furnished the seeds of life for the mush and bread on which they depended.

The Northern Paiute, the last group of Indians concerned in this study, lived west of Winnemucca to Walker and Pyramid lakes. Most knowledgeable people estimated their numbers in the early 1860s at slightly over 8,000, with perhaps 6,000 of them living along the Humboldt River and west to the lakes; the other 2,000 or so were located in the south-central region of Nevada. Richard F. Burton, in his celebrated journey from Salt Lake City to California in 1860, listed the following twelve bands:

> 1. Wanamuka's; 2. San Joaquim, near the forks of that river in Carson Valley, numbering 170; 3. Hadsapoke, or Horse Stopper band, of 110, in Gold Kanyon on Carson River; 4. Wahi or Fox-band, on Big Bend of Carson River, 130 in number; 5 and 6. Odakeo, "Tall man band," and Petodseka, "White Spot band," round the Lakes and Sinks of the Carson and Walker Rivers, numbering 484 men, 372 women, and 405 children; 7. Tosarke, "Grey head band," their neighbours; 8. Tonoziet, "Woman helper band," on the Truckee River below Big Meadows, numbering 280 souls; 9. Torape, or "Lean man band," on the Truckee River near Lone Crossing, 360 souls; 10. Gonega, the "Dancer band," 290 souls, near the mouth of the Truckee River; 11. Watsequendo, the "Four Crows," along the shores of Pyramid Lake, 320 souls; 12. The second Wanamuka's band, 500 in number, along the shores of the Northern Mud Lake.[11]

The Northern Paiute who lived in the Walker-Pyramid Lake region were more numerous and better fed than those scattered from that region to Winnemucca.

The seven major Shoshoni groups just described, comprising about 17,000 people, have been for years an enigma wrapped in a mystery. In the early years of white penetration of the Great Basin and Snake River areas, most travelers and settlers just lumped the Indians of Snake River together as "Snakes," while farther south, in western Utah and eastern Nevada, the natives became "Diggers."

Even today, except for a few scholars and a few knowledgeable attorneys concerned with aboriginal land claims, many people still throw up their hands in dismay and talk about a general population of Shoshoni Indians with little appreciation for their differences and the geographical boundaries of their tribal homelands.

Although the various Shoshoni groups spoke a similar language, visited with other Shoshoni in friendly exchange, occasionally hunted together, and rarely went to war with each other, they, nevertheless, were quite aware and jealous of the lands they claimed, and they understood the cultural differences between various tribes. From the Eastern Shoshoni and the Fort Hall Shoshoni and Bannock, who were considered the aristocrats of all the Shoshoni because of their large herds of horses, their easy mobility, and their proclivity to war with other Indians, there was a perceptible gradation to a more precarious existence for the Shoshoni in the western regions of the Shoshoni nation (or to a less "noble" Indian in the eyes of ethnocentric whites). While the eastern tribes lived on buffalo meat, their western cousins ate whatever could be found in desolate desert areas. Nevertheless, before the coming of the white man, all the Shoshoni lived rather well. Buffalo were available in Idaho and northern Utah areas, salmon and trout thronged the streams, and camas roots abundantly covered the prairies. In western Utah and throughout Nevada, grass seeds for flour, piñon nuts, and small game provided plentiful food. Emigrants along the trails and Mormon farmers in the Great Basin quickly destroyed what had once been a mostly comfortable existence.

———————

While the above population figures for the various tribes are based on a variety of estimates made over the years by travelers and government officials, Indian numbers may have been sharply reduced by contact with exotic diseases introduced by the early fur hunters. Even though the fur trade era was, in many respects, a golden age for the mountain and desert Indians with the advent among them of iron utensils and firearms, the many written accounts of decimation by cholera, smallpox, and lesser afflictions emphasize the dangers associated with the coming of white men. In 1849, for example, Almon W. Babbitt recorded the effects of cholera among the plains tribes "with many dead Indians lying about and their bodies torn and half eaten by wolves."[12] And closer to the people of this story, Mormon pioneer David Moore reported, in 1850, that the Northwestern Shoshoni along the Weber River were dying of measles, with many of those that remained being nursed by the settlers.[13] An 1853 emigrant, Harriet Sherrill Ward, met some Bannock near the Bear River Ferry north of Great Salt Lake who had "suffered much from the ravages of Small Pox the present season, and indeed have been nearly destroyed by it."[14] All three diary entries were typical incidental comments by casual observers.

The destruction of food supplies as whites penetrated Indian country was of greater importance. The large game, vital to the subsistence of the Eastern, Fort Hall, Lemhi, and Northwestern Shoshoni, and to the Bannock, had disappeared or had been greatly reduced in the mountain regions by the 1840s. Osborne Russell reported during his visits to Salt Lake Valley in 1841 that "the buffalo had long since left the shores of these lakes" but added that Wanship, a "Eutah" chief, remembered when the "buffalo passed from the mainland to the [Antelope] island [in Great Salt Lake] without swimming."[15] As late as 1833, however, buffalo were still numerous on the Snake River plains, where Captain Benjamin Bonneville hunted among "immense herds . . . slaying and cooking, and feasting . . . [in] an enormous carnival."[16] But by 1840 the buffalo were gone, and in 1860 F. W. Lander noted that the "Salt Lake Snakes, . . . as a class more civilized than Washikee's band . . . ," were forced to go "to Buffalo" through the lands of the Bannock and the Eastern Shoshoni.[17]

An equally important loss to all Shoshoni was the destruction of the magnificent grass cover that enveloped mountain meadows and the lower hills of much of the region from South Pass west to Carson Valley. When Mormon leader Wilford Woodruff first caught sight of Salt Lake Valley, he "gazed with wonder and admiration upon the most fertile valley . . . clothed with a heavy garment of vegetation . . ."[18] Thomas Bullock, another 1847 pioneer, was more specific— the Wheat grass grows 6 or 7 feet high, . . . some being 10 or 12 feet high," and "after wading thro' thick grass for some distance" he found "a place bare enough for a camping ground, the grass being only knee deep, but very thick."[19] As late as 1862, Chaplain John A. Anderson of the California Volunteers was amazed that between Ruby Valley and Camp Floyd "in some valleys it [grass] is higher than a man's head, and all over the numberless hills grows the best of bunch grass."[20]

Grass seeds were an important part of the Shoshoni and Northern

Paiute diet, especially west of the big game country. When F. W. Lander described the food habits of the Eastern Shoshoni, he sharply observed that "their principal subsistence is the roots and seeds of the wild vegetables of the region they inhabit, the mountain trout, . . . and wild game."[21] Grass seeds were gathered in flat tray-like baskets by raking them with beaters and then storing for winter use. The seeds were either boiled as a nutritious mush or soup or ground into flour to be baked or mixed with jerky.[22] The Gosiute, for example, used seventy-nine different species of wild vegetable foods: forty-seven of that number yielded seeds, twelve provided berries, eight gave them roots, and twelve were used for greens. [23]

Julian Steward, famous for his 1930s anthropological study of the Shoshoni, described their seasonal subsistence activities. In the spring, when stored foods had been exhausted, the Indians eagerly gathered the stems and leaves of early edible plants to be eaten as "greens."[24] Peter Skene Ogden thought it "incredible that human beings can live on grass, but it is a fact. . . ."[25] By early summer the Indian women traveled to the moist hills to collect ripening seeds for a winter supply. In late summer, roots were dug and, with berries, provided food during this season as well as for winter use. Nuts of the piñon pine were taken during the fall and added to the larder. Wild game could provide large food supplies with less effort than the backbreaking task of beating seeds into baskets, but in its absence, especially among the desert tribes, grasses and roots were essential to existence.

Indian anger mounted as the settlers' large cattle herds began to devour the grasses. As early as 1855, Mormon church herds were pastured in Cache Valley in such large numbers that 2,300 died during the hard winter.[26] And while the grass was still luxuriant at this time, the process of depletion had begun. In the following years, Utah Indian agent Garland Hunt reported that the Western Shoshoni along Humboldt River "claim that we have eaten up their grass and utterly deprived them of its rich crop of seed which is their principal subsistence during winter. . . . Now there is nothing left for them to eat but ground squirrels and pis-ants."[27] And in 1860, the Northern Paiute of the Pyramid Lake area complained that "the cattle they [whites] bring with them eat the grass which their squaws gather for making bread."[28] These typical comments emphasized the hunger and degradation forced on the Shoshoni and Northern Paiute until the Mormon Jacob Hamlin could report in 1862, only fifteen years after the Mormons had settled in Utah, that grazing had so destroyed native seeds that the Indians were starving.[29]

Before the coming of the white man, the Shoshoni and Northern Paiute were one of the most ecologically efficient Indian groups in North America. They had maintained a delicate balance with nature, but overgrazing and destruction of game rapidly transformed the western Shoshonian groups of Utah and Nevada into poor Indians who inherited the Digger stereotype. George C. Yount announced, "There is not in all the world a race of human beings more low and degraded than the Diggers."[30] Suggesting existence may have been a living hell, Peter Skene Ogden wrote, "What will be the reward of these poor wretches in the next world I cannot pretend to say, but surely they cannot be in a more wretched state than in this."[31]

Perhaps it was impossible for white settlers to realize that they were responsible for the degraded condition of the Gosiute, Western Shoshoni, and Northern Paiute. And although members of the eastern bands of Shoshoni and Bannock may have looked more noble and romantic astride their pinto ponies, these warriors could have stomachs as empty as their pedestrian cousins farther west. Sooner or later, all of them would be forced to choose between starvation, begging at the doors of white farmers, or raiding their aggressive white neighbors. From the beginning of white occupation, the drama of Indian and white friction was played out on the desert stage of the western valleys and along the emigrant trails, becoming more intense as time and American civilization advanced.

As historian Earl S. Pomeroy points out in a seminal book on territorial government, American political administration was discordant, confused, and fumbling, making many mistakes as it evolved. This was especially true in the supervision of Indian affairs in the Shoshoni region, and this ineptitude, especially on the Snake River plains, did little to maintain peace.[32] Prior to June of 1846 and the division of Oregon Territory along the forty-ninth parallel by the British and American governments, the Shoshoni had been left to a relationship with fur traders and trappers from both nations. Another three years elapsed before the United States Congress established Oregon Territory on March 3, 1849, and placed the territorial capital at Oregon City, hundreds of miles from the Boise and Bruneau bands, the Lemhi at Salmon River, and the Shoshoni and Bannock at Fort Hall.

The Oregon superintendent of Indian affairs was responsible for a vast area with many tribes and had little time to attend to the Shoshoni in the far eastern corner of his district. Because of insufficient funds and because the closer tribes demanded more attention, the various superintendents just allowed Indian affairs on the periphery to drift without direction. Oregon officials were galvanized to dispatch military units only when massacres of emigrant parties along the lower Snake and Boise rivers or attacks near Fort Hall attracted national attention. The establishment of Washington Territory in 1853 failed to relieve the Oregon superintendent of his many arduous tasks, and when the Oregon and Washington superintendencies were reunited into one agency in 1857, Superintendent James W. Nesmith complained, "The duties in either Territory while the offices were distinct afforded ample business for the Superintendents. If any change was originally necessary it was that the country east of the Cascade Mountains should have been erected into a separate district. My apparent neglect or omissions in the discharge of my official duties can very properly be attributed to an excessive amount of business."[33] Then, in May of 1861, a new Washington superintendency was separated from Oregon to include also what is now Idaho. To the Indians along Snake River, Olympia, Washington, was even farther removed from them than Oregon City or Salem. Finally on March 3, 1863, with the establishment of Idaho Territory, a government official was appointed who could understand Indian conditions in the Snake River area.

In 1847, the Fort Hall Shoshoni and Bannock looked to Salt Lake City and Utah Superintendent of Indian Affairs Brigham Young for guidance and help. The Indians could not comprehend an imaginary forty-second parallel cutting them off from Superintendent Young, who seemed to take good care of Washakie and the Eastern Shoshoni. As for the Boise and Bruneau bands, they had no one to look after them but occasional army patrols—and their help usually consisted of shooting first and asking questions later.[34]

Initially Utah Territory was too large for an efficient administration of Indian affairs, and superintendents were further handicapped by insufficient funds and few personnel. While Washakie's tribe, the Northwestern bands, and the Gosiute received some attention because of their proximity to Salt Lake City and the importance of the trails near which they lived, the widely scattered Western Shoshoni, extending from Deep Creek to Carson Valley, were fortunate to get an annual visit by a single agent. These western Indians did not begin to get attention until Nevada Territory was established on March 2, 1861.[35]

As will be detailed, the Mormon authorities in Utah vacillated between their "cheaper-to-feed-than-to-fight" philosophy and the common frontier belief that the native inhabitants occasionally needed to be chastised. The Mormon settlers of northern Utah certainly did not abhor the tactics of Colonel Connor when he directed the massacre of Bear Hunter's people at Battle Creek. In fact, there was rejoicing throughout the land and thanksgiving in Mormon church services for the intrepid courage of the California Volunteers.

Despite popular belief, the majority of deaths along emigrant routes occurred west of South Pass, not on the Great Plains. John Unruh demonstrated this point in his admirable study of emigrant-Indian interaction, *The Plains Across*, and estimated that ninety percent of all emigrant killings took place beyond South Pass. Often travelers did not meet their first Indians until they reached Eastern Shoshoni country, after which there might be frequent sightings of Shoshoni with possibilities for trade and barter or less friendly exchanges. There were comparatively few Indian attacks along the Oregon and California trails prior to the Gold Rush years of 1849 and 1850, but from then on until the early 1860s, the number of hostile incidents increased dramatically. Perhaps as many as 400 people lost their lives as a result of raids and murders at the hands of Shoshoni, Bannock, and Northern Paiute warriors on the Humboldt and Snake rivers. This was a significant loss, one not taken lightly by emigrants themselves and one historians should not ignore. Furthermore, it was safer to travel the California Trail than to take the more dangerous route to Oregon.

The year 1845 marked the beginning of Indian attacks that were sometimes instigated and led by gangs of white desperadoes who also infested the trails west of South Pass. Accounts mention dangerous stretches of trails haunted by these renegades—especially at Green River, Hudspeth's Cutoff, and the Lander Cutoff. Unsuspecting

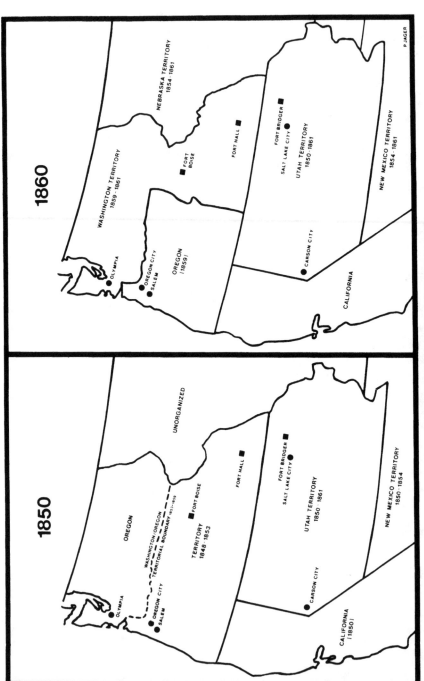

STATE AND TERRITORIAL BOUNDARIES

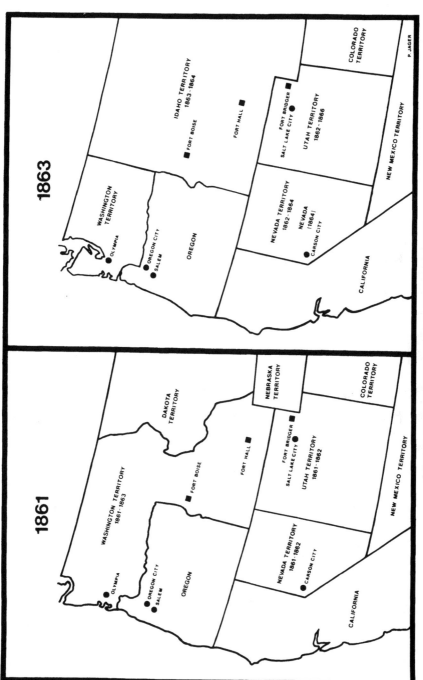

STATE AND TERRITORIAL BOUNDARIES

travelers were extremely vulnerable on the trail along the Humboldt River because the many trading posts were hangouts for both white and Indian bandits. By 1860, the threat of Indian attacks west of the Continental Divide had reached dismaying proportions, a situation caused by many factors including lack of government supervision, the ethnocentric behavior of white emigrants toward native populations, and appropriation of Indian lands by Mormon settlement.[36]

With this overview of the seven major Shoshoni groups west of South Pass, the delicate and precarious ecology of their homelands, the general lack of attention they received from the government (both in Oregon and Utah territories), and the persistence of Indian hostilities that led to the Bear River Massacre, one may ask why this confrontation has not received proper notice in the historical annals of the West. The problem may be put in perspective by considering an article printed in *The American West* magazine of July 1973 entitled, "How Many Indians Were Killed? White Man Versus Red Man: The Facts and the Legend." Author Don Russell accepted the dictionary definition of a "massacre" as being a " promiscuous wholesale slaughter, especially of those who can make little or no resistance." He then considered the five Indian massacres that "have received the most attention from historians and which produced the most casualties." First, there was the notorious Sand Creek Massacre of November 19, 1864, when Colonel John M. Chivington and his volunteers killed 130 Cheyenne, "two-thirds of them women and children."[37] Chivington later wrote that several days before his attack on the Indians, he had met in Denver, Colorado, with General Patrick E. Connor, who had said to him, "I think from the temper of the men that you have and all I can learn that you will give these Indians a most terrible threshing if you catch them, and if it was in the mountains, and you had them in a canon, and your troops at one end of it and the Bear river at the other, as I had the Pi-Utes [Shoshoni], you could catch them, but I am afraid on these plains you won't do it." Chivington replied that he was confident he could corner the Cheyenne.[38]

The second Indian killing listed was the Washita Massacre of November 27, 1868, with Major General George A. Custer in command, at which approximately 103 of Black Kettle's Cheyennes died. In a third incident, on January 23, 1870, Colonel Eugene M. Baker destroyed 173 Piegans at the Marias River in Montana Territory. The Camp Grant attack of April 30, 1871, by a group of vigilantes on a band of Aravaipa Apaches resulted in the deaths of a maximum of 150 Indians. Finally, the most notorious of all the Indian massacres occurred at Wounded Knee on December 29, 1890. Here 84 Sioux men, 44 women, and 18 children—a total of 146—were killed. Russell's "reasonable total" for the five massacres was 615.[39]

The affair at Bear River of January 29, 1863, was not listed. Nevertheless it resulted in more casualties than any of the five described by Russell. The reasonable figure of at least 250 Shoshoni deaths at Bear River makes the massacre one of the most significant Indian disasters in western American history. This seems a somewhat grisly way of assigning importance to a historical incident, but it is difficult to come up with either a more precise or compelling criterion.

Selecting only a few of the general and specific histories on Indian warfare in the West from Robert M. Utley's comprehensive bibliography in his recent work, *The Indian Frontier of the American West, 1846–1890* (1984), soon makes it apparent that Don Russell reflects at least one reality—the Bear River Massacre has not received attention from historians.[40] Paul I. Wellman in his 1947 *Death on Horseback* lists four of the five Indian disasters mentioned by Russell, omitting only the Marias River attack.[41] Oliver Knight describes the adventures of newspaper reporters among the Indian campaigners in *Following the Indian Wars* (1960) and emphasizes the Washita and Wounded Knee incidents but omits mention of the lone correspondent who reported the Bear River encounter to his[42] California newspapers. The military historian S. L. A. Marshall, in his 1972 *Crimsoned Prairie*, discusses Sand Creek and Wounded Knee at length but apparently was not aware of the Shoshoni slaughter at Bear River.[43] These three are typical of the general histories.

There are specific monographs devoted to descriptions of some of the five massacres noted by Russell. Two by Stan Hoig treat *The Battle of the Washita* (1976) and *The Sand Creek Massacre* (1961).[44] The most widely publicized is probably Dee Brown's *Bury My Heart at Wounded Knee: An Indian History of the American West* (1970), which describes the five attacks on Indians mentioned by Russell and even spends one sentence on Connor's destruction of the Northwestern Shoshoni at Bear River, although he mistakenly calls them

"Paiutes," probably taken from Connor's advice given to Colonel Chivington as already quoted.[45] Brown could have obtained more accurate and detailed information about Bear River from apparently the only general history of western Indian wars that deals with the subject, Robert M. Utley's well-known *Frontiersmen in Blue: The United States Army and the Indian, 1848–1865* (1967). Utley also follows this initial account with explanations of the Bear River Massacre in his *The American Heritage History of the Indian Wars* (1977) with coauthor Wilcomb E. Washburn and in his most recent and admirable bestseller, *The Indian Frontier of the American West, 1846–1890* (1984).[46] Of course, Fred B. Roger's *Soldiers of the Overland* (1938), the story of Patrick E. Connor and his California Volunteers, has been in print for a long time, but few except Robert M. Utley seem to be aware of it.[47]

The dramatic bloodletting at Bear River on January 29, 1863, has been lost to history perhaps, first of all, because the Mormon people have not been overanxious to highlight an approved slaughter of Indian men, women, and children. The salvation of all native Americans is of concern to the Saints under the Book of Mormon declaration that American Indians are descended from Israel. The paean of thanksgiving from the Cache Valley settlers after the Bear River engagement that the "victory" of Colonel Connor was "an intervention of the Almighty"[48] and the regret of a *Deseret News* reporter that Chief Pocatello and his gang had not also been wiped out[49] indicated a sharp break with Brigham Young's long-standing policy of peace. Also, coming only a little over six years after the infamous Mountain Meadows Massacre, the least said about Mormon exultance over another wholesale killing of innocents the better, even though in this instance Indians were on the receiving end. The very fact that Utah historians, with few exceptions, have continued to call this encounter a battle rather than a massacre may have some significance in this respect.

The cavalier unconcern for Indian bodies left on the banks of Bear River reflected the attitude of most whites of the time. What was considered a battle in 1863 might be taken for a massacre today as historical perspectives change. Hubert Howe Bancroft, twenty-seven years after the engagement, wrote, "Had the savages committed this deed, it would pass into history as a butchery or a massacre."[50] His comments came just a few years after Helen Hunt Jackson had written *A Century of Dishonor* and the Dawes Act had attempted to make white farmers and citizens out of the Indians in a burst of American guilt and penitence after years of mistreatment and betrayal. Of course, if army troops were killed by "savage" Indians, as in "Custer's Last Stand" of 1876, there was little reluctance in reporting it as a massacre.

As most students of the past recognize, the historical significance of an event or its appearance in history at all often depends on reporters at the scene and their perceptions and skill at describing a confused and chaotic situation. Although the engagement at Bear River was big news in the West, and especially in California and Utah, it attracted little notice where attention was focused on the Civil War. A single newsman braved the below-zero temperatures of late January 1863 to accompany Connor's Volunteers to the ice-choked Bear River and write a dispatch for journals in California. New York newspapers like the *Times*, the *Tribune*, and the *Herald* devoted short paragraphs to the incident, but apparently none of the Chicago journals paid any attention at all.[51] January headlines in the East were more concerned with the recent Emancipation Proclamation issued by President Abraham Lincoln, his firing of General Ambrose Burnside and the appointment of General Joseph Hooker to replace him in the eastern sector of the war, and the dispatch of Ulysses S. Grant to take personal command of the forces before Vicksburg.[52] A fight with western Indians, no matter how desperate the conflict or how high the casualty rate, seemed insignificant compared to thousands of Union and Rebel soldiers engaged in a contest to decide the fate of the United States.

If the Bear River struggle had occured after the Civil War, it probably would have received the same attention as have other major Indian engagements. Oliver Knight's *Following the Indian Wars* (1960) demonstrates the avidity with which newspaper correspondents, egged on by editors eager for increased circulation, followed army commanders in their pursuit of recalcitrant Indians in the postwar years. A glance at the newspapers of the day illustrates the wide coverage given Indian massacres to satisfy the curiosity and sympathy, or lack of it, of the American public. But in 1863 the American people were caught up in a bloody war with daily casualty figures that promoted a calloused view towards death. The destruction of unknown Indians in the Rocky Mountains did not raise many eyebrows at the time.

Nevertheless, the killing of 250 Northwestern Shoshoni at Bear

River was a national catastrophe. It deserves to be listed with other Indian massacres in American history, but, even more important, it has significance as the culmination of over twenty years of increasing Indian-white violence on the various major western trails. The massacre was probably inevitable. That the encounter took place when and where it did was a happenstance of time and geography. Bear Hunter's people, camped on Battle Creek and within easy reach of aggressive volunteers from California, provided the target that could just as easily have involved the Fort Hall Shoshoni and Bannock or any of the other Shoshoni tribes. The spilling of Northwestern blood provided a catharsis and object lesson that helped bring to a close a long chapter in Indian hostility west of South Pass. There were to be a few more years of decreasing violence until the establishment of reservations forced most of the tribes off the trails, but the sanguinary Bear River conflict was a climax.

The story of Indian-white relations in the Great Basin and on the Snake River, culminating in the slaughter at Bear River, was a preview to the drama played out on the Great Plains from 1860 to 1885. It puts the plains wars in perspective, allows us to examine the role of the press, the influence of the Civil War, the character of Mormon-government relations, the incongruity of federal Indian policy, and the brutality of the frontier spirit. This look at the Shoshoni frontier will, it is hoped, fill a gap in the history of the West.

In the succeeding chapters, the heightening tensions and deteriorating relations that developed from 1840 on are traced, examining year by year the agonizingly slow and ineffective government supervision of the Shoshoni peoples, the most significant Indian attacks on emigrant parties and mail stations, and especially the Mormon-Northwestern Shoshoni interaction that led to January 29, 1863. The five treaties signed in 1863 with the Shoshoni demonstrate that, in the main, the agreements did bring some peace to the Snake River plains and the Great Basin.

TWO

Mormons and Forty-niners Invade Shoshoni Country

As the Shoshoni people watched the first emigrant parties hurry through tribal lands on the way to Oregon and California, few realized that these travelers signaled the end to a way of life that had been good for native inhabitants. Within a few years the Mexican War would take place, thousands of Mormon farmers would occupy the fertile and well-watered spots, and thousands more gold-hungry argonauts would begin to exploit Indian food supplies. In the coming years, the first fumbling attempts by the federal government to administer Indian affairs would result in almost hopeless confusion. Mormon leaders, sincere in their initial attempts to appease the Northwestern Shoshoni and Ute tribesmen by feeding rather than fighting, would soon reveal that they could be as ruthless as other frontiersmen if native recalcitrance got in the way of saintly objectives. Forty-niners would show less patience and would make no pretense to appease or placate the unfortunate Indians. As elsewhere on the frontier, such incidents would point eventually to major confrontation. However, the decade of the 1840s was a period of experimentation as Shoshoni, overlander, settler, and Indian agent alike sought an accommodation between different cultures.

The first pioneers to cross the continent to Oregon and California were so few in number that Indians appear to have shown little apprehension. Early contacts between the two groups were limited. When emigrant William Newby traded with some friendly Shoshoni near Soda Springs in 1843, they were the first Indians he had met in two months.[1] The Indians travelers met were often helpful, sometimes cutting and carrying grass for wagon parties, herding and guarding stock, engaging in mutually beneficial barter, or even agreeing to deliver letters for the homesick emigrants. Indian guides were especially appreciated as they mapped out routes, located springs and water holes, and showed the way to river fords or assisted in stream crossings.[2] For example, the trail marked out by the Stevens-Murphy party beyond the Humbolt Sink could not have been accomplished without the help of a Northern Paiute Indian chief who described the route and then led the way.[3] Similarly, Peter Burnett of the Marcus Whitman wagon train gave credit to a faithful and competent Indian guide who helped steer the party to Oregon.[4] But there were harbingers of hostilities to come. A few early emigrant groups on occasion kidnapped some Indians as unwilling guides to make locating grass and water more certain.[5]

Inevitably, calloused frontiersmen with little regard for Indians accompanied the growing tide of emigrants, and by 1845 relations with Snake River and Humboldt Shoshoni bands began to deteriorate. A brutal Texan named Jim Kinney, for example, decided, while traveling west of Fort Hall in 1845, that he wanted a slave to do chores. Capturing a passing Indian, Kinney handcuffed him, tied a rope around his neck, and hitched the unfortunate man to the rear of his wagon. After whipping the Indian until satisfied that his spirit was broken, Kinney pressed him into service as a driver and to help with other menial duties. Kinney boasted that if his captive escaped "he could follow him" with the help of his family dog, and would "kill him to show the other Indians the superiority of the white man. He said he had killed plenty of negroes and an Indian was no better than a negro." But one night the new slave took off with some hams and Kinney's prized Kentucky rifle. As it turned out, the tracking dog was unsuccessful and the Shoshoni escaped. Other members of the wagon train were afraid to stand up to Kinney but secretly rejoiced when the Indian got away.[6] In a similar incident, a son of guide Caleb Greenwood shot an Indian who accidentally frightened his horse. The animal had almost thrown his rider, much to the amusement of other members of the party. Young Greenwood then left in a hurry to escape his father's anger, and Caleb was forced to order one of the party to shoot the mortally wounded Indian in the head to relieve his suffering.[7]

In a reflection of mounting tensions, Lansford Hastings cautioned emigrants in his 1846 guidebook against the practice of selling or

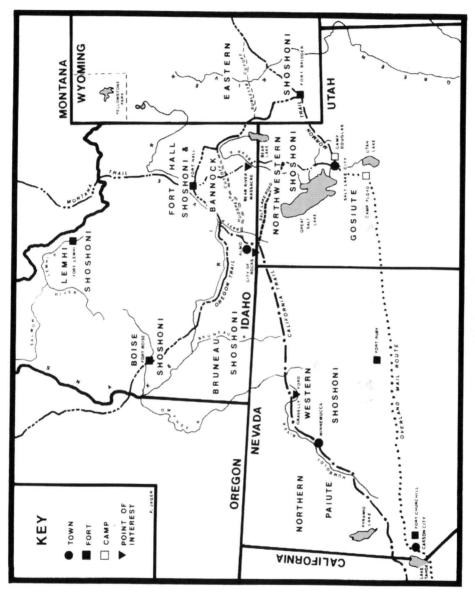

P. JAGER

WESTERN TRAILS

trading weapons to Indians and others on the road near Green River and Fort Hall.[8] Rifles and other arms, he warned, might well be needed for self-defense as the journey proceeded. The Hastings warning was justified. Chester Ingersoll's party lost six animals stolen by Indians on the Humboldt River in 1847. Ingersoll concluded, "After that we shot at every Indian we saw—this soon cleared the way."[9] Ansel McCall, in 1849, came upon three men from Missouri who intended to shoot the first Indian they saw, believing that Indians had stolen their horses. McCall thought "this inconsiderate retaliation upon a whole race for the acts of one of its members leads to half the conflicts that occur."[10]

By 1847 a pattern of white emigrant attacks and Shoshoni and Paiute retaliation was beginning to emerge as a constant in western travel. The encounters would never reach the extremes depicted in western movies or by some fiction writers, where encircled wagons were charged by hundreds of merciless Indian warriors, but would cause enough deaths and suffering on both sides to make western travel and settlement a sanguinary chronicle.

A major intrusion into Indian lands occurred in July of 1847 with the settlement of the Salt Lake Valley by Brigham Young and his followers. Driven from their homes in Nauvoo, Illinois, and seeking a refuge from mob violence, the Latter-day Saints looked forward to a colony in Mexican territory in the desert Great Basin that would be secluded and isolated from the rest of the world. The Mexican cession to the United States placed them once again under American control but left them for a time well beyond the effective bounds of federal influence or protection.

When the Saints entered the valley of the Great Salt Lake, they were fortunate in choosing a spot that was not heavily populated with Indians, although within a week of arrival the pioneers were visited by both Ute and Shoshoni interested in trading. In a fight over a stolen horse, four of the Shoshoni pursued and killed a Ute warrior and then expressed their anger that the Mormons had traded with the Utes. "The Shoshones claimed that they were the owners of the land and that the Utes had come over the line to interfere with their rights. They signified to the brethren by signs that they wanted to sell them the land for powder and lead."[11] Heber C. Kimball, second in command to Brigham Young, was quick to warn against selling guns and ammunition to the Shoshoni, but more important, he expressed strong disapproval of any land purchase. Indeed, he rejected the very "idea of paying the Indians for the lands, for if the Shoshones should be thus considered, the Utes and other tribes would claim pay also." Kimball expressed a special kind of Mormon "manifest destiny," which was not unknown among other frontiersmen, when he continued that the land belonged to "our Father in Heaven and we expect to plow and plant it."[12]

In keeping with this, the Mormons made no pretense of compensating any of the Shoshoni of the Great Basin for their aboriginal lands, although Brigham Young soon announced his policy that it was "manifestly more economical, and less expensive to feed and clothe, than to fight them."[13] There were some exceptions to this, but mostly Young insisted that his people adhere to it despite the later drain on Mormon food supplies by hungry natives whose best lands had been taken over by aggressive white farmers. In a typical statement to the Utah territorial legislature in his position both as governor and as superintendent of Indian affairs, Young later explained:

> We exhort you to feed and clothe them so far as lies in your power; never turn them away hungry from your door; teach them the art of husbandry; bear with them in all patience and long suffering, and never consider their lives as an equivalent for petty stealing; remember that it is a part of their existence, practiced by them from generation to generation, and success in which paved the way to renown and influence amongst them. Induce them from those ideas and notions by your superior wisdom and genial influence and intercourse with them. . . . Finally brethren, be just and quiet, firm and mild, patient and benevolent, generous and watchful in all your intercourse with them; learn their language so that you can explain matters to them and pay them the full and just reward of their labor, and treat them in all respects as you would like to be treated.[14]

Nevertheless, Young's humanitarian policy differed more in degree than in real substance, as he demonstrated in February 1849 when he dispatched a militia company of about forty men to Utah Valley to "chastize" a band of seventeen Indians under Cone and Blue-Shirt, who had been stealing and killing cattle and running off horses from the settlement at South Willow Creek. In a battle lasting almost four hours, the troops killed four of the Indian men and "then warned and fed" the women and children of the band before sending them off to the care of other "Snake Indians."[15]

Yet another Indian difficulty occurred early in 1849 when mountain man Barney Ward was accused by Louis Vasquez of Fort Bridger of being involved in the murder of a Bannock Indian. Vasquez reported that the tribe now "talked of coming to the valley to war upon the whites." Brigham Young was convinced that Jim Bridger was behind the whole affair and "is death on us" because of his jealousy of Mormon trade with the indians. The Bannock who was supposedly murdered was later discovered alive and well at Fort Hall. This ended the scare, but the incident reinforced the pragmatic Young, who was a pessimist about the prospects of saving the souls of the Indians. "As for the old Indians now alive," he wrote, "entering into the new and everlasting covenant, they will not do it, but they will die and be damned. . . . They will not be converted in many years."[16]

A much more important development in 1849 to Mormon and Indian alike as well as for this study, was the passage of thousands of gold-seekers on their way to California. The Gold Rush emigrants transformed the economy of Salt Lake City as they traded their excess baggage and wagons for pack horses to continue the journey. The argonauts also had a tremendous impact on the Shoshoni and Paiute. Only small numbers of emigrants had crossed the continent each year before the California rush, but in 1849 about 25,000 traveled to the coast, and perhaps 45,000 went in 1850. Approximately 10,000 in 1849 and 15,000 in 1850 went through the City of the Saints and followed the Salt Lake Road north around the end of Great Salt Lake and thence to Nevada. From the Salt Lake settlement north across the Bear River and past the Promontory Mountains was Northwestern Shoshoni territory, so these Indians tasted the discouragement of having to deal with hordes of whites moving through their homeland.

Grasses along the trails were destroyed, wild game was depleted, and firewood exhausted creating an immediate and devastating impact on the Northern Paiute and Shoshoni people. Two incidental comments by travelers passing through the Northwestern Shoshoni area emphasized the effect even small groups could have on game. Charles Glass Gray recorded on successive days while nearing Bear

View on Snake River of artemisia plains. Ackerman Lithographers, N.Y. *Idaho State Historical Society.*

Shoshoni encampment on Boise River. *Idaho State Historical Society.*

River Crossing that "several of our men . . . brought in 12 fine prairie hens" and "5 of us today shot 50 *large sage hens.* . . ."[17] Three years later, Mariett Cummings wrote that he was able to catch thirty-two fine speckled trout from Weber River in two days of fishing.[18] Such takes were multiplied many times, soon reducing important Indian food sources.

Nearly all the tribes along the Oregon and California trails insisted, as did the Northwestern Shoshoni, that the Gold Rush emigrants were trespassers on Indian lands and that travelers should pay a tribute or tax for the privilege of crossing. The Forty-niners responded much the same as had Heber C. Kimball. Isaac Lord angrily wrote, "The whole is a gross imposition. The . . . 'idea' that an old Indian should lay claim to a tract of land as large as all the New England States, and levy black mail on all passers, is sufficiently absurd; but when it is done by the connivance of the U.S. government . . . language becomes useless."[19] Sarah Royce thought that a tribute "demand was unreasonable! that the country we were traveling over belonged to the United States, and that these red men had no right to stop us."[20] Major Osborne Cross of the Mounted Rifle Regiment of 1849 argued, "If these people really deserved compensation for the wood used, which was of itself too absurd to think of for a moment, it was a proper subject to lay before the Indian department."[21] However, a few emigrants like James Hutchings, acknowledged Indian land ownership and recognizing the justice of a crossing fee willingly paid up.[22] The Shoshoni and Northern Paiute never acknowledged the right of white men to usurp the land. It was not until the twentieth century that the government agreed to compensate the western tribes for some of their aboriginal lands.

It was the indiscriminate killing of Indians by white travelers that contributed most to retaliatory attacks by the natives. The twenty-five member Colony Guard outfit of New York City was so apprehensive about the Indians that they provided each man of their Forty-niner group with a large knife, a Colt revolver, and a hair-trigger rifle. When the order of rifles came, they were rejected as "being too light in weight," and heavier weapons were requisitioned.[23]

With such fears, it is little wonder that night guards sometimes fired at anything that had the slightest resemblance to a lurking warrior. When "an Indian of doubtful appearance" entered the camp of

James A. Pritchard looking for something to eat, Pritchard took his gun, ordered him to stop by the fire, and warned that he would be instantly shot if he moved at all before sunrise. The next morning the Indian was given breakfast and sent on his way.[24] Captain Howard Stansbury took extra precautions for his expedition when he learned that "a mortal offence had been taken by the Shoshones or Snake Indians . . . arising from a gross and wanton outrage which had been a short time before inflicted upon them by a company of unprincipled emigrants, by whom their women had been most brutally treated, and their friends murdered while attempting to defend them."[25] Bands of white robbers, often disguised as Indians, sometimes raided the Gold Rush parties, adding to the numbers of unprovoked attacks by the travelers on innocent Indians. Mormon John D. Lee wrote about a group of ferrymen who left the Platte River ferry ten days early to escape one such band hiding in the Wind River Mountains.[26]

Trail fights in 1849 were inspired by both emigrant parties and Shoshoni and Northern Paiute raiders. The Foster Company of California pioneers rallied its fifty men just west of the Malad River north of Great Salt Lake when they observed smoke in the mountains because a group of emigrants under a Captain Walker had murdered Indians for their horses. The Foster party expected an attack any minute.[27] Another emigrant train met a company of eighteen young men between the Goose Creek Mountains and Humboldt River who had been embroiled in "quite a fight with the Indians. Two men were killed and four wounded—one died afterwards from his wounds. . . ." The survivors returned to winter in Salt Lake Valley after their wagons were burned and their provisions were destroyed.[28] In late October 1849, Brigham Young's secretary recorded that some Snake Indians had attacked a party of gold-rushers.[29] Farther west, Elijah Howell came upon a physician who had been camped for a week after he had lost his cattle on the Humboldt to Indian marauders.[30] And Alonzo Delano reported that one wagon train had lost twenty-seven mules on the Lassen trail. Bereft of their draft animals, the men had to leave their wagons and start walking the rest of the way to California.[31]

Indian strategy was often oriented to the trails. Emigrant cattle and mules were killed or disabled by shooting arrows into the animals. After the emigrants passed, the Indians harvested the meat.

Elijah Farnham rejoiced that his group was able to put one over on the hungry natives by using "up the flesh of the dead cattle so clean that the diggers did not get a morsel for their pains."[32]

Larger horse- and cattle-stealing raids were mounted by the Indians along the trails in 1850. The *Deseret News* of July 13, 1850, advised its readers to be careful when trading horses with the Indians because an animal might be reclaimed later by the emigrant from whom the horse had been stolen. In the same newspaper dated October 5, 1850, a group of Mormons arriving in Salt Lake City from California reported that a band of Indians was holding a herd of no fewer than 1,000 stolen animals in a secure canyon near the head of the Humboldt River. Emigrants sometimes blamed Mormons. Charles Bush, for example, was sure they had instigated Indian depredations by exciting the natives "against us so they kept us in continued alarme both night and day. . . . Often time the grass was fired by night thereby endangering our lives and property."[33]

Instead of such overt attacks on wagon trains, the Shoshoni and Paiute more often visited the emigrant camps to trade for goods and convinced many a would-be gold-digger that Indian skill at swapping was not to be underrated. Finley McDiarmid, on his 1850 trip, was impressed that the Shoshoni were "very sharp traders. . . ."[34] A member of W. S. McBride's party sold a good rifle to a Shoshoni and received in return eight five-dollar gold pieces that later turned out to be a Cincinnati hardware merchant's tokens.[35]

There can be no doubt that the growing numbers of gold-seekers who thronged through their homeland north of Salt Lake City aroused the Northwestern Shoshoni during 1850. The California-bound travelers found it necessary to stand guard every night "against surprise by Indians who are said to be very thievish and treacherous on this route." Calvin Taylor thought that despite their horse-stealing proclivities the Shoshoni were friendly "owing no doubt to the proximity of the Mormons of whom they stand in dread."[36] Adam M. Brown described the "Digger Indians they met near Bear River Crossing" as the "most miserable specimens of the red race our eyes ever rested upon. They subsist upon roots, carrion, and a species of cricket, . . . and frequently do immense injury to the crops of grain."[37] It was the Indian propensity to raid farmers' fields

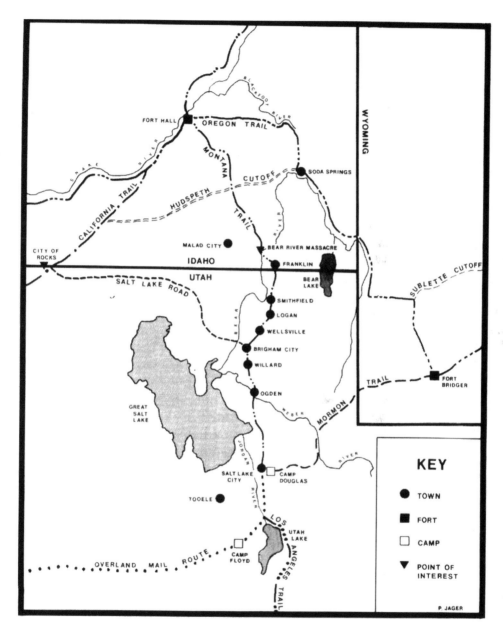

GREAT SALT LAKE AREA

that caused the chief difficulties between the Mormon people and the Northwestern bands in 1850.

In a prelude to later Shoshoni troubles, settlers at Fort Utah (now Provo) encountered problems in January 1850 when three young Mormons shot and killed Old Bishop, a Ute who refused to give up a shirt he claimed he purchased from one of the Saints. The three men then disemboweled the Indian, filled the body cavity with stones, and sank it in Provo River. Old Bishop's tribesmen soon discovered the corpse and began to kill the settlers' stock and to fire on people outside the fort, taunting them when they forted up by calling the Mormons "old women and cowards . . . [who] were afraid to fight them."[38] Fort Utah Saints asked Brigham Young to allow them to fight the Indians, and the Mormon leader "decided to grant the brethren their request."[39] Anticipating friction, Young had warned the Utah Valley settlers the autumn before to stop mixing with Indians "promiscuously." "If you would have dominion over them, . . . you must not treat them as your equals. You cannot exalt them by this process. If they are your equals, you cannot raise them up to you."[40]

With the concurrence of his council and after assurances of military aid from Captain Howard Stansbury, Young dispatched a force of 150 men from Salt Lake Valley to help the Utah Valley settlers chastise their native adversaries. In a three-day seige, eight Indians were killed. Another nineteen "ceased to breathe" when they were hunted down by horsemen on the ice of Utah Lake.[41] John Hudson, the schoolteacher at Fort Utah, assisted in the battle, explaining, "Hostilities were concluded after the annihilation of the Indians in which we were much assisted by the measles & the severity of the weather. . . . "[42] Only one white man was killed in the engagement. In this instance, as on numerous future occasions, the feeding policy yielded to fighting Indians who made bold to challenge the Mormons because, as Captain John W. Gunnison explained, the white settlements had "encroached on hunting and fishing grounds, and the usual winter camping places, and scared off the game."[43]

Hostilities also developed during 1850 when Shoshoni winter camps were usurped by small Mormon settlements along the Weber River, at North Ogden, and at a few scattered sites in Box Elder (present Willard and Brigham City). A band of "Weber Utes" (actually Shoshoni) with about sixty-five warriors under their chief, Little Soldier, camped on the south side of the Weber River, while another band of Northwestern Shoshoni numbering about eighty-five warriors under an old chief, Terrikee, camped at the big bend of the river. Mormon leaders were uneasy about the number of Indians near their homes and in February 1850 organized a militia company of thirty-five men that included about fifteen Gold Rush emigrants wintering in Ogden. When the latter resumed their journey in the spring, the company was reduced to only twenty members.[44]

Both Shoshoni groups also left in the spring, but Terrikee led his people back to Ogden in August. They began acting "very bad," riding "through grain fields and melon patches . . ." and Chief Terrikee soon sent his people away again and intended to leave shortly himself. But on the night of September 17, when he tried to retrieve his ponies out of Urban Stewart's cornfield, he was "killed dead on the spot" by Stewart who thought he was stealing corn. Stewart sought help from his neighbors. When they refused, feeling it too "dangerous to do so,"[45] Stewart asked a furiously anti-Mormon emigrant, Reverend J. W. Goodell, for help, but Goodell also turned him down.

The frightened Mormon farmers and their families and Goodell sent for help and crowded into the settlement to wait. While the militia was gathering, word came that Terrikee's band had pursued two settlers and butchered one, an emigrant, who, according to Goodell, had joined the Mormon church only the day before. The new convert, a "Broth Camel" (Brother Campbell), left a wife and family in the States but had also been planning to take a second wife under the Mormon law of polygamy.[46]

About 150 militia set out immediately for Ogden, the news of the killing tending "to hasten this expedition very much."[47] A flurry of orders dispatching troops, ordering a fort built, and commanding that the Northwestern Shoshoni be reproved demonstrate how seriously Brigham Young and his military lieutenants took the incident.[48]

Young's military leader, General Daniel H. Wells, then sent old mountain man Barney Ward to bring about peace. Ward was instructed to tell the Shoshoni that any white man who said the Mormons were not friends of the Indians was a "*liar.*"[49] Wells also agreed to negotiate with the Shoshoni about their land claims if "they will stop molesting our people."[50] In Ogden, the militia made a fruitless attempt to catch the guilty Shoshoni and only succeeded in mistaking each other for marauding Indians.[51] General Horace Eldredge, in his final report of the incident to Wells, concluded, "We found some of their seeds on the road which they had spilled and would not take time to gather. It is my opinion that they are satisfied. They have had blood for blood, Campbell for Terrikee, and will return to their tribe contented."[52]

Concerned for the safety of unwary emigrants, General Wells sent out parties to warn wagon trains to be on guard and to talk to the Indians. Five troopers were to read a proclamation to emigrants stating:

> To the Emigration on the Road
> We have sent Master L. Robinson with a small detachment to inform you that a little difficulty having occurred with the Shoshones or Snake Indians, you should be on your guard, you should travel in companies and keep a good watch, especially at nights. We do not know as there is any danger but "caution is the parent of safety" therefore be wise and harken to the counsels of wisdom.
>
> > Yours Respectfully
> > By orders of Brigham Young
> > Gov.[53]

The decade of the 1840s had started out on a note of harmony that persisted until 1845 when travelers' irresponsible and ethnocentric actions and the destruction of grasses and game stirred the Indians to retaliate. A major source of Indian anger was white refusal to acknowledge aboriginal ownership of the land, and Shoshoni anger increased when Salt Lake and other nearby valleys were settled by the aggressive Mormons in 1847 and after. Indian raiders began to shoot and steal livestock and avenge the deaths of their slain people. The most serious hostilities between the newcomers and the native inhabitants occurred, perhaps naturally enough, in the settled Mormon areas in Utah, such as Fort Utah, where a three-day battle resulted in twenty-seven Indian deaths and one Mormon casualty. More far-reaching in its consequences was the death of the Shoshoni chief, Terrikee, and troubles only increased as Mormon farmers continued to press north into Northwestern Shoshoni territory.

Mormon Indian policy in Utah was shaped during the first three years of settlement. Despite the constant pleas of Brigham Young to his people to treat the neighboring Indians as brothers in the gospel, native hostility over white encroachment periodically activated enough resentment on the part of the Saints that Young had to accede to requests for the chance to spill Indian blood. It was significant that in the battle at Fort Utah, federal troops from Captain Stansbury's command fought shoulder-to-shoulder with the Mormon militia, foreshadowing the way in which the aid of United States soldiers would be welcomed in later years against recalcitrant Northwestern Shoshoni. It was also clear that Young entertained the ethnocentric views of the time that native Americans were not the equal of whites and must be treated as inferior people.

The advent of the Forty-niners introduced a complex new dimension to Indian relations in the Great Basin. The gold-rushers were young and impatient to get to the diggings in California, and, as mere passers-by, had little patience with the Mormons, whose sinister hand they could discern in every Indian problem. Their great numbers made busy thoroughfares out of the western trails, cluttering and denuding the watercourses that were the chief resources of the natives. Inevitably they introduced a new and trying era in Indian relations.

Thousands of newcomers to California also made certain the political organization of that area into a territory. Under the Compromise of 1850, Brigham Young became governor and superintendent of Indian Affairs for Utah, but he wasn't sworn in until February 3, 1851. Although Brigham Young's policies as superintendent were influenced by his religious views of the natives as descendants of the tribes of Israel, he frequently fell back upon frontier beliefs about the supremacy of the white man. Nevertheless, he was more knowledgeable about the Indians in his jurisdiction and quicker to act than the Oregon superintendent who was simply too far removed from the Shoshoni in the Boise and Fort Hall regions to be effective and who remained ignorant about these bands for many years.

THREE

Early Territorial Supervision of Indian Affairs

Throughout the 1840s there was no established governmental system to treat with the Shoshoni or Northern Paiute along the western trails, and until the Compromise of 1850, there was no formal government in the vast region that became Utah Territory. After the acquisition of Oregon Territory in 1846, another three years elapsed before a territorial government was proclaimed at Oregon City on March 3, 1849. But the capital city was too far removed for the governor, who was also the superintendent of Indian affairs, to have any control over the Boise and Bruneau Shoshoni and especially the Fort Hall and Lemhi Shoshoni and Bannock.[1] Joseph Lane, the first superintendent, did his best to describe the homelands of the Shoshonis, or Diggers, and the Ponastas (Bannock) and numbered the former at about 2,000 and the latter at 550. Lane initiated some form of supervision by recommending on October 13, 1849, the appointment of one agent for the tribes between the Cascade Mountains and Fort Boise and a subagent for the Shoshoni occupying the area from Fort Boise to the Rocky Mountains.[2] But by February of 1850, the Office of Indian Affairs in Washington, D.C., reported that of the three men appointed as Indian agents to Oregon, all had resigned. The governor then suggested that one agent and four subagents be appointed for the eastern region of Oregon.[3]

A new superintendent, Anson Dart, reported in July 1851 that he had not been able to visit the Shoshoni and Bannock and therefore had no semblance of control over them.[4] He described the Indians to Elias Wampole, a new agent, as having "thievish propensities," and regretted that there was no military force in the territory. He recommended that Wampole go as far east as Fort Hall to warn travelers "of the inevitable consequences" of any depredations. Wampole was also "to persuade, if possible, the Emigrants to treat the Indians kindly . . . [and] to check the reckless spirit that is sometimes observable among the emigrants and other white men passing through their country."[5] September of 1851 found Dart pleading for a small force of troops to be stationed in "the Snakes' country before the emigration of next summer comes over the plains."[6]

The response of the Shoshoni and Bannock of the Snake River area to lack of supervision was to wonder why the Great Father in Washington did not meet with them and give them presents like the ones the Eastern Shoshoni and the Northwestern bands were receiving from Brigham Young. They could not grasp why an imaginary dividing line along the forty-second parallel placed them under the jurisdiction of a government official in Oregon City when Salt Lake City was so close.

After the Territory of Utah was proclaimed on September 9, 1850, Brigham Young took the oath of office as governor on February 3, 1851, and began to administer the Indian affairs of his new jurisdiction, which included all of present Utah, all of Nevada except for the southern tip, the western third of Colorado, and the small southeastern corner of Wyoming with its frontier post of Fort Bridger. To supervise this immense area, "larger than Texas,"[7] Superintendent Young divided it into three districts: (1) Henry R. Day was to direct the Parvan Agency "west of the Shoshone nation," which included the "Weber," "Timpanogos," and "Lake" Utes, and "Parvants," "Sanpitch," and "Diggers to the rim of the Great Basin"; (2) Stephen B. Rose was to head the Uinta Agency, which included "all of the Snakes or Shoshones, . . . [and] the Uinta and Yampa & all other tribes South and east of the Eastern rim of the Great Basin"; and (3) Jacob Holeman was to direct the Parowan Agency, which included "all the country lying west of the eastern rim of the Great Basin and South of the South line of the Parowan Valley to the Western bounds of the Territory," "the home of the Piedes," "Piutes," and the "Cumembahs" (Western Shoshoni).[8] Young's simple organization to supervise the Indians gave him an advantage over the Oregon agents, but the Western Shoshoni and Northern Paiute were almost as distant from his headquarters as the Snake River Shoshoni were from Oregon City.

In a report to the commissioner of Indian affairs, Brigham Young

Brigham Young, President of the Mormon church, Governor of Utah, and Superintendent of Indian Affairs in Utah Territory, 1853. *Utah State Historical Society.*

described the Indians under his jurisdiction. The Eastern Shoshoni were the "chivalry of the tribe, and generally have horses and arms, and are always friendly to the whites." The Western Shoshoni, whom he called Cumembahs, "are so-called snake diggers . . . [and] live in small excavations in the ground with grass and brush pulled up around to break off the wind, with perhaps no cover but the canopy of heaven." They "had no clothing, arms or anything else. . . ."[9]

When emigrant troubles with the Indians did flare up in 1851, they centered not in Utah but around Fort Hall.When the John L. Johnson Company split over whether or not to post a night guard at their camp near Bannock Creek, one group decided to forgo the onerous task, while the other established a night watch. The first group, just a hundred yards away from the second, lost all of their oxen while the second camp lost only a few animals. The fortunate ones joined in trying to retrieve the stolen oxen for their sleepyheaded companions who had dreamed away their draft animals.[10]

On July 18, 1851, while camped on the Portneuf River, P. V. Crawford's wagon train was warned that the Indians of the neighborhood were "expert in the business [of stealing horses]." That night the guard surprised "some Digger Indians" near the horses and "fired after them but the villains were too far out of the way."[11] Most travelers might shoot at any natives who happened along after horses or oxen were stolen rather than determine the particular Indians guilty of such indiscretions. "The innocent suffer for injuries done by others," wrote Agent Jacob Holeman.[12] Charles Howard Crawford explained how one old emigrant "mad at the Indians and chaffing his loss [of a horse] 'swore' he would kill the first Indian he saw." Near Salmon Falls the white man spied an Indian spearing salmon in the Snake River and "placed himself behind a rock, leveled his gun at the Indian's breast and fired, killing him instantly as he tumbled into the river."[13]

An Oregon Indian agent claimed that thirty-two whites had been killed by "Snake" Indians during the summer of 1851. The chief provocation for these deaths occurred when a Dr. Patterson, leader of a company of emigrants, ordered a band of Indians to vacate a campsite he wished to use. Perhaps not understanding his command, the Indians remained where they were until Patterson fired his shotgun over their heads, and then he and other members of his party pursued them on horseback to see how fast they could run. The next day the

Indians shot three of the whites in revenge and one died of his wounds. A member of the group later concluded that this was the cause of "the whole trouble with the Bannock tribe of Indians that year."[14] In the severest attack of 1851, a band of warriors ambushed a pack train near Fort Hall, broke up the party, killed eight of the men, and took $1,000 in cash, $2,000 in property, and twelve horses.[15] Lacking the protection of government officials and troops, emigrants along the trail in eastern Oregon suffered these reprisals.

Utah territorial officials, on the other hand, were persuaded by newly appointed Indian Agent Jacob Holeman to try to achieve some accord among the Eastern Shoshoni, the Northwestern bands, and other tribes. Holeman suggested to Brigham Young and the commissioner of Indian affairs that the Eastern Shoshoni and other Utah tribes should be included in negotiations that were to take place with the plains Indians at Fort Laramie on September 1, 1851, to strike a peace and secure safe passage for overland travelers. In a letter written from Fort Laramie to officials in Washington, D.C., Holeman mentioned Indian dismay over white settlers destroying the game and driving off the Indians. "The greatest complaint on this score," he said, "is against the Mormons; they seem not to be satisfied with taking possession of the Great Salt Lake, but are making arrangements to settle other, and principally the rich, vallies and best lands in the Territory. This creates much dissatisfaction among the Indians; excites them to acts of revenge; they attack emigrants, plunder and commit murder. . . ."[16] Holeman's comments underscored Indian discontent with Mormon settlers, which had first surfaced as early as July 3, 1851, when Northwestern Shoshoni took seven horses from Weber County and were unsuccessfully pursued by two Mormon expeditions.[17] Brigham Young, unaware of his new agent's charges against the Mormons, agreed with Holeman's suggestion to invite the Utah tribes to attend the Fort Laramie meeting.

On November 10, 1851, Holeman reported the results of the Fort Laramie negotiations to Brigham Young. He explained how the killing of two members of the Eastern Shoshoni tribe by Cheyenne had discouraged leaders from taking the whole tribe to Fort Laramie, but that a delegation of eighty men had finally agreed to proceed. Once at Fort Laramie, peace had been made between the Eastern Shoshoni, Cheyenne, and Sioux. Holeman felt assured that the Shoshoni would now treat the emigrants with kindness and would protect and assist them. In the past the Shoshoni had been blamed for attacks on emigrant parties that occurred during intertribal wars, but the Cheyenne and Sioux were "the principal disturbers of the peace. . . . " Holeman cautioned that because the Shoshoni were not admitted as full participants in the Laramie treaty, another treaty should be signed the next year with Utah tribes, and some assistance should be given to them or other bloodshed would occur. The important Fort Laramie Treaty, which emerged from this conference, was the first major attempt on the part of the government to try to stop intertribal wars in the general Wyoming and eastern Utah areas, and it provided for the construction of more roads and military posts in Indian territory. The treaty also initiated the long process, which eventually continued after the Civil War, to settle the western tribes on reservations. Attracted by the presents to be awarded and the promises of more goods in the future, the Eastern Shoshoni bands willingly signed the agreement. Holeman finally advised Superintendent Young that the Office of Indian Affairs should pay the Indians for the rights-of-way through their country, for the destruction of game and food, and for the timber used by the whites. If something were not done to allow the incoming emigrants "to settle the lands, quietly, the Indians may resist, and the consequence will be the shedding of much blood."[18]

Mormon pioneers continued to reconnoiter the valleys of the Wasatch Mountains in 1852 while other emigrants from the east looked forward to new opportunities in Oregon and California. Starting west brought the usual apprehensions about Indian attacks, as noted by Caroline Richardson—"we are continually hearing of the depredations of the indians but we have not seen one yet."[19] Many of the emigrant parties were more casual. Benjamin Ferris recorded that when an Indian scare occurred, only one effective weapon could be located in the entire company.[20] Brigham Young thought that such inattention to security was all right when travelers reached friendly Eastern Shoshoni territory, for they could then "relax their vigilance and usually dispense with their guard."[21]

A new phenomenon, "white Indians," became an increasing problem as "all the blacklegs in the universe" and criminals from the east and west found easy pickings from emigrant wagons.[22] The San Francisco *Alta California* of July 27, 1852, reported that a "systematically organized band of thieves" was plying the trade of murder and pillage between Salt Lake and Carson valleys. Even greater thieves, perhaps, were white traders who rivaled the Digger Indians in robbery exploits.[23] Brigham Young was incensed, too, with traders who "recklessly put the liquid fire to the lips of the untutored savage" with often fatal results.[24]

Minor difficulties occurred similar to Abigail Scott Duniway's experience when a young white man roughly pushed an Indian away from their camp, whereupon the Indian and his friends refused to accept anything offered them and left the white party, who then felt considerable uneasiness.[25] There were the usual attempts to shoot Indians stealing stock,[26] and predictable threatening gestures as Indians appeared from behind willows armed and ready for a fight. Brigham Young excoriated travelers who engaged in "the wanton and murderous practice of shooting them [Indians] whenever they show their heads,"[27] while his mouthpiece, the *Deseret News* of June 12, 1852, denounced a party of emigrants who had burned the grass "and like some quadrupeds and amphibropeds, covering with their foreaft filth all they left behind them, shot some of the Snake squaws, for the sake of a few ponies. . . . " The editor thought that a few presents and "*true talk*" would quiet the Shoshoni more than $10,000,000 in powder, lead, buckram and epaullettes. . . ." White disregard for Indian lives was common. When Abigail Duniway's party discovered a half dozen dead Indians hidden in a thicket near an emigrant camp at Fort Boise, inquiry at the fort revealed that "some emigrants had poisoned some dead oxen in order to prove a disputed point about whether or not the Indians would *eat* cattle left dead by travellers." The experiment was considered a success—nearly twenty Indians were killed by strychnine.[28]

While both Governor Young and Agent Jacob Holeman deplored the indiscriminate slaughter of Great Basin Indians and sought to achieve a better life for the natives, the two men differed sharply on the means to accomplish these ends. Holeman, as a zealous defender of Indian rights, was prepared to protect their interests at all costs. Brigham Young, more farsighted and realistic, understood that the Indian way of life had to be reconciled to the expansionism and colonization of whites and that teaching the tribesmen to settle down as farmers meant that Mormon occupation of some of their lands was actually a benefit, as they learned from their white neighbors how to plant and sow. To add to Holeman's discomfort in his relationship with the governor, his private letters to the commissioner of Indian affairs, highly critical of Young, failed to get any response. Holeman, like most Indian agents of the time, was left to chart his own course, much to his irritation and frustration.

The first accurate information about the Western Shoshoni and Paiute in the western part of Utah territory resulted from a summer trip initiated by Agent Holeman to Carson Valley. But even before Holeman left on May 12, 1852, news came in that Absalom Woodward, who held the mail contract between Sacramento and Salt Lake City had been killed. He had left California the preceding November with the mail and a four-man escort. Woodward's body was discovered about forty miles west of Salt Lake City; the other men had been killed at a spot on the Humboldt River.[29] Holeman explained to the commissioner that little was known about the "Cumembahs," the western tribes, "except that they are murdering and plundering every train that passes the road."[30] At Tooele, west of Salt Lake City, citizens were being compelled to "repel them [Indians] and seek to break up their haunts by force."[31]

Holeman was convinced that three different groups of white men were exciting the Indians and causing ill will: the traders and trappers, who cheated them or took their possessions by force; the Mormons, who usurped their land, destroyed the game, and killed many of the Indians; and, finally, the emigrants, who committed depredations through the mistaken idea that all Indians were treacherous.[32] His tentative conclusions were confirmed by the time he reached Carson Valley in late June—"the great, almost the sole cause of all the difficulties, the destruction of life and property on this route, is owing to the bad conduct of the whites, who were the first to commence it. . . . they manage to have it charged to the Indians." Some white men were in the habit of enticing Shoshoni and Paiute into camp only to shoot them down, while others shot the natives whenever and wherever they could find them. The Indians, of course, retaliated until a war existed on both sides along the 700-mile stretch of road from Salt Lake City to Carson Valley. The Indians had been so badly treated by whites that they refused to talk to white men, and Holeman had difficulty conversing with them. Game and other foods were so scarce that the Indians were "almost in a state of starvation." Those who would sit down in council with the agent still doubted his sincerity and that of the "Great Father" but said they would be very happy if government officials "walked straight, and had not forked tongues."[33]

At Carson Valley, Holeman found the Paiute also wishing for peace. The Indians charged that they were forced to retaliate when attacked by whites. "They said they had killed as many whites as the whites had killed Indians, and taken as many horses from the whites as the whites had taken from them, and no more." They were now satisfied and hoped the whites would leave them alone. On his return trip to Salt Lake City, Holeman discovered that the White Knives on the upper Humboldt and at the Goose Creek Mountains were especially troublesome but still not as flagrantly antagonistic as the whites.[34]

Both Young and Holeman recommended that a treaty be signed with the Western Shoshoni and Paiute to stop the depredations and to ensure some governmental help for the starving natives. Holeman also advised establishing two military posts, one on the Humboldt near the mouth of the south fork and one in Carson Valley.[35] Young did not agree with Holeman about stationing soldiers in the Humboldt area, believing that white settlements "would be far more productive of good, and better subserve the interest, and purposes of the Government."[36] To try to assuage the hunger and destitution of the tribes, Young authorized two men, Christopher Merkley and John P. Bernard, to serve as traders with the Indians on the Humboldt River and "in the Northern District of the Territory."[37]

By the time Holeman returned to Salt Lake City in September 1852, his relations with Young were frosty. Young had read Holeman's earlier report to the commissioner about the Mormon people dispossessing the Northwestern Shoshoni and was now in "ill humor with me." The agent was also in trouble with the commissioner, having been somewhat "*pestiferous*," as he admitted, and because he "had been reported to the President" for failure to render his accounts. Young wrote the commissioner to respond to some of Holeman's complaints.[38]

Some twenty years ago the Shoshonees claimed a small tract at the mouth of Weber upon which there is now a settlement, but abandoned it as the Buffalo receded. No Indians have ever been driven off these lands that I have ever heard of. The Shoshonees and Uintas, . . . have at various times solicited settlements to be made in their respective lands in order that they might be benefited in the articles of clothing and provisions, as the game spoken of affords . . . but a very precarious dependence for subsistence [exists]. . . . Are not the Indians better fed, better clothed, and more peaceably disposed towards the whites than before their settlement among them? An affirmative reply must be made to all these queries.

Brigham Young added that his people were helping to feed the Indians even though these *"involuntary contributions"* were "rather too *burdensome"* at times. Furthermore, Indians needed to be chastised occasionally when punishment was "richly deserved." In conclusion, he expressed the hope that Holeman's longer residence in Utah and his better acquaintance with conditions would correct his earlier views.[39]

Although Young's defense of Mormon settlement as being beneficial to the Indians might seem specious reasoning today, frontiersmen of the 1850s believed that transforming unoccupied land into productive farms was a wholly righteous and noble objective, and Young was very much in tune with his times. Brigham Young, as the Mormon prophet, was caught in the dilemma of trying to nurture and convert the Indians while also being obliged to occupy native lands so that he could achieve his main purpose of building the Kingdom of God on earth.

According to Agent Henry R. Day, assigned by Brigham Young to the Parvan (Pahvant) District with the Gosiute and central and southern Utah Indians under his jurisdiction, the natives expressed a wish to cultivate the soil "provided the Mormons would not drive them off from their lands." In a later council meeting, Agent Stephen B. Rose reported, "The Chiefs said they claimed all the lands upon which were settled the Mormans, and that they were driving them further every year, making use of their soil and what little timber there was, and expressed a wish If their Great Father was so powerful, that he would not permit the Mormans to drive them out of the Vallies into the Mountains, where they must starve."[40]

Early in 1852 Superintendent Young dispatched Holeman and Rose to Box Elder to investigate complaints from the citizens that some unscrupulous whites were violating the laws concerning trading with the Indians.[41] The two agents discovered that these friendly Shoshoni had a large quantity of American gold pieces that they claimed they had received as a result of trading horses with emigrants and in other ways, all of which Holeman thought suspicious but could not be sure the Indians had been involved in any of the depredations along the California and Oregon trails. The affair with the traders was "amicably settled,"[42] but Holeman's doubts about the Northwestern group were reignited later in the year when he found the band in the Goose Creek Mountains adjacent to the California Trail, although they assured him they were merely on a hunting excursion.[43] The incident was an early recognition by Indian agents that the Northwestern Shoshoni of the Box Elder and Cache Valley areas might well be involved in attacks on emigrant parties and was a forerunner of later events that led to the bloody encounter at Bear River between these Indians and troops in 1863.

Brigham Young warned Aline Martin, who wrote from Monroe, Michigan, for information about trail conditions, that "vigilance is a virtue" and that the Shoshoni and Bannock on the northern route near Fort Hall were apt to attack trains.[44] Young did his best to try to quiet the northern Indians, even though they were the wards of Oregon Territory and met occasionally with delegations from Fort Hall.[45] To James Palmer, writing from Salt Lake Valley, the Indians were anything but friendly in 1852—"This season there was repeated agreshone by the Indians . . . stealing cattle and horses from our people caused a feeling of indignation to arise in the minds of the sufferers. . . ."[46]

Sporadic Indian attacks continued through 1853 and especially along the Snake River in Oregon Territory. The Oregon superintendent of Indian affairs requested $67,350 for presents and treaty negotiations for all the Indians in the territory of which $13,000 was to be used in dealing with the "Snakes, Bonach and Indians on Boise River," but apparently no money was ever voted for this purpose.[47] With no agent assigned to the area east of the Cascade Mountains, Captain Benjamin Alvord, in command of troops in the territory, took it upon himself to intercede for the eastern tribes, recommending that treaties be concluded so that reservations could be set aside for the Indians. Alvord hoped to prevent white settlements in the area and warned squatters to maintain good relations with the Indians because most of the tribes had been friendly to whites since the time of Lewis and Clark.[48]

When a new superintendent of Indian affairs for Oregon, Joel Palmer, reached his post at Milwaukee, Oregon, in May 1853, he found that Anson Dart, the previous official, had departed two weeks earlier. Palmer started from scratch and asked first for a subagent to be assigned to the Indians east of the Cascade Mountains to gain their friendship and "guard the interests of the passing emigrants."[49] After securing the services of Joseph M. Garrison, Palmer instructed his new man to go to Fort Boise and travel on to Fort Hall if he had reason to believe "the safety of the emigrants will be promoted by your visiting the Indians along the road. . . ." The records do not indicate if Garrison ever made the trip.[50] The Shoshoni and Bannock of the region continued to travel to nearby Salt Lake City for conferences with Brigham Young and to receive presents.[51]

Most Indian encounters along the Snake River in 1853 concerned the time-honored Indian custom of stealing horses. While encamped at Goose Creek, D. B. Ward recorded how a member of his party was so concerned about the safety of Ward's prized $1,500 stallion that he decided to stay up all night guarding the horse at the end of a thirty-five-foot rope. While his attention was distracted, an Indian cut the rope about six feet from the halter, mounted the animal, and rode off. Ward philosophized that his well-bred animal and others like him stolen by the Indians accounted for a great number of fine horses found among the Shoshoni years later.[52] When one wagonmaster finally decided he was among friendly Indians and posted no guard, his party lost all its horses.[53] In another rather typical incident, two packers were followed for ten miles by eight Indians intent on stealing their mules. One of the Indians shot at the packers, who returned the fire, killing an Indian. Soon, almost 300 friends of the murdered Indian gathered and began searching for the two packers in the camps of emigrant trains, peeking into wagons to see if the two men were being hidden. The packers escaped by joining a large party of well-armed men.[54]

In Utah Territory, Brigham Young continued to request that a commission be appointed to treat with the Indians, to buy portions of their lands, to provide annuities that "they may not on the one hand fade rapidly from the earth by neglect and starvation, nor on the other hand be induced to plunder our citizens," or become a burden on the settlements.[55] Another trip by Agent Holeman to survey conditions along the Humboldt and in Carson Valley emphasized the need for a treaty. He met with several bands of Indians: a Shoshoni group of 600 individuals under Too-ke-mah (the Rabbit) at Thousand Spring Valley, a friendly group who intended to winter in the neighborhood of Fort Hall where there was more game; a tribe of 500 people under Ne-me-te-kah (Man-Eater), who informed the agent that if certain bad Indians along the Humboldt did not stop stealing from the whites he would "collect his band together and make them"; a small party of 200 under Paut-wa-a-vante (the Drowned Man) at the first crossing of the Humboldt; another Shoshoni group of 450 under Oh-hah-quah (Yellow Skin) at Stony Point; and a group of 600 Bannock under Te-ve-ne-wena (the Long Man) about seventy-five miles from the sink of the Humboldt.[56] All the chiefs and their people professed friendship with the whites.

On Holeman's return trip to Salt Lake City, he learned that some California traders had killed the son of Chief Ne-me-te-kah and five of his "braves" and had taken their guns and horses without any cause. The chief's heart was sick, his men were angry, and the entire band meant to kill all the whites who passed along the road. They attacked two emigrant trains, wounded four men, and took much of the stock and one wagon. With some difficulty and with the gift of all the presents he had left, Holeman was able to restrain Ne-me-te-kah by explaining the difference between unscrupulous traders and innocent emigrant parties.

Holeman told the commissioner that the California Trail was lined with trading posts liberally stocked with liquor but with few of the necessities required by the emigrants. The stations operated merely as bases for the traders to prey on Indian and emigrant alike, usually charging neighboring Indians with the depredations that occurred. Holeman met with some of the traders to try to stop their activities, but "they laughed at me; they defied me and the laws; they told me there were so many of them that they could and would do as they pleased, law or no law." He concluded that such whites were far more troublesome than all the Indians in the Humboldt region.[57] The Marysvale, California, *Daily Evening Herald* called on government authorities to put a stop to the depredations of what the editor thought was a group of about 150 white men and perhaps some Paiute who were conducting their nefarious operations along the Humboldt River and at the sink of Carson River.[58]

The Mormon settlers north and east of Salt Lake City had their share of troubles in 1853 with the Shoshoni bands who were still attempting to hold on to their aboriginal lands. In an early spring visit to the Box Elder area, Holeman met with a friendly Shoshoni group, gave them some presents "which pleased them very much, and they promised a great deal in the future."[59] The Indians at this place were so friendly that three of them were mustered in as privates in the local militia. Brigham Young attempted to continue peaceful relations with the Shoshoni by issuing passes to such *"good"* Indians as See-nâh-gee (the Beaver) and by advising his church members not to molest the Indians, "to trade fairly, & not pass bad money upon them. . . ."[60]

These halcyon days were rudely interrupted in late August when Indians killed John Dixon and John Quail in Parley's Canyon. Brigham Young immediately ordered all the settlers into forts and considered building a wall around Salt Lake City. Sarah D. Rich, whose husband was in California, slept with a loaded gun at her side, believing she would "be good for one Indian" at least.[61] But a more critical situation was developing in the Box Elder region where David Moore reported that, at Willow Creek [Willard], tension mounted when 150 Shoshoni and Bannock warriors swept into the settler's camp "at full speed, whooping & yelling & singing their war song. . . ." When Moore arrived, he found the farmers poorly prepared for defense and ordered the erection of makeshift forts at both Willow Creek and Box Elder. The Indians turned their horses loose in the grain, corn, and potato fields while the warriors themselves also harvested some of the crop. Moore thought the Indians "very bold & saucy. . . ."[62]

The day after these activities, the Shoshoni warriors suddenly descended on Willow Creek and challenged the settlers to fight. The Indians had been excited by an Indian woman who lived at the home of a white man named Crandall and who had told her people that the "ammericans were going to kill them." After a talk, the Shoshoni left. Moore reported, "The Shoshones are very bitter against us & say that this is their ground & they intend to have it. I cannot see how we can avoid a fight with them much longer. . . ."[63] In spite of Moore's concerns, a battle never materialized. Militia officials advised the settlers to be careful and avoid arousing the natives over light and trivial causes, and this no doubt forestalled a violent encounter at this time.

After the two main Gold Rush years, the character of western migration to California and Oregon changed dramatically. Parties composed mostly of men hastening to the gold field gave way in 1851, 1852, and 1853 to groups of families on their way to seek new homes. Only about 4,700 traveled the California and Oregon trails in 1851, but emigration jumped to 60,000 in 1852, and 27,500 in 1853. Of the total of 92,000 travelers, about 77 percent (71,000) chose to go to California rather than Oregon.[64]

One of the major results of increased travel along the Humboldt River was the proliferation of outlaw gangs composed of white desperadoes, the dregs of the Gold Rush who had failed to strike it rich in the diggings and who now sought easy wealth from raids on emigrant trains. Most operated from the protection of trading posts along the trail and sought at every opportunity to throw the blame for their attacks on neighboring Shoshoni and Northern Paiute. White hostility toward native tribesmen increased because of the traders' machinations, and groups of young warriors retaliated in revenge for the murders of their kinsmen. As Agent Holeman discovered on his two trips to the Humboldt, the Utah superintendency was too far distant and deficient in personnel and funds to oversee the diverse bands of Western Shoshoni and Paiute.

Likewise along the Snake River, the situation was explosive because the Oregon superintendent of Indian affairs had almost no funds and few agents to supervise the Shoshoni tribes between Fort Hall and the Boise River. The Oregon superintendent was ignorant about Indian conditions in this far-off eastern section, but Brigham Young occasionally sent an agent to observe conditions along the California Trail. The Boise and Bruneau bands were almost entirely overlooked, but the Fort Hall Shoshoni and Bannock received nominal supervision from Brigham Young and enjoyed a friendly relationship with Washakie's tribe and the Northwestern Shoshoni. However, at Box Elder and Ogden, the dispossessed Northwestern Shoshoni began to strike out at Mormon settlements, foreshadowing the serious problems to come in the 1860s.

It cannot be overemphasized that most of the Shoshoni problems stemmed from the location of the tribe astride the main western trails. It was not until late in the 1860s and 1870s that the Blackfeet, Sioux, and other plains tribes encountered as much exploitation by whites, since the buffalo herds they based their lifeway on stayed mostly north of the Oregon Trail. The Shoshoni could not avoid the main routes of travel and could not deter white travelers from destroying the grass seeds, roots, and small game they relied on for survival. Their problems with the white man were at hand, and the intruding white government was not sufficiently interested or equipped to deal with the question of native survival.

FOUR

The Ward Attack and Continuing Starvation

Disinterest among policy makers in Washington, D.C., regarding Indian problems continued to inhibit the ability of territorial officials to address the needs of Indians in the western region. The changes brought about by the influx of whites into the West increased between 1854 and 1856. A brutal massacre near Boise aroused the Oregon superintendent and military authorities to police the Snake River route, and the angry Shoshoni along the Humboldt were increasingly unwilling to continue to put up with emigrant attacks and the destruction of native food sources. Early Mormon interest in Cache Valley aroused suspicions among the Northwestern Shoshoni of northern Utah that this prized spot would soon fall to the plow of energetic Saints. As white incursions increased, the Shoshoni expressed dismay at not receiving compensation for their lands, and settlers were anxious to have native claims extinguished so they could establish clear title. Traditional Indian lifeways could not respond to the white invasion, and displacement continued rapidly. Efforts initiated to teach Indians to farm were not entirely successful. White leaders at all levels failed to develop consistent and coherent policies to deal with these predicaments, and this exacerbated dissension between whites and Indians and within the official bureaucracy established to deal with the problems.

In 1854 the eastern Indian tribes were still relatively unknown to the Oregon superintendent in spite of ongoing requests for more money to hire agents to supervise and inform him about the Snake River region. The Shoshoni and Bannock of Fort Hall still looked to Salt Lake City and Brigham Young for presents and an opportunity to talk to someone in authority. In February a deputation of seven Bannock visited Salt Lake City and were housed in the agent's office for several days while a winter storm raged outside. They professed friendship for all whites but complained on "several occasions the Emigrants had treated them badly. . . ."[1]

Lack of interest in Snake River Indian affairs took a sharp turn in August, however, when news arrived of a cruel massacre twenty-five miles east of Fort Boise. A large emigrant train had split into three sections. The last section, made up of four families in four wagons and two unattached young men, fell several miles behind the lead sections. A band of Indians stopped the wagons and indicated they wanted to trade for whiskey but were told there was none. The Indians shook hands and appeared friendly but suddenly opened fire, killing George Lake, and wounding Empson Cantrell and Walter G. Perry, both of whom died later. After taking five horses, the warriors left, having suffered two casualties themselves. A survivor subsequently testified that the Indians were led by two white men dressed and painted as Indians.[2]

The next day, August 20, 1854, the distraught party caught up with the advance sections led by Alexander Ward and discovered that Ward's group had been almost annihilated. About thirty Indians (probably Boise Shoshoni) had approached the five wagons in the Ward train. One Indian attempted to take a horse by force, cocking his weapon and aiming it at a man in the group. The white man thereupon shot and killed the Indian, starting a battle that ended in the deaths of eighteen of the party of twenty. Thirteen-year-old Newton Ward was shot in the side with an arrow and then knocked unconscious and left for dead. He was picked up by a group of seven other emigrants under Alex Yantis who came up shortly after the attack. Newton's brother, fifteen-year-old William, was shot through the right lung with an arrow that protruded through his back. He hid in the brush until the Indians left and then, unable to extract the arrow, started down the trail. After five days of wandering, he arrived at Fort Boise where the arrow was cut out. Both boys survived.[3]

Alex Yantis and his seven men came upon the Ward trail while the Indians were still plundering the wagons. The whites attempted to rescue the women and children who were still alive, but lost a young man named Amens who was killed in the fight that followed. They were forced to withdraw and to leave the women and children to their fate. Two days later an eighteen-man force from Fort Boise reached the site of the massacre to find that the women and young girls had been ravished. A piece of hot iron had been thrust into one woman's body; the pregnant Mrs. Ward had been raped and her body dismembered; a third woman had been scalped. The children were hung "by the hair of the head over the blazing fire, untill burned to death, while the poor distracted mother was reserved [as] a spectator to their barbarous cruelties." Evidence from later investigations proved that the Indian women were responsible for mutilating the bodies. In addition to killing eighteen people, the Indians took the five wagons, forty-one head of cattle, five horses, about $3,000, and several guns and pistols.[4]

By September 6 Agent R. R. Thompson was ready to accompany troops into the Snake country on an Indian-hunting expedition, but suggested that "winter and spring would be the time when they would be least able to make resistance, as they are then half famished, and would not find the same protection in the brush as they do in summer when the leaves are on"[5]—a similar consideration would later influence General Patrick Connor when he attacked the Northwestern Shoshoni at Bear River in 1863. While Thompson was making preparations, Superintendent Joel Palmer offered the position as agent to Nathan Olney, expecting him to direct the Indian affairs of the new district of Southeastern Oregon. In a long letter Palmer outlined Olney's duties, including bringing the perpetrators of the Ward Massacre to justice and becoming acquainted with the various Snake River tribes so that better control could be exercised over them. But Olney did not get to the Snake country in the fall of 1854, and it was left to Thompson to accompany Major Granville O. Haller's troops to awe the Indians and capture the murderers of the Ward party.[6]

The military expedition was at Fort Boise by September 12, 1854. Thompson reported to Palmer that one squad of six men shot down three of four captured Indians when they became frightened and broke away. A band of Bannock under Chief Oete were subsequently taken prisoner and given a stern lecture about how they were to behave toward all whites. The troops killed two more Indians, gathered in about twenty Indian horses, gave forceful speeches to other bands, and visited the Ward Massacre site.[7]

In Utah Territory, ill-feelings between Agent Jacob Holeman and Brigham Young were resolved when the commissioner of Indian affairs appointed Edward A. Bedell of Warsaw, Illinois, to replace

Holeman. In spite of Holeman's abiding interest in bettering the conditions of the Indians, whose care he was charged with, and regardless of requests for treaties with the tribes, he received little official encouragement from his superiors in Washington, D.C. With the arrival of Bedell on August 15, 1853, Brigham Young divided Utah Territory into two districts—the western area from the border of California to approximately present U.S. Highway 91 under Stephen B. Rose, and the eastern area from there to the Continental Divide under Bedell. Young asked for four subagencies—one for Carson Valley and the Humboldt River area, a second for the Green River region, a third for the country around the confluence of the Green and Grand rivers, and a fourth for southern Utah in Washington, Iron, and Millard counties—but as usual there was no response to this request. When Bedell died at Green River on May 3, 1854, and Rose returned to New Jersey, Dr. Garland Hurt was appointed to replace Bedell, and a Mormon, George W. Armstrong, replaced Rose.[8]

Young asked his agents to post a notice to emigrants on the California Trail that "little danger is apprehended until after passing Goose Creek Mountains" and asked emigrants to treat the Shoshoni kindly because they had been very friendly. He was no doubt referring to the Northwestern bands from Box Elder and Cache Valley who frequently hunted in the Goose Creek Mountains.[9] But Charles Kleinsorge's party found that depredations could occur even at Goose Creek when Indians drove off fifty head of cattle. Only a determined charge by six of their party led to a recovery of the stock.[10] And the theme of white bandits masquerading as Indians recurred again in an editorial by Brigham Young in the July 13, 1854, edition of the *Deseret News*, which warned of "a numerous and well organized band of *white* highwaymen, painted and disguised as Indians" who murdered and robbed emigrants of their stock "by wholesale."

The Indians along the Humboldt could expect little mercy from companies who had suffered casualties on the western journey. One train of 172 well-armed people carried twelve scalped travelers with them and thereafter "shot and killed every Indian they met on sight. . . ."[11] The Humboldt natives retaliated against such indiscriminate killings by seeking revenge on innocent parties. In one instance, a group of seven travelers was attacked near the Humboldt River and four were killed. The remaining three were stripped of their clothes and forced to trudge along naked in search of help.[12]

Intertribal fights also occupied the Utah superintendent. In September 1854 about eighty Shoshoni attacked a camp of Utes near Provo in an altercation over some stolen horses. Five of the Utes were killed. In frustration and anger, the Utes swore vengeance on all citizens of the territory, whereupon the sheriff of Utah County requisitioned the governor for troops to "kill every damned Rascal" in both tribes.[13]

Even friendly Chief Washakie had his troubles with white men. The commissioner of Indian affairs received a request to settle the question of whether or not ferrymen had a right to operate on Green River when no treaty had been signed with the Eastern Shoshoni. The Shoshoni contended that until some agreement was made, the land, timber, and rivers legally belonged "to them until purchased of them by treaty. . . ."[14] There is no record of any action taken to meet Washakie's demands. Brigham Young did his best to keep peace with the Eastern Shoshoni,[15] inviting the tribe to visit Salt Lake City "when the moon will be full, to give good light," and suggesting that the Indians camp at Parley's Park where the grass was good and where beeves would be given to Washakie's people. Young concluded, "I love the Shoshones very much. They have always been good, and friendly to us, and we think a great deal of them."[16] The superintendent advised Washakie to settle his people on Green River at Brown's Hole where men would be sent to teach them to farm.[17]

Superintendent Young also met with seven chiefs and their bands of Northwestern Shoshoni about five miles north of Ogden and advised them to go to the buffalo country for the winter since they had not raised any grain and the game was gone. He promised to send men to teach them to farm the next year.[18]

In his annual message given December 11, 1854, to the territorial legislature, Young gave a detailed comparison of the Ute and Shoshoni peoples. He thought the Shoshoni were "rather superior to the Utahs, and provide better for their own living, although a large party of *them* have quartered upon the settlements north during the past summer." He indicated that the settlers had been very helpful in ameliorating the difficult condition of the Shoshoni, furnishing them with provisions, clothing, guns, and ammunition, and even raising grain for them and building houses for some of the chiefs. But he pointed out that these helpful services were "a severe tax and burden upon the people" and looked forward to signing treaties with the Indians so that the settlers would be secure against future depredations. He nevertheless warned the white farmers to be on their guard always and to prepare for their own defense. Young praised the experiment being conducted in Weber County, where the citizens were adopting Indian families into their homes and providing food and shelter in exchange for labor. He was aware that "a vast deal of patience and forbearance would be required to carry out this policy" but hoped for its success so that it could be applied to the whole territory.[19]

As 1855 opened, Oregon Superintendent Palmer explained to the commissioner of Indian affairs that he had sent Major Haller and a military expedition to secure the punishment of the "retches" who had brutally massacred the Ward party. Initially, Haller was to remain in the vicinity of Fort Boise throughout the winter since Agent Nathan Olney would not be able to start his duties in the new Snake country district until spring.[20] In instructions to Olney, Joel Palmer warned against lavishing too many presents on the Indians of the Snake and Salmon rivers, asked him to compile an accurate description of the various tribes of "Banacks and Mountain Snakes" together with a proper census, and advised him to prepare for the signing of treaties "for the extinguishment of their title to the Country. . . ."[21]

By April Major Haller's troops were accompanying Agent Olney to the Fort Hall area to avenge the murders of the Ward party. Dimick B. Huntington, Indian guide and interpreter for Brigham Young, brought in a report from a half-breed that the Indian attack on the Ward wagon train had been instigated "to avenge the ravishing of one of their squaws and the stealing of their horses by a company of whites passing through the country. . . ."[22] Olney's late August report summarized his summer activities. Olney and Haller's troops visited Fort Hall, Camas Prairie, and Shoshone Falls without finding any large Indian encampments because most of them had gone to the "Buffelow" country. The agent distributed a few presents to the wandering families he did find, and then he and the major returned with most of the troops to Fort Boise. Lieutenant Edward H. Day was sent with a small command to check out the Salmon River area and captured six of the murderers of the Ward group, but Olney did not explain how Day determined the Indians were guilty of the Ward Massacre. Day and his men "shot dead" three of the captives, two escaped, and the last one was hanged. Day was ordered to remain at Fort Boise long enough to escort a train of twenty-five emigrant wagons through hostile Indian country before rejoining the main command at winter quarters at The Dalles, where Olney also went for safety.[23]

Lieutenant Day incidentally reported that while at Salmon River he had met a party of Mormons who were "makeing preparations to commence a settlement on that stream."[24] At a General Conference of the L.D.S. Church on April 6, 1855, Brigham Young had appointed twenty-seven men to establish a mission station among "the buffalo-hunting Indians of Washington Territory." The group finally established Fort Lemhi on a principal branch of the Salmon River. By late October the missionaries had erected a stockade, harvested some crops, and baptized fifty-five Indians. The Bannock and Shoshoni were friendly. Chief Le Grand Coquin of the local tribe expressed the wish that the Mormons would show his people how to farm because the traders were not allowed to sell the Indians ammunition so they could hunt. To the Shoshoni and Bannock of the Fort Hall and Salmon River area, there was finally some hope that white settlers might help them learn how to survive in the new environment.[25] More realistically, there was also the threat of encroachment from an established white settlement.

In Utah Territory Dr. Garland Hurt was turning out to be as much of a trial for Brigham Young as Jacob Holeman had been. Hurt arrived in the territory on February 5, 1855, determined to approach Mormonism and its leaders with an open mind, but by May 2 he wrote the commissioner of Indian affairs that, in his opinion, Brigham Young was turning the Utah Indians against the United States. The Mormon missionary program was creating a distinction in the minds of the Indians that there was a difference between the Mormons and the "Americats" or "Mericats," the other citizens of the nation. Before the year was out, Hurt made another major decision —the way to deal with the Indians was to settle them on "reservation" farms. Without official authorization, he established agricultural colonies at Corn Creek, Twelve-Mile Creek in Sanpete Valley, and near the mouth of Spanish Fork Creek. After the fact, and to the consternation of the commissioner, he then asked for a congressional appropriation of $75,000 to $100,000, which was not forthcoming.

Throughout his tenure Agent Hurt continued to support these Indian farming ventures in central Utah, effectively appropriating almost all district funds for the projects and for some reason excluding the Northwestern Shoshoni or Western Shoshoni from the experiment—an oversight the Indians did not understand.[26]

Holeman had promised some presents to the Indians of the Humboldt River area to keep them from attacking emigrants prior to Hurt's arrival, so Hurt left Salt Lake City on July 16 for a two-week trip to honor this commitment and met with 400 Indians under Chief Nemeticky, or Nim-ah-tio-cah. After distributing the presents, which included some cattle to assuage the hunger of the starving Indians, Hurt presented a treaty composed of eight articles he hoped would bring a lasting peace with the assembled "Sho-sho-nee nation of Indians (commonly called Snake Diggers)." The Indians were to receive the sum of $3,000 by September of 1857 in return for granting a right-of-way through their homeland, allowing white farmers to settle in their country, and promising to stop depredations on travelers and white settlers. There was no stipulation about paying for Indian lands, and the very general terms of the simple agreement did not receive the support of the Office of Indian Affairs, which never submitted it to the Senate for ratification.[27]

On the return trip to Salt Lake City near the Goose Creek Mountains, Hurt and party sighted an Indian some distance away and sent a horseman to bring him in for questioning. The frightened native took "off at a rapid rate," but was overtaken and escorted to talk with Hurt, who "gave him a lecture for running away. . . ." The Indian explained that he thought "they were *Californians and Would Kill Him.*" He was given a dinner and released. A member of the Hurt delegation mentioned that the region surrounding the junction of the Sublette Cutoff and the Salt Lake Road was neutral ground between the Shoshoni and Bannock tribes.[28] It is, therefore, difficult at this date to determine which Shoshoni group was responsible for specific emigrant attacks at the junction and offers one explanation for the many Indian-white encounters that took place in this no-man's land.

In 1855 Washakie sent word to Superintendent Young that his Shoshoni people wanted to learn to farm and asked Young to select a piece of arable land on Green River because the chief "could not trust his own judgment." The superintendent reported to the commis-

Washakie's band. *Smithsonian Institution.*

sioner that there was some dissatisfaction among the tribe because the government had failed to compensate them for their lands and mentioned that the Indians had benefited from the Mormon settlements,[29] but on October 12, 1855, Young was compelled to issue a warning that the Shoshoni and Utes had begun hostilities at Green River by killing Edward Edwards, William Behunin, and Wiseman Hunt. Governor Young dispatched troops and pleaded with citizens "to omit no opportunity for conciliating the Indians and securing their friendship."[30]

On his July trip to the Humboldt, Garland Hurt had met with two groups of Northwestern Shoshoni and dispensed tobacco and shirts to Little Soldier's band and gave presents to a small party of Washakie's tribe fishing at the mouth of Bear River.[31] About a month later, a report came in from Box Elder that some Shoshoni from Fort Hall "under pretense of gleaning, are committing great depredations on the wheat still in the fields."[32] Lower Bear River was a favorite hunting and camping spot for the Shoshoni, and Brigham Young had granted licenses earlier in 1855 to I. Hockaday and J. M. Hockaday to trade with the Indians to keep them supplied and to reduce the drain on the settlers. But not all the Shoshoni were satisfied with "gleaning" presents from the agent or goods from traders. On Garland Hurt's return from the Humboldt River, he met a "rough looking set of fellows" on the Salt Lake Road east of the Deep Creek Mountains who had obviously been stealing because they had four or five head of horses with freshly cut ears. Hurt gave the Indians some presents but "lectured them severely" about stealing horses from the white people.[33]

In early September Dr. Hurt held a grand council meeting in Salt Lake City with a large number of "Snake Indians" (probably Eastern Shoshoni) under Ti-be-tow-ats, another band of "northern Snakes" (Fort Hall Shoshoni) under Ka-tat-o and several groups of Ute Indians under the chieftains, White Eye, An-ta-ro of the Yampa Ute, Tia-tick of the Timp-no-quint band, Sow-i-ett's son, Tab-ba of Arrapeen's band, and Pe-teet-neet of the Spanish Fork band. The Shoshoni came after hearing rumors that government officials were to sign a treaty with them. While the Shoshoni assembled in a line opposite the Tabernacle, the Utes appeared near the Deseret Store painted black and prepared for battle. It took all of the ingenuity of interpreter Dimick B. Huntington to prevent an attack on the unarmed Shoshoni. The

Utes finally laid down their guns, although a few braves still tried to conceal bows and arrows under their blankets. Eventually, there was much handshaking and embracing between the two tribes before they settled down to smoke the peacepipe and to partake of refreshments furnished by Hurt.

The Shoshoni complained "that they had permitted the white people to make roads through all their lands and travel upon them in safety, use the grass and drink the water, and had never received anything for it, although the tribes around them had been getting presents." Agent Hurt, in agreement, argued that it was unprecedented in the history of United States' relations with Indian tribes not to extinguish native title to the land by purchase before allowing white settlers to move in. His contention cannot be sustained as one reviews the many instances in American history in which frontiersmen just moved onto Indian lands with no intention of paying for the privilege. The important issue for the Shoshoni was that they were not receiving annual presents as did their plains neighbors. Hurt explained further, "This delay is not only unjust to the Indians, by depriving them of their wanted hunting grounds, without paying that respect to their claim which is due them, according to our usage with other tribes, but it is equally so to the pioneer settlers, who are forced to pay a constant tribute to these worthless creatures, because they claim that the land, the wood, the water, and the grass are theirs, and we have not paid them for these things." Hurt implored the commissioner to ask for a congressional appropriation so that he could negotiate treaties with the Indians of Utah Territory.[34]

Pioneer encroachment on Indian lands without compensation was highlighted in August of 1855, when Mormon ranch hands drove about 2,400 head of "Church" cattle into Cache Valley, for generations a prized camping and hunting area for the Northwestern Shoshoni. By fall another bunch of about 600 head belonging to private owners had joined the church herd. The industrious settlers then fenced one hundred acres of land and put up over two hundred tons of hay before welcoming the first two families of settlers into the valley before winter set in.[35] John Clark Dowdle recorded, "During summer became acquainted with a great many of the Shoshone Indian, and learned a great deal of there language, which has since been very useful."[36] He also came to know Ben Simons, a Delaware Indian who had married two Shoshoni women and exercised some

influence with the various bands. Brigham Young had warned the
new settlers to pacify the Indians. Keziah Warner remembered the
Prophet's words: "There were lots of Indians and squaws here. President Young told us to be very kind to the Indians and feed them, or
else they would kill us. This we did until we had very little left for
ourselves."[37]

To secure title to all of Cache Valley, the territorial legislature, on
December 13, 1855, granted all of the valley to "Brigham Young,
Trustee in Trust for the Church of Jesus Christ of Latter Day Saints,
and those whom he may associate with him; together with all the
products and benefits arising therefrom, for a herd ground and other
purposes." During the time that Brigham Young held the post of
governor for Utah Territory, the legislature routinely assigned different valleys as herd grounds and farming areas to such prominent
leaders as Young, Heber C. Kimball, and many others. These acts
never mentioned any compensation for the aboriginal inhabitants.
One typical grant concluded with the phrase, "The said Heber C.
Kimball and William McBride shall have exclusive use and control of
said grant [Tooele Valley], during the pleasure of the Legislative Assembly. Approved Jan. 3, 1857."[38] Federal officials may not have
been aware of the practice, or if they were, chose to ignore it, realizing that the legislature of Utah was under the firm control of the Mormon leaders.

On January 5, 1856,[39] the legislature created Cache County.
Cache Valley, swarming with Indians when the first settlers moved in,
thus became the stage for a confrontation between the aboriginal inhabitants and the Mormon farmers.

─────────────── •• •• ───────────────

Along the Oregon Trail in 1856 hostilities between Shoshoni and
Bannock raiders and emigrant parties continued mainly with horse-
stealing raids against wagon trains. Although Washington Territory
had been carved out of Oregon Territory by this time, the hard-
pressed superintendent of Indian affairs in Oregon City had not
noticed much diminution in his duties as his minuscule staff of agents
tried to conciliate the tribes west of the Cascades while continuing to
allow the Indians east of the mountains to run free as they always
had. Superintendent Young, in Utah Territory, could not forbear
some criticism of what was going on in the two territories north of

him and in the process pinpointing the chief causes of problems along the Snake River and elsewhere in the region:

> The accounts of Indian hostilities in Washington and Oregon are truly painful. . . . When will the people learn to treat Indians as they themselves would like to be treated, . . . to make allowance for their ignorance, habits of life, traditions, and instead of treating them like dogs and wolves, learn to treat them kindly, and like human beings, to abstain from gratifying their own inordinate and hellish lusts with the squaws, and from destroying the reason and intellect of the Indian with their bitterest foe—the fire water, and from plundering him of his effects under the name of trade? When will the whites refrain from shooting them down for mere pastime? rather expensive sport they begin to find out, though the guilty are not the ones that most generally suffer in consequence of all these criminal practices. But who can blame the Indians for resenting such injuries.[40]

Superintendent A. F. Hedges of Oregon wrote the commissioner on October 10, 1856, regarding a renewal of hostilities among the Snake Indians and expressed concern that the powerful Nez Perce nation had joined in the war. Agent R. R. Thompson was trying to persuade twenty lodges of Snakes to winter at The Dalles in an effort to change their attitude through kind treatment during the winter months. Hedges asked for an appropriation so that he could sign treaties with the Shoshoni of the Snake River and place them on reservations.[41] As usual, nothing was done.

There was no money for treaties with the tribes along the Humboldt River in Utah Territory either, but Agent Garland Hurt continued his annual visit to the tribes to award presents. Hurt left on May 17, 1856, and met first with a group of sixty Shoshoni at Thousand-Spring Valley, about 140 miles northwest of Salt Lake City between Wells, Nevada, and the Goose Creek Mountains. These men, women, and children were "very destitute and degraded." Their chief, Sitaski, responded to questions about a reported massacre of the Carlos Murray family by admitting that it was probably true, "for he had understood that Murray was a very bad man, and had killed an Indian the year before. . . ." The next day Hurt met about forty warriors "dressed and painted in the most fantastic style" whom he suspected of being the perpetrators of the murders but secured from them only a gold pencil and earring having belonged to Mrs. Murray. The entire band numbered about 150 people composed of "Utahs, Cum-um-pahs, Snakes, Banacks, and Diggers, who had evidently col-

lected here for the purposes of plunder." From this point on, the
Hurt party found the road thronged with Indians. Hundreds of them
gathered around the expedition's camp at night hoping for handouts
of food. They were starving and said that many of their children had
died of hunger during the winter.[42]

At the Sink of the Humboldt, about fifteen miles south of present
Lovelock, Nevada, Hurt was visited by 200 Paiute, as destitute as the
Shoshoni, but able to speak English, apparently because of an earlier
residence in California. He also encountered another band of about
150 Paiute and a small band of Washoe Indians who had been attempting without much success to collect rent from the settlers. On
his return trip Hurt reached the Sink of the Humboldt to discover 200
or more Paiute harvesting a species of grass seed, "somewhat re-
sembling the millet in size and taste of its grain, and [which] grows in
great abundance upon the shores of the lake. . . . This seed consti-
tutes an important article of food with them, and large quantities of
it are stored in deposits underground for winter."

Beyond a place he designated as Stony Point, Hurt and his companions met emigrants almost hourly who said that the Indians had
become treacherous and were attacking wagon trains day and night.
The emigrants had found the bodies of three white people buried
near Gravelly Ford, a crossing of the Humboldt River about forty-five
miles east of present Battle Mountain, Nevada. A band of 150 Indians under To-sow-witch, when questioned about the burials, refused any information. Many emigrants were camped along the river
with 2,000 head of cattle and horses among the trains. During the
night an attack was made on a camp of Missouri emigrants, but only a
horse was killed. The next day Hurt learned from some Indians that
they had fired the shots because the cook of the company had hit one
of the Indians on the head when he had asked for some bread.[43]

When Hurt met Chief Nim-ah-tee-cah, the Indian leader said the
whites were to blame for making his young men "to-buck [mad],"
because the emigrants refused to sell powder so that the Indians
could hunt game. One band of Shoshoni under Shocup had farmed
the season before under the guidance of a white settler and had
grown large crops of wheat, potatoes, and squash. These Indians were
certainly unique because the rest of the Shoshoni along the road were
involved in depredations on emigrant trains in an attempt to get am-

munition and food. Hurt thought the Indians between the head of Humboldt River and Bear River had been the most troublesome during this travel season—"We scarcely met a train who had not had some of their property stolen, or, been fired upon. . . ." Hurt estimated that 300 head of cattle and 60 or 70 horses and mules had been destroyed or stolen on this section of the road adjacent to neutral ground between the Bannock, Snakes, and Cum-um-pah tribes. In the opinion of the agent, if the government did not take some kind of action, the merciless deeds of these Indians would surpass any recorded in the "history Indian barbarity."[44]

The Eastern Shoshoni under the firm hand of Washakie persisted in friendliness toward travelers and farmers even though they were the only tribe that had not received presents among the ten tribes participating in the Treaty of Fort Laramie in 1851. In August 1856 Young sent William Hickman and two other men as temporary agents to distribute $3,756.50 worth of presents to the tribe to insure peace.[45] The three agents reported that not only was Washakie friendly but that he was also willing for whites "to occupy as much of his land as they want or any other favor his country affords."[46] Young advised the Eastern Shoshoni to settle down, build homes, farm, and to learn to read and write.[47]

Brigham Young solicitously retained his friendship with the Eastern Shoshoni, and Garland Hurt pursued his promises to the Indians of central Utah to provide reservation farms,[48] but neither official did anything special for the Northwestern bands at Ogden or Box Elder, Utah. These groups provided for themselves by begging or stealing from the settlers when they were not away on a hunt or haunting the California Trail.

Mormon pioneers in northern Utah were busy occupying the Northwestern Shoshoni lands in Cache Valley. A bitter winter in 1855–56 almost wiped out the large cattle herd Mormon ranchers had driven into the valley, but the presiding elder at E.T. City near Tooele, Utah, Peter Maughan, received permission from Brigham Young to try his luck in the frozen north of Cache Valley. On July 21, 1856, Maughan and four men left to make a reconnaissance and selected a site in the southwest corner of the valley. There was some trepidation among them about the reaction from Shoshoni bands to this incursion.[49]

In August seven men with their families and two other men left for Cache Valley where they began cutting hay and built two rows of houses facing each other in "fort style." During the first winter, the small settlement, named Wellsville, experienced no trouble from the Indians of the valley.[50]

Sporadic Indian raids by Shoshoni, Bannock, and Paiute continued along the Oregon and California trails between 1854–56, but the Ward Massacre of 1854 brought an immediate response from territorial officials; however, efforts to exercise control were still extremely erratic. Conflicts along the Humboldt section of the road west were increasing, as desperate Indians struck back in an effort to get ammunition for hunting and to obtain food from emigrants. Garland Hurt's expeditions into this area provided information about the tribes but did little to protect emigrants traveling the route or provide relief for the starving natives.

In spite of ongoing neglect from the government, the Eastern Shoshoni remained friendly. The Northwestern Shoshoni were also neglected, but mainly by territorial officials, as Hurt turned his attention to solving the problems of Indians in central Utah. The infant settlement at Wellsville was a portent of future conflict but was as yet only a small dot on the Cache Valley landscape.

A policy regarding the Indians was still lacking both on a national level and a regional level. Brigham Young's responses were inconsistent and opportunistic—reacting to situations, Young based his next move on the success or failure of his last response. He would encourage his Saints to feed the Indians and would just as easily send troops to punish the Shoshoni when three men were killed at Green River. He supported spending time and energy on the reservation farms for the Utes but ignored the Northwestern Shoshoni who were not as near substantial Mormon settlements. Oblivious to a conflict of interests, Indian Superintendent Brigham Young had the legislature grant Cache Valley to him and his associates as stewards for use as a herd ground. Clearly Indian rights had given way to personal profit for the citizens of the territory.

Inexorably, the destitution of the Northwestern and other Shoshoni began to increase as Cache Valley and other lands fell under white control. A confrontation was building due to converging forces —the advance of Mormon farms, the commitment of Indians to a lifestyle that no longer worked in an environment being rapidly denuded of aboriginal food supplies, and the failure of officials to understand an increasingly tense situation.

FIVE

The Utah War and
the Mountain Meadows Massacre

In the period after 1856, the Shoshonean peoples were increasingly swept into the net of white affairs as interest in mail and freight contracts grew and an administrative bureaucracy evolved to support increasing numbers of emigrants and settlers in the West. As North American wars had always done, the Utah War entangled Indians in a clash between quarreling white factions and aggravated Indian-white tensions. In its way, the Utah War was to Shoshonean relations what the Civil War would later be to the larger Indian frontier. As with the Civil War to come, the Utah War set the stage for greater discord and an eventual final resolution that would see the Shoshoni tribes permanently subdued in 1863 and 1865 just as plains tribal insurrection would be crushed in the middle and late 1870s.

In Oregon Territory as 1857 opened, Superintendent of Indian Affairs James W. Nesmith was faced with the dismal prospect of too many Indians and too few agents to supervise them. When Washington Territory was organized in 1853, the Oregon superintendent rejoiced that he now had only half as much area to administer. However, cost-cutting officials in Washington, D.C., made the decision to combine the two jurisdictions once again under one head at Oregon City, Oregon. Nesmith traveled to Olympia, Washington, picked up Governor Issac Stevens's Indian records, and returned to Oregon City to complain to the commissioner: "The duties in either Territory while the offices were distinct afforded ample business for two Superintendents. If any change was originally necessary it was that the Country east of the Cascade Mountains should have been erected into a Separate district. Any apparent neglect or omissions in the discharge of my official duties can very properly be attributed to an excessive amount of business."[1] He asked for $45,500 for the Indians east of the mountains but had little expectation of receiving it. He had no agents to send to the tribes of the Snake River area anyway.[2]

A. P. Dennison was finally assigned to supervise the entire region from the Cascades to the Continental Divide but explained, in his annual report of August 1, 1857, that because of the "multiplicity" of his duties and the great extent of the area under his supervision he had been unable to visit the Snake River country. He wrote: "Of these Indians but very little is known. They are considered an indolent thieving people. . . ." He noted that the description Agent R. R. Thompson gave in 1854 was "as near correct as any that can be given at this time."[3]

Consistent with all this, Nesmith recommended that his huge region be divided into three superintendencies: one in Oregon west of the Cascades, another in Washington west of the Cascades, and a third east of the mountains. He explained that the Indians in the eastern area were very different in character and habits from those in the western and coastal districts and would require the "constant and vigilant attention" of a superintendent.[4] Special Agent I. Ross Browne, sent to inspect the Oregon Department, reinforced this proposal because the depredations of the Snake River Indians on emigrant trains over the past several years had definitely retarded the settlement of the two territories. He especially warned the commissioner about the Mormons and their settlement at Fort Lemhi and "the teachings of the Mormon leaders, who are constantly instigating them to acts of aggression." Browne did not want to see this fine cattle country "fall in the hands of a renegade and debased people. . . ."[5]

The Indian mission station of the Mormons on the Lemhi River had been very successful. A large number of Bannock and Shoshoni had been baptized, and conditions were so prosperous and inviting that Brigham Young and a large company of Saints left Salt Lake City on April 24, 1857 to make the long wagon trip to Fort Lemhi to visit the flourishing settlement. Young distributed presents to the Indians of the region and held a grand council with them. The young men of the mission were urged to marry the native women because "the marriage tie was the strongest tie of friendship that existed," but the few who made overtures were rebuffed by their parents who "refused to let their daughters go, or at least seemed not willing."[6]

The Indians of the Fort Hall area became quite used to Mormon wagon trains passing through their homeland to and from Fort Lemhi. In the main, the travel further cemented the strong relationship Young had developed over the years with the Bannock and Shoshoni. Young continued to receive delegations from the natives of the Fort Hall region who came to Salt Lake City to talk, receive presents, and ask for flour and ammunition.[7] However, these interactions between Mormons and Indians led to charges during the Utah War of 1857–58 that the Mormons were indeed forming alliances with the Indians and "stimulating the Indians to acts of hostility. . . ."[8]

Even before becoming president, James Buchanan had decided to replace Brigham Young as governor and superintendent of Indian affairs because of these charges and because it was alleged that the Mormons would not cooperate with government officials. Supposedly the Mormons had destroyed legal records, and non-Mormons could not receive fair treatment in a court system dominated by the Saints. Buchanan was convinced that Utah was being ruled by a despotic theocracy and was in a state of rebellion against the federal government.

Buchanan appointed Alfred Cumming of Georgia as governor and ordered an army to Utah under the command of General William S. Harney to seat Cumming and restore governmental control. Subsequently the military force was placed under the command of Colonel Albert Sidney Johnston. When it became bogged down in winter snows and the troops were forced to dig in at Camp Scott near Fort Bridger, Brigham Young used the technicality that he had not yet been legally replaced as governor. On September 14, 1857, Young proclaimed a state of martial law and sent the territorial militia into Echo Canyon to harass Johnston's troops by destroying supply trains.[9] By fall, the possibility of an all-out war was strong enough that Lieutenant General Daniel H. Wells of the Utah Legion wrote the commander of the approaching United States troops recommending that any ladies accompanying the army be placed in a separate train as the Mormon militia did not "wish to molest defenseless females."[10]

The coming of troops to Utah and the prospect of a war excited and confused the Indian tribes throughout the Great Basin and along the Snake River. Most bands decided to avoid the troubles if possible. Their main concern was to get enough food to stay alive, and they quickly perceived that the Mormons might not be able to supply provisions and presents as before. Chiefs Little Soldier and Ben Simons of the Ogden band of Northwestern Shoshoni assured both the Mormons and government officials that they wanted no part in the conflict.[11] The commissioner of Indian affairs in a sharply worded letter of November 11, 1857, to Brigham Young attacked him for exceeding his appropriations, for going on a trip into Oregon Territory "to give presents to Indians not under your control," and for the fact that Young had "studiously endeavored to impress on the minds of the Indians that there was a difference between your own sect, . . . and the Government . . . [and] that the former were their friends and the latter their enemies."[12]

The news that a United States army was on the way to discipline the Saints in their mountain home was at first overshadowed, at least in California, by steady reports of Indian-white violence along the Humboldt road. A Mr. Gibney reached Mormon Station (Genoa) on August 6 with the information that the Indians were troublesome and forcefully demanding ammunition from emigrant parties.[13] Only one company driving a herd of 1,179 cattle had no difficulties with the Indians, perhaps because the party was large and well prepared.[14]

A serious incident occurred when seven people of the Holloway party of ten were killed near the head of Humboldt River in a dawn attack by a band of Indians on August 13. Three men, one of them wounded, managed to escape. The two-year-old daughter of the Holloways was swung by the feet and her brains knocked out against a wagon wheel. Mrs. Holloway was wounded several times and, while feigning death to escape her assailants, was scalped. Another train of emigrants coming upon the marauders, frightened them away and rescued some of the stock and personal possessions including the scalp of Mrs. Holloway, which had been dropped during the Indian retreat. She recovered from her wounds and fashioned a wig out of the scalp but later lost her mind as a result of the tragedy.[15]

An Englishman named Wood lost his wife and baby when his party was attacked late in August on the Humboldt River. Wood was wounded but was able to escape with the help of two other men in the group. His wagon was looted of all his property including $1,500 in English gold coins hidden in the bottom of the wagon box. The next day three white men, described as mountaineers, came up to the main wagon train and asked permission to accompany the emigrants because the Shoshoni Indians were "very angry at the white people" who were traveling through their lands. When Wood got a good look at the men, he announced that the largest was with the Indians when his wife and child were killed. The three soon announced that the party was in Paiute territory and, no longer needing protection, left the company.

A few days later, they returned, and the big man announced that his name was James Tooly, that Wood had charged him with the killings and that he intended to shoot the Englishman as soon as he could find him. Wood stood in silence among the other emigrants as Tooly made these threats. He finally rode off without identifying Wood. But the other emigrants were angry over the affair, and when the party reached Black's Trading Post at the Sink of the Humboldt, they found Tooly enjoying the liquid refreshments of the wayside inn. Inebriated, he announced to the crowd that he had "done up a lot of Pikers, up the creek." The emigrants resolved to determine his guilt or innocence by appointing a court composed of a judge, sheriff and deputies, and a fair jury. They put Tooly under arrest, convened the court, but from the evidence could not find conclusive proof of his guilt. The judge, as a final resort, ordered the prisoner searched. In a belt under his shirt, the deputies found $500 in English gold coins. Convicted by the find, Tooly was given the choice of being shot or hung from a wagon tongue. He chose neither but broke away from his captors who immediately riddled him with bullets.[16]

The Wood incident once again emphasized the involvement of white desperadoes, many from California, who saw opportunities for plunder among the wagon trains along the Humboldt and who could masquerade as Indians. The *Sacramento Union* of August 12, 1857, reported that a highly organized band of highwaymen composed of Indians, Spaniards, and Americans was operating from a base in Truckee Valley. Three months later, on November 2, the same paper accused certain white men in the eastern California valleys of provoking and mistreating the Indians to start a war whereby these speculators "may make something out of it."

Depredations by white and Indian groups mounted during late September. A company of thirty well-armed men under John Kirk left Marysville, California, to patrol the emigrant road west of Salt Lake City to help travelers in need. The group repelled at least one attack from Indians during the journey. An emigrant train led by John Wiggins was robbed of its cattle and all personal property "except the clothing on their backs." Caroline Jones, a sister of Wiggins, was shot, mutilated, and scalped in an incident at Rocky Ford and was then lying in critical condition at Carson Valley.[17] S. G. Gibney, perhaps the same man who had reported Indian troubles on August 6, was stopped in the road at Stony Point by three Indians who demanded some gunpowder. According to the whimsical editor, Gibney, "thinking that powder was of little use without lead," drew his revolver and killed two of the assailants. Gibney claimed that at least eighty-five men, women, and children had been murdered by the Shoshoni during summer travel on the California Trail and that 1,100 horses and cattle had been taken from the emigrants.[18]

Few whites agreed with an editor of the *Sacramento Union* who pointed out that most of the natives were forced to commit depredations because white farmers and ranchers appropriated their lands and killed off the game. "The Indians rob and kill often because they are starving.[19] All the Indians ask is that they may be permitted to fish and hunt on their old grounds unmolested. . . . They should not be ill-treated for contending for their rights."[20] To the suggestion that a military post be built on the upper Humboldt, the editor thought a reservation for the Indians should be added to provide employment and food. In his opinion, the majority of attacks on emigrant parties were instigated by whites who did not seem to consider Indians as human beings. "Such men think no more of killing an Indian than they would of shooting a buck." He had been notified that the summer attacks by the Shoshoni on passing emigrant parties was caused when one wagon master informed traders that if any of his cattle were found missing the next morning he would hold them responsible. When three head of the stock could not be found, the owner gathered his men and attacked a band of Shoshoni who had just come onto the post. In the fight that followed, eighteen Indians were killed. Such "degraded" white men were responsible for much of the Indian hostility.[21]

In a report to the commissioner dispatched on September 12, 1857, Brigham Young acknowledged that the emigrant route along the Humboldt was the most difficult part of his territory to control. He assigned much of the blame for Indian attacks to a company of about 400 returning Californians who had shot at every Indian they could see. The natives had struck back and the innocent suffered for the deeds of the guilty. The Indians to the north were also committing depredations, but not to the extent of those west of the Mormon settlements. Another cause for Indian unrest was the report of troops coming to the territory, because "the sound of war quickens the blood and nerves of an Indian." Some raids had been made on cattle herds of Mormon farmers so that the neighboring tribes could "begin to lay in a supply of food when they had a chance." Pausing in his feverish preparations to meet Johnston's oncoming army, Young made three recommendations that, if followed, would allow him to control the Indians of Utah Territory: (1) travelers must stop the practice of shooting down Indians; (2) the government should provide more liberal appropriations for presents to the natives; and (3) United States troops should be kept away because "wherever there are the most of these we may expect to find the greatest amount of hostile Indians and the least security to persons and property."[22]

On the very day, September 12, that Young was penning the letter to the commissioner, a group of Mormons under Issac C. Haight in the southern Utah settlement of Cedar City, received a letter from their Prophet telling them to allow a company of Missouri emigrants to proceed in safety on the road to Los Angeles. This was the Fancher train that had passed through the upper Mormon settlements when news of the approaching United States Army was stirring the emotions of the Saints and galvanizing them into a frenzy of preparations to resist this new threat to their lives and religion. Mormon leader Heber C. Kimball expressed their spirit well: "Send 2500 troops here, our brethren, to make a desolaton of this people! God Almighty helping me, I will fight until there is not a drop of blood in my veins. Good God! I have enough wives to whip the United States, for they will whip themselves. . . ."[23]

The Fancher party had brought attention to themselves by flagrant anti-Mormon outbursts and by their failure to control their stock while passing through the Mormon communities. Also the Saints in southern Utah had already been set on fire by the exhortations of Apostle George A. Smith and were ready to defend their families and property against the coming invasion. At Cedar City the Saints refused to sell food to the Fancher emigrants, who, in retaliation, threatened to organized another military force to punish the Mormons when the train reached California. Unsure whether or not the settlers should annihilate the Fancher party before its members could carry out their threat, the Mormon leaders sent a horseman to Salt Lake City for instructions from Brigham Young. The return message from their president to allow the Missourians to proceed in safety arrived one day too late. A band of Indians, encouraged by the local Mormons, had already launched an attack on the Fanchers while they were camped at Mountain Meadows. When this assault was not successful, the Indians turned to their Mormon friends, who, afraid that news would reach California that the Saints were helping the Indians attack emigrant trains, joined in a well-planned massacre of the party. Only seventeen small children were spared. John D. Lee, who led the combined force of Mormons and Indians, later claimed that he had opposed the attack and had proceeded only reluctantly. The federal government was unsuccessful in determining the guilty individuals when the Mormon people adopted a cloak of silence. Federal officials had to be satisfied with the execution of John D. Lee almost twenty years later as the chief perpetrator of the infamous deed.[24] The Mountain Meadows Massacre convinced many Americans of the fanaticism of the Utah Saints and of their propensity to turn savage Indians against helpless emigrant parties.

In California and among most federal officials, rumors were already flying during late 1857 that Mormons disguised as Indians were attacking emigrant parties. In two typical stories, informants insisted that Saints had driven off ninety head of cattle and had killed one man of the McKuen, Dunn & Linton train near City of Rocks[25] and that some families named Dunlap, Cameron, and Frazier had suffered casualties by Mormons whose hands were "stained with this blood. . . . "[26] In the aftermath of the massacre, one correspondent to the November 14, 1857 edition of the *Sacramento Union* even charged that he had seen troops dwelling in Salt Lake City preparing to oppose Buchanan's army and that there were over one thousand Indian warriors just outside the city who intended to support the Saints in their fight against the United States.

At Fort Bridger, the coming of the troops caused much anxiety and excitement among Washakie's people.[27] Brigham Young wrote the chief a letter on November 2, 1857, which explained the superintendent's intentions toward the Utah Indians during the coming war:

> Some of the whites in the United States are very angry at the Mormons because we wish to worship the Great Spirit in the way in which we

believe he wants us to and have more than one wife, and they have sent some soldiers to this country to try to make us get drunk, to abuse women, and to swear and dispute and quarrel as many of them do.

Now we don't want to fight them, if they will only go away and not try to abuse and kill us when we are trying to do right. But if they try to kill us we shall defend ourselves but we do not want you to fight on the side of those wicked men. . . . You know that when the Americans come to you they want to lie with your squaws, but the Mormons do not. . . . And if they lie and swear, you may know they are not Mormons. . . .

I do not want you to fight the Americans nor to fight us for them, for we can take care of ourselves. I am your Brother. B.Y.[28]

By the time this letter was written, Dr. Garland Hurt had already fled the territory in fear of his life and met the troops at the Sweetwater River in Wyoming on October 23, 1857. On March 3, 1857, the Congress, acting on a recommendation of the Office of Indian Affairs, had provided for independent superintendents for the territories of New Mexico, Oregon, Utah, and Washington, and Jacob Forney was nominated for the Utah post on August 27, 1857. He was preparing to spend the winter at Camp Scott along with the other federal officials. As two superintendents in charge of Indian affairs in Utah during the winter of 1857–58, both Young and Forney wanted to keep the natives neutral in the impending war, but each suspected the other was "tampering" with the Indians. Throughout his term as ex officio superintendent of Indian affairs for Utah, Brigham Young's chief concern had always been the welfare of his people, and his supervision of the tribes under his jurisdiction took no better than second place. Many of the problems he encountered stemmed from this narrow focus. Nevertheless, the Indians had come to look upon him as a friend who understood their problems and realistically tried to help them.[29] In exploiting Indian lands as homes for his Mormon farmers, Young followed the typical frontier belief that the valleys belonged to those who could use them. The natives resolutely and persistently opposed the occupation of their homeland.[30]

The excitement and uncertainty introduced by the approach of an American army affected the Northwestern Shoshoni perhaps even more than other Indians because of their close proximity to the Mormon capital. When Dimick B. Huntington visited Little Soldier and his band on the Weber River in mid-August of 1857, the chief insisted that he had heard from a passing emigrant that Brigham Young was "a going to cut all the mens throats & take their women to wife. . . ." Huntington told Little Soldier "to be Baptised & then he could tel when the Gentiles told him a lie. he said Tom had been Baptised & he lied all the time. . . ." The Mormon interpreter rejoined that Brigham Young had been trying to persuade Little Soldier's people to learn to farm, "but they sit down on their buts & Howled like so many Woolvs until he saw it was of no use. . . ."[31] The chief indicated he was afraid of the troops but in late fall had overcome his trepidation long enough to visit Jacob Forney at Camp Scott, where he assured the agent that he had always kept aloof from Mormon delusions and was friendly toward the government.[32]

Later in August, Huntington visited about 400 Shoshoni under Chiefs Pocatello, Pibligand, and Pe- teet-neet at Brigham City, gave them six beeves and three wagon loads of bread and other provisions and then accused them of having stolen some "Calafornians" horses and mules. Pocatello "looked much down" and said he knew something about the incident and hoped Brigham was not mad at him.[33] On the way back to Salt Lake City, Huntington stopped off at Ogden Hole to prepare a feast for 100 more Shoshoni and noted, "The Breathren done first rate by the Indians."[34] A month later Huntington was sent by Young to Weber Valley to minister to the wants of another group of Shoshoni who this time received four beef cattle and four wagon loads of corn and melons.[35]

The Northwestern bands in Cache Valley watched the tiny settlement at Wellsville prosper the first summer as the pioneers raised a good crop despite the prophecies of many that the climate was too cold for successful farming. In the spring of 1857, three men opened farms about four miles to the north of Wellsville, but the isolated colony remained small and weak throughout the entire year.[36]

Peter Maughan, the leading Elder in the valley, began what came to be a running account of Indian difficulties in the Cache district by writing informative and accurate reports to Brigham Young. On June 4, 1857, he wrote his president that the day after Young had left on his trip to visit Fort Lemhi, fifty Indians appeared at Maughan's home "all stripped naked and roade around and yelled like as many fiends against you and Arrapean, and made a demand for Shirts, Flour, Powder & two Oxen, then ground their knives and charged their guns." After doing a war dance around the house, the young chief in command explained that they were mad because Young had not given them any presents, that they were hungry, "and that we were

Peter Maughan, Mormon leader in Cache Valley, Utah. *Edward Tullidge*, Tullidge's History (*Salt Lake City, 1889*), *vol. 2, p. 346.*

liveing on their Land, etc etc." Maughan gave them a cow for food, after which they promised to leave the settlers' cattle alone. Just after they left another group of 250 Shoshoni came in from the mountains and camped one night a half mile from Wellsville before leaving the next morning.[37] Brigham Young informed the commissioner that the Cache Valley bands had received "but little" from the government while being "a Sore tax upon the people. . . ."[38] In late October most of the Northwestern Shoshoni left for the north because of their fear of the United States troops.[39]

The military was active in the Oregon country for different purposes and, by 1858, was sending out expeditions against tribes east of the Cascade Mountains. In August, Lieutenant J. K. Allen surprised and captured seventy-one Indians in the Yakima country but lost his life in the battle. Allen's superior officer immediately hung three of the warriors, who were also recognized as having participated in an attack on a company of miners. The *Oregon Times* thought it "time that the Indians should feel that it is not always with them to dictate when war and peace shall prevail over the country east of the Cascades. . . ."[40] Superintendent James W. Nesmith, at Salem, Oregon, wrestled with the legalities of settlers pushing into the eastern district, which was technically still "Indian country." No treaties with the tribes had yet been ratified, and the Indians opposed white occupation. He was able to make at least one visit to the area to try to quiet Indian fears but found the natives upset about the encroachment.[41]

Emboldened by the presence of army detachments that wintered in the neighborhood, Indians in the far eastern section of Oregon were surly and belligerent in their relationship with the Fort Lemhi Mormons. Thomas S. Smith, the presiding Elder at the mission station, described to Brigham Young how bold and impudent the Shoshoni and Bannock had become and that "Old Rock a Ka the Big Bannock" was especially incensed because the Mormons would not give him some white wives.[42] Events came to a head on February 25 when a combined force of Shoshoni and Bannock descended on the fort, killing two cattle herders, wounding other missionaries, and driving off 220 head of cattle and 35 horses. As soon as he learned of the incident, Young ordered the evacuation of the post, but another man, Bailey Lake, was killed during the exodus to the Utah settlements.[43]

The editor of the *Deseret News* of April 14, 1857 charged that the army had instigated this attack and other hostile actions in the Tooele and Rush Valley areas west of Salt Lake City. The newspaperman recited the current rumor that enemies of the Mormon church had offered "$150 for every 'Mormon' they will deliver to them." He was sure that Johnston's command was in collusion with the Indians since the mildest term used by the soldiers towards the Saints was "the damned Mormons," and concluded, "It is not a difficult matter, for a good arithmetician, to count the toes upon a naked foot, when it is put out." In reply to these accusations, Colonel Johnston denied any complicity in the Lemhi attack and submitted affidavits from mountain men B. F. Ficklin, John W. Powell, and Craven Jackson, who also denied any involvement and alleged that the Indians were enraged at the Mormons because "they had never received any compensation from the Mormons for the land occupied by them. . . ."[44] There was probably some truth in the accusations leveled by both sides, but it seems obvious that the Indians were encouraged to take overt action against Mormon settlements as they observed an American army advancing against the Saints. If the Great Father in Washington was displeased with his white children in Utah, surely no punitive action would be taken against the Indians if they too joined the war against the Mormons.[45] Brigham Young seems not to have taken any notice of the charge that his people had failed to compensate the Shoshoni and Bannock for their Lemhi land, because later in the year he assured Tim-a-poo, the "Big Medicine man of the Bannacks," that he had now forgiven the Indians for the attack on Lemhi and concluded, "I may wish, sometime, to have some of my people settle on some of your land to do you good."[46] It also seems apparent that the army's presence and the rush of business connected with it had not diverted Young's attention from Indian relations.

Throughout the winter of 1857–58, President Buchanan, embarrassed and now concerned by the reports that the Mormon people were mobilized for war and meant to oppose Johnston's forces, decided to support conciliation efforts. Colonel Thomas L. Kane, friend of Brigham Young, responded to the Mormon leader's request for help to end the conflict by traveling to Salt Lake City and then to Camp Scott on March 12, 1858, to meet with the new governor, Alfred Cumming. Kane and the governor then left for Salt Lake City accompanied by a detachment of Mormon soldiers. The governor was received with respect by the leaders of the Saints and forwarded that

Soldiers at Camp Floyd. *Utah State Historical Society.*

intelligence to both Johnston and the president. Despite these promising developments, Brigham Young still did not trust the combative colonel and ordered an abandonment of all the settlements north of Utah Valley. Many Mormon families lived in their wagon boxes or with friends and were prepared to move farther south. At this point, two peace commissioners appointed by Buchanan arrived in Salt Lake City on June 7 and five days later proclaimed that the difficulties between the Mormon people and the government had been adjusted to the satisfaction of both. Brigham Young, in return for an offer of amnesty from the United States, agreed to the establishment of a military post in the territory. On June 26, the army marched peacefully through evacuated Salt Lake City streets and went on to Cedar Valley, forty miles south where Johnston established Camp Floyd. The Saints moved back to their homes, and Buchanan's Blunder, as some called it, ended.[47]

With an army ensconced in Utah Territory, the citizens in the settlements and the emigrants on the trails looked forward to military protection from raids and depredations by the Shoshoni tribes. However, the secretary of war did not consider that the Mormon pioneers needed help. In his first report after Johnston's troops had settled in at Camp Floyd, the secretary wrote, "All other Territories and people upon our vast frontiers suffer from Indian depredations, but the Mormon people enjoy an immunity from their outrages. For the protection of these people against Indians there is no necessity for the presence of a single soldier."[48]

But the Saints thought otherwise, especially when it was rumored that the Utes, Sanpitches, and Pe-ob-a-wats had heard that the Americans and other Indians "were going to use up the Mormons, and they thought they would pitch in."[49] In October a small band of Utes captured and then raped a white woman and child near Spanish Fork. The Indian agent called for help from Johnston, who sent two companies of infantry and two companies of dragoons to capture the guilty men. Most of the tribe were forewarned of the approach of the troops and fled to the mountains leaving Chiefs Tintic and Pinteets and a small group behind. When Pinteets refused to submit to arrest along with the rest and broke away, he was shot and killed. Three of the Indians were released on the promise that they would bring in the guilty men, which they did. The two culprits were placed in jail in Salt Lake City.[50]

Whether it was a matter of calculation or merely of happenstance, this encounter between the army and central Utah's Indians seemed to consolidate relations between the Saints and their Indian neighbors. Angered by Pinteet's killing, Arrapeen, "Great Chief" of the Utes, announced that he was mad at the Americans; that he was in correspondence with the Navajo, Bannock, Shoshoni, and sixteen Indian nations in all; and that he intended to unite with the Mormons to wipe out the Americans. Young advised him that it was not good to shed blood but received the answer that Dr. Jacob Forney had "a little heart and it is dark as night," while Brigham Young had "a big heart and it is white and clean as the sun." Arrapeen explained that three men had come out of the ground during a grand Indian council to tell the tribes that they should not fight the Mormons.[51]

But as it turned out, troops from Camp Floyd were soon to have duties outside the area of Mormon settlement as news came in that the Overland Weekly Mail had suffered attacks from a band of renegade Indians. In an incident of August 16, 1858, a band of Shoshoni attacked four mail guards on the Humboldt. Only one man escaped. Two other mail riders came along later and met a young chief who began to cry and warned them they had better escape while they could.[52] In response to such assaults, the editor of the *Alta California*, on August 17, 1858, attacked Johnston and his troops for "having a pleasant time watching the Mormons" instead of patrolling the mail route and asked that military posts be established on the Humboldt. The *San Francisco Bulletin* of August 18, 1858, chose to censure Agent Jacob Forney for not sending an agent to pacify the natives and for authorizing the mail contractors "to tell the savages for him that they must behave themselves."

A second attack on a mail coach occurred on August 20 at a crossing of the Humboldt. John Mayfield and his two companions held off Indian attackers for a day and a half before taking refuge in the nearby mountains. They finally reached the mail station in the Goose Creek Mountains and traveled on to Camp Floyd. Governor Cumming called upon Colonel Johnston to station troops at the head of the Humboldt River, but the colonel only sent one hundred dragoons and fifty infantry with orders to return by November 1. Captain J. M. Hawes, commander of the detachment, reported back on his return that the Indians were friendly and that he had been unable to capture the perpetrators of the attacks.[53]

Agent Forney visited the Humboldt tribes to offer them presents and engage them in council. He left Salt Lake City on September 12 accompanied by Frederick Dodge, the Indian agent, for Carson Valley. They met a large assemblage of Indians under four main chiefs: Py-poo-noo-yan, Sanpitch, We-ra-goo-tse-mah, and Paw-sha-quin, representing about 600 Shoshoni. Farther down the river at Stony Point he met two large bands of White Knives who told him they intended to winter on the Snake River where there was an abundance of fish. All the Indians encountered were friendly.

After conversing with all the chiefs, Forney was convinced that the Indians had been driven to retaliation by white men. "They have been shot down for trivial causes. They have been robbed, and have received other ill treatment from the whites."[54] He gave presents wherever he went and promised more in the future, which Jefferson Hunt, a Mormon Indian expert, said he "would never fulfil."[55] Forney discovered that the natives were "poor, miserably poor" and suffered constantly from lack of food. They might have agreed with a comment made by Chief Winnemucca of the Paiute in March 1858 that the pine nuts on which his people chiefly subsisted in the winter time were exhausted and, therefore, the members of the tribe were forced to steal cattle or starve.[56]

On the eastern side of the territory, Forney held a council with Washakie and the Ute chiefs—White Eye, Soweat, and Sanpitch—and optimistically declared that all differences had been adjusted between the two tribes after years of bloodshed and fighting.[57] Washakie, however, declared he had no confidence in the Utes, who always violated peace treaties, and within one hour of the conclusion of the treaty the Utes began stealing horses from the Shoshoni.[58]

On another visit Jacob Forney also had several meetings with Chief Little Soldier and his subchief, Ben Simons, of the Weber Utes. Forney and Brigham Young's correspondence reveal that Little Soldier was a wily and devious leader who played Mormons against government officials and vice versa while raiding Mormon cattle herds and managing to get as much as he could from both sides. Forney wrote, however, that he was convinced the tribe "have ever been faithful to the Government & our Citizens."[59]

The evacuation of the settlers from the Box Elder area during the move south in the Utah War had left their homes accessible to the Northwestern Shoshoni. James Bywater reported that when the first

Two Shoshoni chiefs. *Smithsonian Institution.*

residents returned to Brigham City, they found "every house broken open and their contents strewn about." Three weeks later the Indians stole four head of cattle belonging to Bywater's father-in-law.[60]

The Northwestern bands also committed depredations on passing emigrants near the Raft River and Goose Creek Mountains. Craven Jackson, a mountaineer and trader, stated he had purchased two oxen from John Barnard in Malad Valley. Barnard told him that the cattle had been bought from the Digger Indians who lived near the Box Elder settlements and who had stolen the animals from emigrants on their way to California. Barnard showed him four other yoke he had purchased in the same way, while the Indians told Jackson that there were fifteen more at the fort.[61]

On his summer trip to the Humboldt, at Raft River Forney had an opportunity to meet Pocatello, one of the able young Northwestern Shoshoni chiefs who was to gain some fame among the whites. The chief seemed "to exercise complete control over his 'Band'" of 150 people who "acknowledge no chief superior to the one with them." Pocatello assured the agent that they had always been friendly to the whites. They described their summer haunts as being at Deep Creek, Raft River, and neighboring valleys, but during the winter "they approach the northern settlements, and roam among them." They were quite destitute and "many entirely naked." The agent gave them some presents, the first they had ever received from a government official.

Coming back from Raft River, he met another group of 128 Shoshoni at Box Elder to whom he gave food and presents. Forney wrote that he had received complaints about how annoying it was to have these and other Northwestern Shoshoni "loafing about the Northern Settlements. . . ."[62] In complete support, the *Deseret News* chimed in with a three-column editorial about the impoverishing tax levied on the citizens by having to feed the Indians. This curse on the white settler was also not humane or honorable for the Indian, who faced sure extermination unless the government altered its policies toward them. A commissioner should be appointed at once to treat with the natives for "the soil we dwell upon." Only then would peace come to Utah Territory.[63]

Just across the mountains from Box Elder, the few settlers at Wellsville in Cache Valley had received word from Brigham Young in October 1857 to evacuate the valley and had done so in March of the next year. Not until September 23, 1858, did the Mormon prophet write Peter Maughan that now the families could return to their homes if Maughan would take thirty-five or forty men with him first. Young also instructed him to build a substantial post and keep a constant guard of ten or fifteen men because the Indians were very hostile.[64] The settlers did not return to Cache Valley until April of 1859. When they reached the little settlement, they discovered that 1,500 bushels of stored grain had disappeared, no doubt into the empty baskets of the neighboring Shoshoni.[65]

The years of 1857 and 1858 were marked by a continuation of governmental neglect of the Shoshoni and Paiute along the western trails, but also by a sudden interest in the Utah Mormons and their supposed subversion of the Indians. There seemed to be more Indian hostility along the California Trail, especially in the area of the Humboldt River. Agent Jacob Forney visited the tribes along the Humboldt in 1858 and reported the same destitution and involvement of white desperadoes that his predecessors had observed. The terrible Holloway and Wood murders highlighted the increased Indian hostility.

The Utah War and the introduction of United States troops into Utah Territory had an indirect influence on the Shoshoni and Bannock attacks on Fort Lemhi and on the infamous Mountain Meadows Massacre, and had an immediate and direct effect on relations between the Mormon people and the federal government. The presence of United States troops at Camp Floyd guaranteed more clashes with the Shoshoni bands nearby in the years after 1858. Already stirred up by the advancing Mormon farmsteads and excited by the Utah War, the Northwestern Shoshoni allied themselves with their neighboring tribes to begin a series of massacres along the Salt Lake Road and the California Trail north and west of Great Salt Lake. The introduction of a regular mail service directly west from Salt Lake City offered additional opportunities for plunder. In swift retaliation to what was perceived to be the beginning of a concerted Indian attack on emigrant parties and mail stations, the army troops began patrolling the western trails and, in the process, began a series of raids against some of the Shoshoni bands. The Indians were soon to discover that these soldiers were more ruthless and unforgiving than Brigham Young's Saints.

SIX

Mounting Tension along the Trails

In the spring of 1959 settlement and migration, which were never really interrupted by the Utah War, resumed after the winter snows melted. Indians continued to suffer land loss and depletion of resources as whites moved in and took over more country. The subdued friction between the two races showed itself in various forms, and tensions mounted as mail service was established on a regular basis and troops from Johnston's Army interacted with the Indians.

Indian raids and massacres south and southwest of Fort Hall on the road to California increased markedly in 1859, but the western section of the Oregon Trail remained comparatively quiet. Captain H. D. Wallin, reconnoitering a new wagon route from Great Salt Lake to the Columbia River, reported there had been several murders committed by Indians and many wounded along the upper California Trail, whereas on the Oregon road he had heard of only one man being wounded.[1]

Agent Jacob Forney, in Utah Territory, continued efforts to settle tribes on farms or reservations. The secretary of the territory, John Hartnett, supported Forney by forwarding to Congress a memorial asking that Indian lands be purchased and the tribes be located on reservations "at suitable distances from white settlers." Hartnett recommended a site at the junction of the Bear and Little Snake rivers.[2] Agent Forney was more specific, and after explaining again and at length how white appropriation of the mountain valleys had impoverished the natives and how under "the new order of things" the Mormon people were now withholding "the hand of charity," he recommended establishing four reservations: (1) Henry's Fork Valley, forty miles south of Fort Bridger, for the 1,200 Eastern Shoshoni under Washakie; (2) Cache Valley for the 1,500 Northwestern

Shoshoni who had originally ranged from Salt Lake City north to the Oregon line and west to the Goose Creek Mountains, including Malad, Salt Lake, Bear River, Ogden, Weber, and Cache valleys; (3) Ruby Valley for the 1,200 Humboldt (Western) Shoshoni; and (4) Deep Creek in Skull Valley for the 250 Gosiute who presently live "principally by stealing."[3] Although the Saints continued to prosselyte among the Utah natives, Forney's recommendations indicated that white farmers were becoming tired of constant Indian demands for food. Some of the Mormon people were apparently deciding that an occasional diet of fighting should supplant the incessant feeding.

Howard Egan, a Mormon agent for the mail route west of Salt Lake City, echoed Forney's suggestion. He had heard rumors that military posts were to be erected to protect the new mail line and was of the opinion that as long as the Indians "remain scattered far and wide," they would continue to attack the mail stations and emigrant parties for the food and supplies they needed for subststence.[4] To try to exercise control over the Gosiute and the Western Shoshoni along the mail line, Forney dispatched subagent R. B. Jarvis to establish farms in Deep Creek and Ruby valleys.[5]

In his 1859 request for the "articles most desired" by the Snake Indians of the Fort Bridger, Fort Hall, and Salt Lake areas, special agent F. W. Lander ordered for each small family or single half lodge $11.07 worth of goods, including one blanket, one butcher knife, cloth, beads, tobacco, powder and caps, shawls, leggings, crackers, and coffee and sugar. He listed 300 families of the Washakie band, 200 families of the Pannack tribe, and 300 families of the two bands of "Western Snakes."[6] The need for some type of government assistance became clear early in the year. Reports circulated of the theft of cattle from the herd grounds in Tooele Valley and at Grantsville west of Great Salt Lake. A troop of dragoons had to be sent from Camp Floyd to protect government property in the region.[7] The presence of the military at Camp Floyd was disquieting to the Indians as evidenced by the visit of a delegation of Northwestern Shoshoni from Cache Valley who traveled on snowshoes to Salt Lake City because they "had heard that there was going to be a fight, and . . . they came to see about it."[8]

With spring and the end of the Utah War, Peter Maughan and the original settlers of Cache Valley returned to their log cabins at Wellsville even though there was still concern that the Indians might

Howard Ransom Egan, Pony Express rider, born in 1840. *Utah State Historical Society.*

take immediate offense at this reentrance into their homeland. The first party reached the settlement on April 23, 1859.[9] News of the agricultural possibilities of Cache Valley circulated rapidly by word of mouth and in the *Deseret News*. By May another colony had been established at Mendon, and soon two more were built at Providence and Logan. During the summer, Richmond was founded and in the fall, Smithfield, so that by the end of the year there were about 150 families in the valley.[10] Perhaps one-third of the people lived in Logan, with the next most important towns being Wellsville and Richmond. Providence and Mendon were much smaller.[11] Brigham Young announced in the semi-annual conference of his church at Salt Lake City that he believed Cache Valley was able to sustain 200,000 people. Such pronouncements from a prophet encouraged[12] a very rapid settlement of most of the remaining arable land in the valley, which was accomplished the next year.

Two of the church apostles visited the Cache settlements in November 1859 and chose Peter Maughan as spiritual leader, or stake president, of the colonists. He was de facto practical leader as well.[13] To complete the organization of the area, a military command of "Minute Men" was established, but they were used most often in fruitless expeditions after horses and cattle stolen by the neighboring Indians.[14]

As the settlers began to pour into the valley to start crops, the Shoshoni became quite "saucy" and, according to Matthew Fifield, were particularly annoying toward the women; when their husbands protested, the red men "spatted their bare behinds toward them and asked them what they could do about it."[15] Peter Maughan did not like the "movement going on among the Indians" and advised the settlers about the first of June 1859 to move their families and stock to the southwest corner of the valley near Wellsville. Nine lodges of Bannock visited Maughan and told him they hoped the "Salmon River mess [a reference to the Shoshoni–Bannock attack on Fort Lemhi in 1857] could be forgotten."[16] A Shoshoni group then came along to tell the Mormon leader that the "Banackee" Indians intended to attack the settlers and steal their cattle. Maughan ordered half the men to stay and protect the families while the other half worked on the forts.[17] Walter Walters has left a graphic description of what came to be a typical response to Northwestern Shoshoni demands.

During the summer the first hostile Indians came upon us we thought it was the end   They Praded around and danced and Sang   they were all painted ready for war   There were about fifty of them   of us there was not twenty five or thirty   We had not arms worth anything   They was well armed and it would be foly to fight for they could have killed us all without trouble . . . They wanted Beef flower tea and sugar   Tea and Sugar was out of question and we had but little Flower   But every body divided what they had and Peter Maughan Sent a man after a Beef   So the Indians killed the Beef and took what flower they could get and finely went of[18]

These events were only a part of mounting Indian tensions in the region north and west of Salt Lake City during the late summer and early fall. In reviewing the series of "atrocious" murders and robberies of emigrants that occurred during these months, Secretary of War John B. Floyd was certain that white men disguised as Indians were the instigators and that these whites were Mormons "sanctioned, if not directed by the authority of the Mormon church."[19] The general mistrust as well as the shadow of the Mountain Meadows Massacre were still darkening the thoughts of many government officials. Some of the Utah Indians the year before had taken advantage of anti-Mormon sentiment when they gave as their reason for murdering several people in Salt Creek Canyon near Nephi, Utah, that "they understood the Americans and Indians were going to use up the Mormons, and they thought they would pitch in."[20]

The military at Camp Floyd west of Utah Lake were especially suspicious of Mormon involvement with the Indians and responded at once to Governor Alfred Cumming's request on May 9 for troops to be sent to escort any emigrants from the Mormon settlements along the Wasatch front who wanted protection. Colonel Johnston dispatched Major Issac Lynde with one hundred dragoons for an eighty-day expedition and placed an advertisement in the *Valley Tan* of May 17, 1859, advising the emigrants to assemble at a given point so the command could accompany them on the first leg of their journey to California. Delayed because of high water at the Weber and Bear river crossings, Lynde finally left on June 12 as escort for forty emigrant families under the leadership of D. W. Bayless. The major was cautioned to use force only where necessary, but if required, Johnston warned that the Indians should be made to "*feel* the power of the government." Lynde was to travel as far as the Sink of the Humboldt before returning to Camp Floyd.

After receiving two letters detailing depredations by the Bannock of Fort Hall against settlers at Green River, of an aborted attempt by Indians to run off stock on the Malad River, and of fears by drovers that their large herds of horses would be stolen by Fort Hall Indians, Johnston also sent troops to capture the offenders and to "inflict upon them decided and exemplary punishment." If required, Captain R. H. Anderson and the one hundred men of his "Northern Expedition" were to stay in the field. New provisions would be sent to them from Camp Floyd.[21]

The dispatch of the two companies to patrol the east and west segments of the California Trail occurred at the same time Agent Jacob Forney was writing the commissioner that he had no confirmation of rumors that Oregon Bannocks and "other renegade Indians" were combining to annoy the settlements of northern Utah. Forney thought it was easy to blame the poor Indian for thefts and "other improprieties" when most depredations were really committed by white men.[22] Although it is not possible to assess the accuracy of the reports involving white renegades masquerading as Indians and in other ways attacking emigrant parties, the very quantity of the reports from government officials and others suggests a reliable picture of white involvement.

Elijah Nicholas Wilson, an Anglo-American boy who lived with a Shoshoni group for several years, listened to tales by his Indian friends that tended to corroborate the charges made by Forney and other Indian agents. One of the chiefs told Wilson how, in 1859, white mail carriers would steal horses from emigrant trains, turn the animals over to neighboring Indians to herd, and then return for them after the threat of emigrant retaliation had passed. In one incident, the Indian leader related that angry travelers opened fire on his band and killed seven Indian men when the whites discovered their stolen horses in the Shoshoni camp. Washakie warned all the Indians to stay away from the emigrant roads because the white travelers had "crooked tongues." Wilson's Indian friend said that because settlers kept crowding the Indians farther and farther west into the deserts of Nevada where there was nothing but lizards, snakes, and horned toads soon there would be no land left and they would have "to jump off into the great water."[23]

Contemporary reports indicate that there were numerous attacks on wagon trains during the late travel season of 1859. But one assault that has crept into the history books never even occurred. This wholly imaginary massacre illustrates the hold such events have on people's minds and is an interesting story in itself. Purported to be the greatest emigrant disaster of the summer, and perhaps in the history of the West, the so-called Almo Massacre is supposed to have been an engagement of over four days between a party of 300 emigrants with sixty wagons and numerous cattle and horses and a large band of Indians on Almo Creek near the present village of Almo in Idaho by the Utah line. The pioneers were said to be well armed and discounted any trouble from Indians until on August 21 when a large band of warriors suddenly appeared and began firing on the train. The travelers hurriedly circled their wagons, enclosing the horses and stock. For three days the company was under seige and unable to get to the nearest water a mile away. They unsuccessfully tried digging wells. On the third day they were forced to release their thirsty animals, which were immediately captured by the Indians. On the fourth night, the guide and a young woman managed to escape, followed by a man and two women, one with a baby she carried by holding its clothing in her teeth as they crawled away from the encircled wagons. The next day in "a scene too wild and awful to contemplate," the Indians murdered the remaining emigrants. The five who escaped the ring of death made their way to Brigham City, from whence a rescue party came to bury the bodies in the dry wells. In the summer of 1937, some interested citizens in Idaho located the site of the massacre and erected a marker in the town of Elmo to commemorate the imagined tragedy.

Discrepancies appear in the various accounts, with some writers mentioning five survivors and others insisting there were six. The attack took place either in 1859, 1860, or 1861, according to which author is read. The first narrative of the incident appeared in 1926 and was reissued by the same author in another book in 1936, just before the pioneer association discovered the site. Historians connected with the Idaho State Historical Society finally put this western myth to rest after a diligent search of diaries, personal accounts, and newspapers of the time failed to mention the horrible deed. This writer has also failed to find any evidence in contemporary newspapers, which usually devoted many columns over several days to even minor attacks. It is quite possible that the story grew out of real but lesser massacres occurring in the summer of 1852 near Almo.[24]

———————————————•◆ ◆•———————————————

Although the wildly imaginative Almo Massacre did not occur, plenty of hostile action did happen along the route of the mail line west of Salt Lake City. An overland mail bill had been passed by Congress in March 1857 with service initiated along the southern route by way of El Paso to Los Angeles. This Butterfield Overland Mail was successful but did not meet the needs along the northern road from Kansas to San Francisco, so a semimonthly service was established in 1858 through Salt Lake City and was soon improved to weekly trips.[25] The line extended from the Mormon capital to Camp Floyd and from there almost due west across the desert stretches of Utah Territory to Carson Valley.

Mail superintendent Howard Egan reported in July 1859 that depredations were occurring from one hundred miles west of Camp Floyd to the Humboldt. A group of well-armed Indians menaced the stage stations and had already run off forty head of mules. Governor Cumming requested that troops be sent from Camp Floyd to protect the mail line, but the attacks continued.[26] A month later, on August 11, 1859, the *Sacramento Union* quoted Egan as saying that the Indians in the neighborhood of Schell Creek Station, about 200 miles west of Salt Lake City, were particularly troublesome, having several times driven off all the stock from the post.

The first serious Indian attack on an emigrant party during the 1859 travel season occurred on July 27 when a train headed by Ferguson Shepherd was ambushed in a canyon on Sublette Cutoff about eighty miles northwest of Salt Lake City. The Indian hostility was triggered when two Flathead Indians entered an emigrant camp (perhaps the Shepherd train) to trade and were killed without warning by the travelers. In retaliation, a group of eight Indians approached a party of emigrants at Cold Springs while the white men were having supper. After being given some bread to eat, one of the warriors suddenly shot and killed a man guarding the stock nearby and escaped with nine head of cattle and two horses. In an exchange the next morning, two Indians were killed and eight or ten wounded when twenty-five or thirty Indians attempted to run off more of the emigrant cattle and finally succeeded in getting twenty-one head.[27]

Shortly after, the Shepherd train was proceeding about seven miles from Cold spring on Sublette Cutoff. The emigrants stopped to doctor a sick horse and a rifle bullet struck and killed Ferguson Shepherd. Immediately a volley of shots rang out from the bushes on either side of the trail killing Bill Diggs, Clayborne F. Rains, and William Shepherd. James D. Wright was critically wounded but lingered on another nine days before finally succumbing. I. M. Smith was slightly wounded, and Mrs. Wright received a severe wound. Her eighteen-month-old baby had her thigh broken when one of the warriors picked up the child and dashed her against a rock. Four of the remaining white men cut horses out of the traces, and rode off "saying that they would be killed if they remained there another moment." They left the rest of the party to the mercy of the attackers. Mrs. Wright mounted a mule and, with her injured daughter in her arms, escaped with the remaining members of the train. Mrs. William Shepherd became so exhausted she left her eight-month-old infant hidden in the bushes while she staggered on to find a hiding place for herself.

The next morning, July 28, other trains, which had now combined into a train of fifty-two wagons and 200 armed men, came upon the survivors huddled together under a wagon being tended by a five-year-old boy who was carrying water to the sufferers. The rescue party went back along the road and found the Shepherd baby severely blistered by the sun but otherwise uninjured. Mrs. Wright eventually recovered, as did her little daughter, who was "partly deranged" for awhile. The survivors of the massacre were taken on to California by the other emigrants.[28]

The news of the Shepherd tragedy first reached Agent Forney from correspondent Samuel Smith of Brigham City, who, along with other observers, reported that some Shoshoni were attempting to trade horses, mules, and oxen to citizens "in the suburbs of the city" and that one of the natives had turned over to Smith a daguerreotype. With rumors already circulating about the attack at Cold Springs, the suspicious citizens of Box Elder refused to traffic in the stolen property, and Jacob Forney immediately set off for Brigham City to investigate. He issued a proclamation warning all residents of the territory not to purchase or take any of the stolen goods and requested that Governor Cumming send troops from Camp Floyd to locate the guilty Indians and to execute swift and terrible punishment on them.[29]

Colonel Johnston ordered Major Issac Lynde on his return trip from the Humboldt expedition to station his troops at Bear River Crossing and to send out patrols to punish the perpetrators of the massacre at Cold Springs if they could be found. Lunde had had a rather uneventful journey along the Humboldt, although the Shoshoni of the area were reported as troublesome and impudent. The emigrants were as reckless as ever in their treatment of the Indians they met. One *Deseret News* correspondent reported that one train had a quantity of strychnine which they intended to give to any natives met. The writer feared that some Indians would be poisoned to death and that the nation would soon be told that Mormon influence was at the bottom of the trouble. Lynde did report that upon meeting the Shepherd train survivors, they informed him they had recognized at least three white men, "painted and dressed as Indians," who had led the Indians in the attack.[30]

On the same day Lynde received his instructions, Lieutenant Ebenezer Gay was ordered to march his command to the trails west of Bear River Ferry to investigate the massacre and to afford protection to passing emigrants. When Gay reached the Box Elder area, he was told that a band of Indians who had been involved in the Shepherd affair was camped in "Devil's Gate" (Sardine) Canyon between Brigham City and Cache Valley. With forty men and a local Mormon guide, he reached the Indian camp just before dawn on August 14 and immediately charged the Shoshoni, who scattered and took firing positions behind rocks and trees on the steep hillsides. After an engagement of about two hours, Gay returned to Brigham City.[31]

Up to this point all observers agreed on the facts, but the later reports of the battle, or "small fight," vary widely. The lieutenant claimed he had engaged up to 200 warriors; Mormons who kept close accounts of the movement of the Shoshoni said there were 17 warriors involved. Gay claimed that his men had killed 20 Indians with only 6 wounded among his troops; the Mormon inhabitants, according to both the *Deseret News* of August 24, 1859, and the *Sacramento Union* of September 17, 1859, reported that one Indian man was mortally wounded and a woman slightly hurt. The army officer charged that his Mormon guide had deserted him, and when the soldiers found an Indian boy riding the army horse that had been assigned to the guide, they shot and killed the youth. The *Deseret News* reporter wrote that he was a "tame Indian boy" who lived with a Mr. Hunsaker and was, at the time, peacefully engaged in herding some horses.

As soon as the troops departed, the Indians robbed Hunsaker's house of $1,000 worth of property and drove off forty or fifty beeves. The lieutenant felt vindicated because one of the twenty horses he captured from the Indians had been taken from the Shepherd train. Gay and his command went on to join Lynde's forces at the crossing of Bear River, "having a disrelish for kanyons," as the *Deseret News* phrased it. The officer reported, finally, that 200 Bannock had just joined about 300 other Indians in Cache Valley and that they were a threat to emigrant parties only twenty miles away on Bear River. Colonel Johnston responded by sending two companies of infantry and one of dragoons to strengthen Lynde's forces. The Mormon settlers at Brigham City reacted by holding an "indignation meeting" to protest the killing of the Indian boy.[32]

As the Northwestern bands withdrew to Cache Valley, "bold, and ignorant," according to one white report, they sent word that if the soldiers "wanted to fight, to come on . . . [that] they were prepared . . ." for any dragoons sent against them.[33] Peter Maughan wrote Brigham Young after the Gay fight in Box Elder Canyon on August 17 that a band of Shoshoni shot four horses and stole twenty from the settlers, "which makes the boys feel pretty hard towards them."[34] Maughan thought the raid was in "retaliation for Cutler piloting Lt. Gays Company to the Indian camp in Box Elder Kanyon. . . ."[35]

The Shoshoni also ran off about one hundred head of fat cattle from Ogden and Box Elder canyons. A company of mounted troops was sent to Box Elder but took good care not to get within musket shot of any warriors, according to the sarcastic editor of the *Deseret News*. The newspaperman continued that the six or seven companies of troops camped at Bear River Crossing meant to starve out the Indians, "certainly a novel way of conducting an Indian war." He joined Peter Maughan in warning the settlers to guard their stock night and day.[36] The Northwestern bands were so threatening in northern Utah Territory that most of the emigrants began to take the new mail route south of Great Salt Lake past Camp Floyd.[37]

The dust had hardly settled on the Shepherd massacre and on the battleground of Gay's attack when another massacre captured newspaper attention. A company of nineteen emigrants under Edwin A. Miltimore, consisting of six men, three women, and ten children, was attacked on August 31, 1859, about twenty-five miles west of Fort Hall between the Portneuf Bridge and Snake River. The Indians assaulted the rear wagons first, where most of the casualties occurred. At the sound of firing, the people in the lead wagons took cover behind the bushes alongside the road and used the only two rifles in the company to try to defend themselves. In the melee the Indian leader in charge of the raiders was shot and killed, which dispersed the rest of the band and saved the remainder of the Miltimore party. Five men, one woman, and two children were killed, the bodies being "horribly mangled and scalped. One little girl five years old had both her legs cut off at the knees; her ears were also cut off and her eyes were dug out from their sockets, and to all appearance the girl, after having her legs cut off, had been compelled to walk on the stumps— for the sole purpose of gratifying the hellish propensity of savage barbarity."[38] Three days after the murders, the survivors met the troops of Lieutenant Henry B. Livingston who was on patrol from Lynde's command at Bear River Crossing. The emigrants were escorted to Camp Floyd, where they spent the winter before returning to their homes in Wisconsin.[39]

Frederick W. Lander reported that the attackers were about thirty warriors of the "Salt Lake or Southern Snake Indians" under a chief named Pag-e-ah (the Man Who Carries the Arrows), and other principal Indians Lander designated as Sow-wich (the Steam from a Cow's Belly), Ah-gutch (the Salmon), Pah-win-pooh (Water Goes in the Path), Pag-en-up (the Mist After the Rain), and Wah-me-tuh-mah, "which hardly bears translation." Lander gained this information from a fourteen-year-old boy from Chief Pocatello's band of Northwestern Shoshoni who came into the government camp carrying a blanket he had been given by one of the attackers. The boy assured Lander that Pocatello's tribe had had nothing to do with the murders, although the government confirmed that Northwestern Shoshoni must have been the perpetrators because property taken from the Miltimores was recognized among Indians near Salt Lake City.[40] Lander's mention of Pocatello was an early indication that this Northwestern Shoshoni leader and others, like Bear Hunter of Cache Valley, were becoming central figures in the mounting hostility along the western trails. The peaceful Washakie no longer commanded as much attention from Mormons and Indian agents.

Lander, who plays an important part in the Shoshoni story, was a civil engineer, surveyor, and an army officer. He had already made a name for himself as the result of his 1854 survey of a projected road from Puget Sound by way of the Columbia and Snake rivers to the Mississippi. Congress was so impressed with the report of his reconnaissance that the House of Representatives authorized the printing of 10,000 copies. From 1855 through 1859 he was engaged as the chief engineer and superintendent of the overland wagon road and began advocating a main railroad line from Salt Lake City to San Francisco with a branch to Puget Sound. It was during these four years that he became involved in various incidents with the Indian tribes in Idaho and Nevada, often offering his forces to help maintain order along the Oregon and California trails. He died on March 2, 1862, while on active duty with Union troops in Virginia.

Utah territorial officials were convinced that some of the Indians in the assault of the Miltimore party were actually disguised white men. Judge D. R. Eckels reported that in the first attack of the season on emigrants, one white woman had been ravished by five men and then shot but lived long enough to identify all of them as white men. Nelson Miltimore testified that the men who had attacked his father's train spoke good English, that some wore long beards, and that at least one had light brown hair. Two other witnesses swore that three of the raiders had yellow hair.[41] Judge Eckels indirectly accused the Mormons of being involved in the massacre, and Lander stated, "It is my opinion that these marauding bands are stimulated by inhabitants of Utah territory to steal cattle, horses, and mules for their (the whites) benefit. . . ."[42]

Another aftermath of the Miltimore tragedy was an inconclusive military engagement by Lieutenant Gay in Malad Valley with fifteen lodges of Northwestern Shoshoni who, he was certain, had participated in the murders of the Miltimore family. After firing at each other from a long distance for about three quarters of an hour "without any damage on either side," the two parties withdrew. But Gay reported he had put in irons an Indian who had agreed to guide his expedition. The Indian turned out to be Chief Pocatello, who later was ordered released. Lander thought the military had committed a serious error in arresting Pocatello, whom the government agent invited to his camp for a talk. The chief regarded Lander with respect and consideration. Pocatello declared that "his tribe had received what he termed in the Indian language, . . . 'assaults of ignominy'

from the white emigrants . . .; that one of his principal men had his
squaw and his children killed by the emigrants recently; that the
hearts of his people were very bad against the whites; that there were
some things that he could not manage, and among them were the
bad thoughts of his young men toward the whites." Pocatello concluded he would be a kind friend to the Americans when the Great
Father of the whites in Washington would treat him as well as Big-um
(Brigham Young).[43] The chief's home at the junction of the Salt Lake
Road and the California Trail, near the famous City of Rocks, seemed
destined to thrust him into more confrontations with emigrants and
the military. The young Shoshoni leaders rather than Washakie were
beginning to occupy center stage.

Northwestern Shoshoni were evidently involved in yet another
massacre of 1859, which occurred August 20 on Kinney's Cut-off
about seven miles west of Marsh Creek north of Cache Valley. The
train of five wagons, led by Milton Carpenter, was ambushed by
about sixty Shoshoni Indians who ran off sixty-eight head of cattle
and one mule, killed A. L. Root, and seriously, perhaps mortally,
wounded Jacob W. Paulling and two other men. The warriors found
refuge for a time at a trading post kept by a man named Graham on
Marsh Creek. The company continued their journey to California
with other trains and the wounded men were taken to Lynde's camp
at Bear River Crossing.[44] Chief Little Soldier of the "Weber Utes," a
Northwestern Shoshoni band, told Jacob Forney that only "bad Indians" were now on the northern roads.[45]

While the accounts of Indian raids on mail stations and emigrant
parties seem to indicate an all-out war, an examination of the massacres shows more of a series of small, impromptu attacks by male Indian war parties. Even one incident of murder along the trail could
strike fear into the hearts of travelers and settlers alike. When there
were three or four such events, plus the theft of many horses and cattle, imaginations and terror created a panorama of rapine and destruction that the frontier news editors exploited for their own purposes, not only to narrate the facts but also to include all rumors and,
incidentally, to increase the circulation of their newspapers.

As the seasonal emigration for 1859 came to a close, western newspaper editors settled down to a mostly critical examination of the un-
satisfactory performance of Colonel Johnston's troops in protecting
western travelers and mail stations. The editor of the *Deseret News* of

September 21, 1859, quoted a Mr. Long, who charged the United States troops at Camp Floyd with "eating Uncle Sam's rations and doing nothing." The newspaperman also thought that the presence of troops at the crossing of Bear River only served to incite the natives. He did point out that both Agent Forney and the troops were handicapped by not having the legal authority to operate in Washington Territory, although the editor's comments about the soldiers were somewhat sarcastic: "It will account for the seeming reluctance by the detachment at Bear river ford to getting into a higher latitude; and inactivity and cowardice should not be imputed to them by passers-by unacquainted with the circumstances on that account." The *Alta California* of September 28, 1859, used an utterly unsubstantiated report that a train of twenty-four wagons was attacked north of Bear River and sixty men, women, and children annihilated to charge the army with gross negligence and to call for the formation of a citizen's volunteer force to punish "these infernal red devils." And when Lieutenant Thomas Hight returned to Camp Floyd after a summer of patrolling the western trails with a report that he and his command had had the unfortunate task of burying the bones of twelve emigrants murdered on Marsh Creek in June, the *Valley Tan* of October 26, 1859, reported, *"He found no Indians but friendly ones."*

Despite the Overland Mail Company's policy of not permitting the abuse of any Indians by employees,[46] a correspondent to the *Deseret News*, on November 4, 1859, quoted a station keeper at Deep Creek as saying the local Indians were "impudent and insubordinate" and had stolen the wheat the company had raised for them for winter use. At Schell Creek station some Bannock sent word that they were coming to steal all the stock. And at Egan Canyon, when an emigrant party lost most of its horses to a marauding band, one intrepid but unwise member of the company started out by himself to retrieve the animals, swearing vengeance. The Indians "took him and stripping him naked, sent him back to his camp in rather a forlorn and ludicrous condition." If it had not been for the intervention of the friendly Shoshoni Chief Shocup, the warriors would have killed the white man. The *Deseret News* correspondent could see no hope of reformation for most of the Indians he met on his trip, deeming them "hard hearted, relentless, vindictive, cruel, and insensible to the emotion of gratitude." He ridiculed the "masterly inactivity" of the 3,000 soldiers at Camp Floyd who spent most of their time protecting the lives of gamblers around their post while American citizens were being plundered and murdered by "bloodthirsty savages." He called for the organization of a small volunteer force of 25 men who would do more to stop Indian depredations between Salt Lake City and California than 3,000 United States troops.

Perhaps sensitive to such criticisms and aware that Utah Governor Stephen S. Harding was advising the establishment of military posts along the Oregon and California trails, Colonel Johnston recommended to General Winfield Scott that "fixed points" be set up from which roving patrols could be sent out to protect emigrant parties and chastise wayward Indians. He intended to establish temporary posts during the summer months, one at the Portneuf River near the junction of the new Lander road and the Soda Springs route and another at Goose Creek near the Goose Creek Mountains. Escorts would be furnished every five days from the Portneuf station to accompany the wagon trains as far as Raft River, where a contingent from Goose Creek would take over the assignment and would continue as far as the Humboldt River. Johnston intended to patrol the Oregon Trail only as far as Salmon Falls, believing it impractical to send troops beyond this point because of the scarcity of forage and water. A small force was stationed at Fort Bridger and a larger company of troops at the crossing of Bear River. He asked for agents to be appointed to deal with the Fort Hall Shoshoni and Bannock and warn them to stay away from the emigrant trails. He also made the very sensible suggestion that the military department of Utah be extended to the forty-fourth parallel to include the Snake River country of Washington Territory. Finally, he advised Oregon authorities to place a force at Fort Boise to guard the trail as far east as Salmon Falls. It was a good plan and one that many Utah residents and western travelers hoped would solve the problem of Indian raids in the region for the next tourist season in 1860.[47]

Some Fort Hall Shoshoni and Bannock, Gosiute, and Western Shoshoni were involved in the troubles that centered in the area just north of Salt Lake Valley and along the California Trail southwest of the junction with the Oregon Trail, but the Northwestern Shoshoni bands seemed to have been the main participants. Their attempts to barter stolen emigrant goods in the Mormon Box Elder settlements testify to the part they played.

Two new elements introduced into the drama that caught the attention of western editors were the establishment of more regular mail service by the Overland Mail Company along the route south of Great Salt Lake and, of course, the presence of some 3,000 troops at Camp Floyd. Colonel Johnston attempted to protect emigrant parties by sending out on patrol his Humboldt and northern expeditions but soon discovered that Indian hostility lay closer at hand at Goose Creek and Marsh Creek. With the Shepherd, Carpenter, and Miltimore massacres stirring up criticism of his command, he was forced to station troops at Bear River Crossing, from which Lieutenant Gay was able to win some glory at little fights in Box Elder and Malad valleys.

One of the main reasons for Northwestern Shoshoni anger was the movement of over 150 Mormon families into Cache Valley. Hostility toward the settlers mounted after the Gay engagement, and Peter Maughan and the other Mormon leaders were forced to increase guard activities and to complete forts for protection.

By year's end, the military was coming under increasing pressure for their apparent inability to stop Indian raids and particularly because renegade white men seemed to be leading many of the attacks. An undercurrent of charges directed at the Mormons (especially from the Pacific Coast) suggested that the Saints were behind Indian depredations and were probably instigating the natives to murder Americans. The only puzzling circumstance was that Mormon settlers were also being assaulted by the northern Indians.

The mounting Indian-white tension in Shoshoni country was matched in other areas of the West with some battles pointing up once more the inability of officials in Washington, D.C., to arrive at a consistent and workable national policy for the western tribes. For example, in the May 13, 1859, battle of Crooked Creek near the Cimarron River in Texas, Captain Earl Van Dorn's troopers entrapped a band of one hundred Comanche and killed forty-nine warriors and thirty-two women while losing only two of their own force. Later in the summer, troops had to be used in Texas to protect other Indian encampments from white settlers. The two events did not demonstrate any more benevolence toward the Texas natives than the Northwestern bands were to receive four years later at Bear River.[48]

In another typical display of army ruthlessness, Colonel Benjamin L. E. Bonneville, in command at Santa Fe, organized a "punitive expedition" against the Pinal Apache during late 1859. Arizona settlers had been raising fears about possible Apache attacks in order to bring army money and supply contracts into the area, and Brevet Colonel Isaac V. D. Reeve was appointed to direct the expedition. With command of 176 dragoons and riflemen, Reeve conducted a fifteen-day hunt in Pinal country and captured seventeen children, two women, and one man. In December the troops engaged in a small skirmish that resulted in the deaths of eight Indians and the capture of twenty-three. While the army seemed pleased with the two sweeps through the Pinal area, the superintendent of Indian affairs at Santa Fe, James L. Collins, thought that the Indians had not provoked such stern measures and that the indiscriminate attacks would only arouse the hostility of other Apache groups.[49] Arizona and Texas were far removed from Camp Floyd, Utah, but these incidents demonstrate that army aggressiveness was not limited to assaults on unsuspecting Indians like Lieutenant Gay's attack against the Northwestern Shoshoni.

The presence of Johnston's army, the increase in western travel along the mail line and on established trails, the shift in attitude toward the natives among Mormons, and a reduction in proselyting were forces arousing increasing native antagonism. Now the settlers and the army were forced to pay attention to the wily and independent Chief Pocatello and other leaders like him who were no longer content with handouts from Brigham Young's Saints. The center of Indian activity had shifted from Washakie's eastern location to the trail aresa west and north of the Great Salt Lake. The inevitability of a major confrontation somewhere in Shoshoni country seemed to be drawing nearer each year.

Troops at Camp Floyd and their aggressive tactics against the neighboring Shoshoni bands accounted for some of the increase in Great Basin Indian attacks in 1859. However, traffic along the trails and, especially, the addition of stage stations along the now regularly operated mail line, brought further exploitation of Indian food sources and offered inviting targets to young warriors whose "bad thoughts" their chiefs could not control. It seems likely that white renegades were involved in inciting the marauding bands, although it is difficult to assess the accuracy of news reports about white involvement. The frequency of accounts suggests that organized bands of white outlaws were at work along the trails taking advantage, with the Indians, of the numerous possibilities to plunder hapless travelers. And, of course, the settlement of Cache Valley by Mormon farmers was an extreme irritant to the local Northwestern Shoshoni.

SEVEN

The Pyramid Lake War and the Otter Party Tragedy

Colonel Albert Sidney Johnston's strategy to guard parties along the Oregon Trail near Fort Hall as far as Salmon Falls was complemented by Oregon military authorities. Major Enoch Steen issued orders to his command "against the Snake Indians" on March 28, 1860. Orders to Captain A. J. Smith to construct a new road from Lake Harney to a point on the California and Oregon trails near Raft River were also included, but Smith was unable to complete the assignment because of an attack by "Snake or Shoshonee Indians" against his troops on June 29, 1860, just east of the Des Chutes River. All of Steen's units abandoned attempts at road making to hunt for the marauders. Part of Steen's command came upon the remains of a miner's camp that had been assaulted by Indians on June 13, 1860, a "truly melancholy and heartrending scene."[1] The *Sacramento Union* of July 7, 1860, set the location at about eighty miles from Fort Boise. The fight lasted a day and a half, and the miners killed five Indians but had two men wounded and lost forty-three horses and mules worth $7,500. The miners thought the Indians were of the "Snake tribe," but the natives had hailed them in "good English."

Two months later one of the most tragic Indian massacres in the history of the Pacific Northwest occurred west of Salmon Falls. The Otter train, with thirty-nine people in eight wagons and about fifty head of loose stock, had been escorted by troops from Fort Hall to the Raft River, where the troops left them. Four army deserters and a "civilian" then joined the train. On September 9 Alexis Van Orman in the lead wagon noticed a cloud of dust ahead and gave the alarm to circle the wagons and enclose the stock. Soon a band of Shoshoni Indians appeared. When they were unable to stampede the stock, they made friendly gestures and accepted food offered them by the frightened travelers. The Indians then left. The company proceeded only a short distance before they ran into another ambush. They were forced to circle their wagons atop a dry ridge miles from any water. The warriors continued an incessant fire for the next thirty-six hours while the emigrants defended themselves as best they could. There were plaintive cries among the children asking for water. During the siege, the four ex-army men and their civilian comrade deserted the embattled wagon train, leaving the emigrants on their own.

Six of the men, including Elijah Otter, plus his daughter, were killed in a hail of bullets and arrows; Mrs. Otter and her three remaining children refused to leave the bodies of their family members. They were never seen again. The twenty-eight survivors—seven men, five women, and sixteen children—left the train while the Indians were ransacking the wagons and took cover among some willows along Snake River. They were without food, but as they traveled down river they came upon an old Indian and bartered a gun for about fifty pounds of dried salmon. Two brothers, Joseph and Jacob Reith, had left on the evening of the second day of the battle to find help, and they eventually reached the Umatilla Indian Agency on October 2 with the first news of the attack. At the end of the tenth night of the ordeal, the survivors reached the Owyhee River and, utterly exhausted, settled down in a camp prepared to await whatever fate offered them. An eleven-year-old boy, Christopher Trimble, volunteered to seek aid and traveled about fifteen miles to the Malheur River where he came upon two of the deserters. He obtained some horse meat and returned to the camp. The boy later visited an Indian camp several times to get food but was finally killed when the natives heard that soldiers were coming to avenge the sufferings of the emigrants. Alexis Van Orman, his family, and ten others decided to make a last desperate effort to avoid death by starvation and left the camp.

At Umatilla the Indian agent alerted army authorities, who dispatched Captain F. T. Dent with a hundred men to rescue those still alive. One unit, under Lieutenant Marcus A. Reno, came upon the mutilated bodies of six of the Van Orman party; the remaining four children apparently were taken away as captives. Lieutenant R. H. Anderson's men found the survivors at their camp. Five were dead; the twelve emaciated people still alive revealed that they had sustained themselves by eating the flesh of those who had perished.[2] The persistent assault on the emigrant train was different from the usual hit-and-run tactics used by other Indian raiders and prompted Colonel George Wright, commanding the Department of Oregon, to request $150,000 for the construction of a military post at Boise to sustain five companies of troops.[3]

The Oregon superintendent of Indian affairs instructed agent John Owen of the Salmon River area to make every effort to rescue the four captive children whose fate created concern all over the Northwest. While industriously pursuing all leads to discover the whereabouts of the children, Owen could not forbear to point out that

> These Indians [Shoshone and Bannock] twelve years ago were the avowed friends of the White Man   I have had their Young Men in My Employment as Hunters Horse Guards Guides etc etc   I have traversed the length & breadth of their Entire Country with large bands of Stock unmolested. Their present hostile attitude can in a great Measure be attributed to the treatment they have recd from unprincipled White Men passing through their Country. They have been robd Murdered their women outraged etc etc and in fact outrages have been committed by White Men that the heart would shudder to record.[4]

In the spring of 1861, Owen convened a council with some Fort Hall Shoshoni and Bannock who denied any complicity in the Otter Massacre and blamed the Indians of the Humboldt Sink region.[5]

Without any government officials to supervise the movement of the Snake River Indians, Colonel Johnston at Camp Floyd again advised the secretary of war of the necessity for appointing agents to treat with the Shoshoni and Bannock in the Fort Hall area.[6] No action was taken. Johnston dispatched three companies of dragoons to patrol the emigrant roads from South Pass to Salmon Falls on the Snake River and as far as the Humboldt on the California Trail.[7] When the troops passed through Salt Lake City on their way north, the *Deseret News* of June 13, 1860, suggested that they would be much safer from attack at Fort Hall than among the troublesome warriors farther west toward the Humboldt.

But emigrants like James A. Evans discovered the Indians at Fort Hall could be more than just annoying. He reported that his party had to mount a tight guard every night because fifty horses had been stolen from another company. In a revealing aside about the army's attitude toward the Mormons, he quoted soldiers from Camp Floyd he met on the Portneuf River as saying the Saints were worse than the Indians being the "d—ndest ragged, filthy, dirty, thieving, God-forsaken set that ever lived. . . ." Evans was reassured to have an escort of soldiers for his train of thirty-three wagons. He thought that most of the emigration would abandon the California Trail from Fort Hall and would take the mail route past Camp Floyd and south of Great Salt Lake.[8]

A series of attacks did occur at City of Rocks on the Raft River where the California Trail approached the northern boundary of Utah territory for about seventy miles beyond Fort Hall, but, sighting no Indians, the guard turned back. The next day, September 7, Indians made a night assault on the emigrants, fought for about an hour and a half, and drove off thirty head of cattle. On the morning of September 9, about one hundred warriors renewed the attack and forced the travelers into the bushes and took control of the rest of the stock and wagons. Two men were able to reach a camp of troops whose commander sent a company of twenty-five soldiers to relieve the beleaguered party. The military met the frightened travelers on Marsh Creek and found one traveler still hiding, after four days, in the bushes near the site of the attack. The nineteen emigrants in the company lost 150 head of cattle and horses and all other property. They were fortunate to escape with their lives.[9]

The same band of Indians, probably Northwestern and Fort Hall Shoshoni and Bannock, battled another emigrant train near City of Rocks on September 12. At first the Indians appeared friendly and offered to sell some beef from among their herd of four or five hundred head of cattle. But as the company proceeded, a group of thirty-five or forty Indians suddenly fired on the wagons from ambush. After a running fight of twenty miles, the travelers took refuge behind some rocks but lost six killed and two wounded in the engagement. The seven survivors made their way toward the Mormon settlements at Box Elder. After five days without food they reached another emigrant camp and then went on to Brigham City and Salt Lake City.[10] The *Deseret News* of September 24, 1860, reported that it was the fifth or sixth company of emigrants attacked in the region of City of Rocks in the past six weeks.

Farther on, near Thousand Springs on the Humboldt, a train of twenty-five wagons under a man named Crawford was set upon by Shoshoni Indians. One man was wounded, and the party waited for reinforcements from another fifty wagons before moving on. The united party then proceeded to Virginia City.[11] The Shoshoni soon learned to anticipate the strategies and movements of troops along the emigrant trails and struck the wagon trains almost at will when the military escorts turned back to Fort Hall. In early October the soldiers returned to Camp Floyd.[12]

In summing up the summer's activities of the Fort Hall troop contingent, Colonel M. S. Howe reported that "ninety-nine one-hundredths" of the emigrants traveled with their unloaded firearms in their wagons and laughed at the idea that it was necessary to unite in large companies for protection. Most of them said "they were not afraid, they could whip the Indians." Howe gave the number of westward-traveling emigrants who were registered at the Portneuf River Bridge during the 1860 travel season: 769 men, 325 women, 474 children, with 359 wagons, 1,045 horses, 4,075 cattle, and 3,415 sheep. He recommended that troops be stationed at City of Rocks for the next year.[13]

Indian troubles in 1860 in the Fort Hall and Snake River areas, while serious, did not reach the critical stage of those at Carson Valley at the other end of the California Trail. The Paiute of the Pyramid Lake district watched with fear and anger as thousands of whites poured into the region after the discovery of the Comstock Lode in 1859. As the *Sacramento Union* of May 21, 1860, pointed out about the Paiutes, the Pyramid Lake area was their "favorite resort, and the spot they have always valued highly." The appearance of white ranchers with their large cattle herds threatened the very existence of the Indians. In addition, irresponsible whites continually harassed Indian families, stealing their horses, and occasionally killing inoffensive members of the tribe.[14]

Two incidents finally precipitated the Pyramid Lake War of 1860. A man named Tom Anderson, who owned a station on the lower Humboldt, shot an Indian and was forced to flee for his life to Honey Lake Valley when other Indians began to kill cattle and threaten other stations.[15] A few days later, in early May, some white men at Williams station "caught one of the Indian women and Ravished her & whipt one or two of the Indians." The next day, May 7, about thirty friends and relatives of the Indian victims passed by several ranches, took four white men prisoner at the Williams ranch, tied them up and set the dwelling on fire, and then "retired quietly without doing any further damage. . . ." Another account stated that David and Oscar Williams and a man named Sullivan were killed outside the building while two other men, Fleming and Dutch Phil, were shot inside the station.[16]

The Indians may have been satisfied with this revenge, but the white inhabitants of the region immediately gathered in hastily formed military units to castigate the natives. On May 12 the poorly organized volunteers charged a group of Indian warriors a few miles from Pyramid Lake. There were 105 white men and from 150 to 1,000 Indians, depending on the newspaper account one reads. In the two-hour battle, the white militiamen at first held their own until they ran out of ammunition, although those armed only with shotguns were no match for the warriors who carried Sharps rifles. The last hour of the battle turned from fight to flight as the panic-stricken whites threw down their weapons and ran for their lives. The Indian warriors disdainfully reported later, "White men all cry a heap; got no gun, thro 'um away; got no revolver, throw 'um away too; no want to fight any more now; all big scare, just like cattle, run, run, cry, cry, heap cry, same as papoose; no want Injun to kill 'um any more." Seventy-six whites were killed and most of the twenty-nine survivors suffered wounds. The majority of the Indians involved were Paiute, although a number of accounts insisted that "Salt Lake bands" also participated in the engagement.[17]

The terrible loss of life in the Pyramid Lake War led to the region being "nearly depopulated" as the citizens sought refuge in California settlements.[18] At Placerville meetings were held with patriotic speeches and resolutions asking for money for arms and ammunition to be forwarded to the scene of the battle. The people of Silver City went so far as to construct a wooden cannon but fortunately never attempted to fire it.[19] Colonel Jack Hays organized a force of 549 volunteers and was soon joined by 144 regular troops from California under command of Captain Joseph Stewart. In a brief engagement on May 29 near Williams Station, the troops killed 6 or 7 of a band of 150 Indians. On June 2, with 200 mounted men and about 100 other soldiers, and accompanied by Lieutenant Colonel F. W. Lander, Hays engaged a large group of warriors near the mouth of

the Truckee River. The estimates of the Indian force ranged from 800
to 3,000 but was probably much smaller. The battle lasted three
hours and resulted in 25 Indians killed and 3 soldiers killed and 5
wounded. The volunteer force was soon disbanded while the regular
troops occupied a temporary post on Pyramid Lake until August 7
when Fort Churchill was founded on the Carson River.[20]

The verbose and ambitious Colonel Lander assumed a prominent
position in Indian hunting when he listened to the supplications of
citizens to use his surveying expedition to help castigate the natives in
the Pyramid Lake area. A correspondent with the pen name of
"Oro" kept the local press informed about Lander's exploits. On
June 20 he reported an attack by 300 Indians on a dozen prospectors
near Keep Hole Springs on the road from Honey Lake Valley to the
Humboldt River. The would-be miners lost all their wagons and
equipment. The marauding natives were so starved that the prospectors watched them "eat the flour raw from the sacks" as they took
provisions from the wagons.[21] A force of about seventy volunteers
started out under the command of Lander to find and punish the
offending Indians. In a minor encounter at Mud Springs, Alexander
Painter of the citizen force was killed while standing a few feet away
from Lander whom the warriors were trying to kill.[22] Lander indicated
in his report of the year's operation that the Bannock and Shoshoni
were "better fighting Indians" and more to be feared than the Paiute
and recommended that these Fort Hall Indians be "thoroughly chas-
tized."[23]

Along the mail line, William Russell of Russell, Majors & Waddell organized the Central Overland California & Pike's Peak Express
Company on November 23, 1859, to gain control of the central mail
route. He also inaugurated the famed Pony Express to demonstrate
that this more northerly route was feasible. The Pony Express initiated service on April 3, 1860, and was soon carrying mail halfway
across the continent twice a week. Stations were established every 10
or 15 miles; each rider traveled 75 miles; and the first mail was
delivered in 10½ days from Missouri to California. On May 11, 1860,
the postmaster general also awarded the COC & PPE the contract for
carrying bulk mail and passengers by stagecoach over the central

route. After midsummer of 1860, however, coach service west of Salt Lake City was discontinued for the next six or eight months, and the mail was shifted to pack mules.[24]

From South Pass to Salt Lake City, Russell, Majors & Waddell established the following Pony Express stations: Green River (then a post operated by Michael Martin), Ham's Fork, Millersville, Fort Bridger (a quick stop, but no station), Muddy Creek, Bear River, Needle Rocks, Weber Station at the mouth of Echo Canyon, Carson House, Dixie Creek, Big Canyon or Snyder's Mill at the western base of Big Mountain, and Salt Lake House on Main Street in Salt Lake City. From here across the dangerous wastes of western Utah and eastern Nevada, stations were built at Traveler's Rest, then Rockwell's, Joe's Dugout at the foot of the road leading to Cedar Valley, Camp Floyd, Pass Station or Faust's or Rush Valley, Point Lookout at the edge of the western desert, Fish Springs, Boyd's Station, Willow Creek, Deep Creek, Antelope Springs, Spring Valley, Egan Station, Butte or Robber's Roost, Ruby Valley (which was halfway between Salt Lake City and Sacramento), Diamond Spring, and then Roberts Creek about 300 miles west of Camp Floyd. After Roberts, the Pony Express riders could look forward to Dry Creek Station, then Simpson's Park, Reese River, Smith's Creek, Cold Springs, Williams, Fort Churchill, and finally Carson City Station. Some of the stations were soon to receive newspaper attention as the scenes of Indian attacks.[25]

From March until October of 1860, the main travel season, Gosiute, Western and Northwestern Shoshoni, and probably some Bannock, hit the mail stations in search of food and in the time-honored profession of horse stealing. The Overland Mail coach was attacked near Eight-Mile Station just south of Great Salt Lake as early as March 22, and driver Henry Harper was killed.[26] At the other end of the mail line, Indians burned the Cold Springs Station buildings and murdered the agent on May 12.[27] A week after this assault and after the Pyramid Lake disaster, the *Territorial Enterprise* of May 19, 1860, reported, "nearly all the stations on the emigrant road are now closed and it seems that an Indian War has commenced in earnest."

To the station keepers along the Pony Express route, fear and caution were the bywords. John Fisher reported "Great Excitement" as a result of the killing of James Ouldcart and the burning of Simpson's Park Station, the murders of Ralph M. Lozier and John Applegate at

The Deep Creek Station near the Utah-Nevada border was painted by Utah primitive artist Francis L. Horspool. *Utah State Historical Society.*

Dry Creek, and the abandonment of the Robert's Creek post—all within a few days.[28] The attack on Dry Creek was precipitated when the station keeper, Si McCanless, refused to return a Shoshoni woman with whom he was living to her tribe. Her relatives stormed the station, killed two of the four men, and chased McCanless and Little Baldy, the pony rider, who stripped to their underwear in a desperate attempt to outrun their pursuers. They were successful, and McCanless later moved to Salt Lake City where he married the Shoshoni woman and raised a large family.[29]

Service along the mail line was interrupted at several points by late May, including the section between the Carson Sink and Diamond Springs. Brigham Young excoriated Johnston's command for their inactivity, writing that he would prefer five hundred citizen soldiers "than all the lazy, worthless do-nothing troops in Camp Floyd"[30] Howard Egan tried to "restore the links" broken by Indian depredations.[31]

The *Deseret News* of May 30, 1860, was of the opinion that the reckless massacre of some Pitt River Indians in California had stirred up the natives east of the mountains to retaliate against whites. The editor reported the abandonment of all stations between Ruby Valley and Carson and considered that the few soldiers along the line only served to "fan the war-flame. . . ." He also did not have a high regard for the people of the "so-called Territory of Nevada" who were generally without arms and ammunition to defend themselves.

Troops were sent out to patrol the mail line, but citizens petitioned officials at Camp Floyd to establish permanent posts at strategic points, rightfully arguing that the Indian hostiles merely waited for the dragoons to pass and then assailed a station.[32] Meanwhile the attacks continued. The Deep Creek post was struck and one man shot and several horses taken.[33] From thirty to fifty Gosiute threatened Schell Creek on June 8 and were fired upon by three white men who killed three or four of the natives. Lieutenant D. D. Perkins found these Gosiute in "a destitute condition, . . . utterly indifferent to everything but the taste of food." The Indians burned the Schell Creek Station[34] and two weeks later set fire to the Butte Valley post.[35] The Shoshoni seemed determined to allow no white men to travel through Indian territory.[36] Pony Express rider Elijah Nicholas Wilson found that the rider who was to meet him at Deep Creek Station had been killed out on the desert. While Wilson was resting at the Willow

Creek post, seven Indians came in asking for something to eat. Not satisfied with the twenty pounds of flour offered them by Agent Peter Neece, they shot a cow, which so angered the station keeper that he shot and killed two of them. The four white men then prepared for the attack they knew would come from about thirty Indians camped nearby. After a night of fighting, the Shoshoni withdrew, but not before losing three more of their number.[37]

By August, as Indian hostility mounted, some of the Camp Floyd troops engaged in battles with the Indians. While William Rogers was camped at Spring Valley with an escort of several soldiers, Indians fired on them and wounded a horse belonging to one of the dragoons.[38] The action then switched to Antelope Canyon. Express riders were shot at, and later an emigrant train was struck.[39] The only casualty was one dead horse.[40] By this time, emigrant parties were very apprehensive about entering Antelope and Schell Creek canyons. Camp Floyd troops attempted to give protection, and on August 11 Lieutenant Stephen H. Weed and twenty-seven men rode to the relief of the station in Egan Canyon where a band of about seventy-five Indians had "been bullying the station men. . . . " In the fight three Indians were killed and three soldiers wounded. One later died. The Indians were very bold during the engagement, and the soldiers "found it anything but *fun* to fight well-armed Indians," at least according to the reporter for the *Deseret News*.[41]

At about the same time, four soldiers hid under some hay in a wagon at Deep Creek hoping to surprise some Indians. They were successful in killing two. On the following day the Indians assaulted Schell Creek Station and kept up a deadly fire for about an hour until Lieutenant Stephen H. Weed arrived with his troops. In the subsequent fight, seventeen Indians were slain with no loss to the troops. Four other Shoshoni were killed on the same day by three soldiers escorting the express through Schell Creek Canyon.[42]

In his annual report dated October 9, 1860, Lieutenant Weed announced that twenty-five Gosiute had been killed during the engagements but did not venture an estimate of other Shoshoni deaths.[43] A final encounter significantly increased the Indian casualties. Eighty Paiute struck Egan Station in early October. After exhausting their ammunition, station keeper Mike Holt and a rider named Wilson were forced to allow the Indians into the building. The chief spoke only one word, "bread," and, hoping to save their lives, the two

white men built a fire and baked all the bread they could. After satis-
fying their hunger, the Indians tied the two men to a wagon tongue
driven into the ground and began piling sagebrush around their feet
to roast them to death. At this point, rider William Dennis came into
the station and, unnoticed in the excitement, turned and rode off for
help. He met Lieutenant Weed and sixty dragoons on their way back
to Camp Floyd. The soldiers arrived in time to save Holt and Wilson
and killed eighteen of the Indians in the battle.[44]

———————— ·•· ·•·————————

The continuous raids on the mail stations and emigrant parties
and the obvious destitution of the Indians along the western routes of
travel prompted various government officials in Utah Territory to
plead for a change in Indian policy. First, Governor Cumming, Surveyor General S. C. Stanbaugh, and Indian Agent Jacob Forney all
recommended that the various Indian farms in the territory be abol-
ished as expensive nuisances supporting only a few individuals in idle-
ness.[45] Washington, D.C., officials should especially have listened to
Cumming, who was experienced in Indian affairs, having served as
Indian superintendent at St. Louis before becoming governor of Utah
Territory. The consensus was to establish two large reservations, one in
the southern and one in the northern part of the territory. Washakie's
people, the Bannock, and "the Shoshones roaming in Salt Lake,
Ogden, Weber, bear river, Cache, and Malade vallies" would be
placed on the northern reserve.[46] The government would then sign
treaties with the various tribes to compensate them for their lands,
and this would protect white citizens in their homes and along the
routes of travel.[47] As usual, nothing was done as a result of these
official requests.

The Mormon settlers north of Salt Lake City would have welcomed some government action, as they, too, suffered from Indian
hostility during 1860. Chauncey W. West, in charge of the local
militia at Ogden, wrote Brigham Young on April 16 reciting a whole
litany of depredations by a band of Northwestern Shoshoni passing
through the northern counties. The worst incident involved Charles
Miles, who was intercepted by three Indian warriors while hunting for
his oxen. One tried to ride his horse over Miles; a second shot twelve
arrows at him, eight of them lodging in his body; then the other two
attacked him with their spiked war clubs. One Indian lost his grip on

his club and Miles picked it up and defended himself so successfully that the Indians whipped up their horses and rode away, hurried by the sight of a rider coming toward them. The local doctor treated Miles's wounds and thought he would survive though "badly injured." General West found the Northwestern Indians "very saucy and overbearing" and asked Young if it was necessary to suffer "their abuse and acts of violence and depredation and pass them off the best we can, or whether we shall stand up and chastize them as their acts and the magnitude of their crimes shall deserve." The very question indicated the answer West desired from his leader.[48]

Jacob Forney visited the northern bands to see if he could quiet them, but the Indians refused to talk to him or accept presents and said "that they had plenty of shirts and blankets" and did not need any gifts from Forney. The Shoshoni continued their hostility in the northern valleys, displeased, one man thought, because three of their number had been jailed at Ogden on a charge of stealing, "a propensity that a majority of the aborigines in this country have to an indefinite extent, according to the *Deseret News* of June 27, 1860.

In verdant Cache Valley, the Indians looked on with some dismay in early spring of 1860 as hundreds of covered wagons, carrying not emigrants but Mormon farmers, rolled into their mountain retreat. The rush to the valley came partly as the result of Peter Maughan's chamber of commerce announcements to the church newspaper that Cache was the "best watered valley I have ever seen in these mountains" and because overcrowding and the lack of water resources in the southern counties prompted many Saints to look for new homes.[49] The older settlements grew in population and five new villages were established: Hyrum, Millville, Paradise (south of Logan), Hyde Park, and Franklin (to the north). The federal census of August 1860 listed 2,605 people in 510 households in Cache Valley, for a total of almost 7 percent of the total population of the territory. Many Mormon families also moved to Carson Valley during the year, and Brigham Young, in a sermon at Wellsville on June 7, 1860, said he had noted that some of the home seekers did not seem to care which way they went "and had written on their wagons, 'To Carson or Cache valley, we don't care a d—n which.'" But the Northwestern Shoshoni did care and looked with some concern at the newcomers in northern Cache Valley's Franklin, which was in the very heart of Indian country. The pioneers were aware of the fact and mounted a strong guard from the very beginning of settlement. At first the newcomers were welcomed by the natives. Chief Kittemare offered the land of his people freely to the founders of Franklin but expected beef, wheat, and potatoes in return. He and his band soon became "great beggars," according to Samuel Handy.[50] Mormon settlers tried to adhere to their policy of giving food to the natives rather than fighting them, but Shoshoni demands and needs rapidly exceeded the willingness and resources of the settlers to support the Indians.[51]

Mormon Bishop William B. Preston of Franklin wrote Brigham Young in March that "Lemuel" was friendly. Peter Maughan was more specific. In one incident he asked the settlers for a beef "for our *friends*" and was offered two or three animals "where one was enough. . . ."[52] When one group of Indians threatened a raid on the livestock herd at Logan, the residents surrounded the warriors, had a treaty talk, gave the natives a beef, and then had a feast on the tabernacle square to ensure peace and tranquillity.[53]

F. W. Lander was certain that many of the Indians pillaging along the California Trail and mail line were from bands wintering in Cache Valley where they were on good terms with the Mormons and were fed by the Saints. He identified Mopeah's group of forty-five lodges, or about three hundred souls, as one of those hanging around Cache Valley. They were among the "very bad Indians" responsible for many attacks on emigrant parties. There was a second band of fifty lodges of "Salt Lake Diggers" who lived by hunting and plunder but also were supported by the Mormons.[54] It was easy for government officials to conclude that Mormon settlers were maintaining Indian raiders. The troops at Camp Floyd were positive that Mormon officials were deliberately supporting hostile bands. The Saints, however, saw feeding the Indians as necessary to their own survival.

But Brigham Young's insistence on this benign policy toward the Indians did not exempt his people from occasional hostility. The "bad and saucy" Shoshoni drew butcher knives on Mormon housewives, threatened cattle and sheep herds, and in other ways kept the frightened settlers continually on guard.[55] On May 1, Peter Maughan reported that Indians had stolen fifteen hundred dollars' worth of horses, which "seems to be hard on us after feeding them all winter. . . ." He warned the natives that thefts must cease or the pioneers would not feed them and that "we would use them up if it took us all summer to do it." He thought that Weber Tom was the leading culprit and expressed appreciation that a brother of Washakie intended to tell the "Big Chief" about Weber Tom's hostility towards the Saints.[56]

Maughan and others decided to organize a company of one hundred minute men. The militia held frequent drills and endured many night guards and occasional chases after Indians.[57] Brigham Young complained that the federal government was not taking effective measures to reconcile the natives toward peace and advised his followers to build strong stockades in the main settlements of Cache Valley.[58]

The most serious Indian difficulty for the Cache Valley settlers in 1860 occurred on July 23 when Chief Pagunap (or Pug-weanne, the One-Eyed Indian) of a small band of Northwestern Shoshoni was arrested at Smithfield for stealing a horse. He was shot and killed while trying to escape when ten of his friends urged him to make the attempt because the "white men were cowards and would not shoot." One of the Indians then shot Samuel Cousins "through his lights so that he breathed through a Bullet hole." In their retreat toward a nearby canyon, the ten natives shot and killed John Reed and wounded James Cowan. Farther up the canyon, the warriors killed Ira Merrill and wounded his brother, Solyman Merrill. A company pursued the attackers but only succeeded in shooting one from his horse before nightfall stopped the action. During the evening an Indian man and woman were taken captive when they came into the Logan fort. The two denied any complicity, and when about twenty of their friends tried to force their release, they were met with "probably 100 guns" from the citizens. The Mormon leaders proposed that these natives bring in the four who had shot the "brethren, so that they might be killed. . . ." The Indians refused and proposed, instead, that they go and kill the guilty ones themselves. The Saints insisted on the first alternative because they "wanted to know that they were used up." As Maughan explained the situation, "we are in a worse condition than if an open war was declared, because if we meet an Indian we have to wait their motion. . . ." Three days later the Indians returned to report they had been unable to find the murderers. Maughan replied the Indians would get nothing more from the white men until the murderers were delivered up.[59] The *Deseret News* of

August 1, 1860, thought the use of force and arms in dealing with the Indians of Cache Valley should be a "dernier [last] resort."

Almost two weeks after the event, Bear Hunter, "the War Chief," came in to talk. Maughan asked the leader to return the murderers for punishment "for we could not endure it any longer." The chief was reluctant but finally agreed to try to find the culprits. He did not want to fight the settlers and announced that he and his band would leave the valley. Maughan distributed four beeves among the Indians in a peace gesture. As for the three wounded white men, all recovered including Cousins, whose bullet hole was "closed up so that he don't breathe through it anymore." War Chief Bear Hunter never returned with the four guilty Indians,[60] and the Saints of Cache Valley were left to deal with the Indians on their own.

The tragic Otter Massacre received the most attention, followed by the Pyramid Lake War, during the 1860 Indian depredations in Shoshoni and Paiute territory. Concentrated and continuous attacks occurred along the Pony Express and Overland Mail line where the natives were starving and, throwing off all restraint, assaulted one station after another. The military in eastern Oregon and Johnston's troops at Camp Floyd and Fort Hall patrolled the emigrant trails, but, with the exception of the minor expedition into eastern Nevada led by Lieutenant Weed, did not engage in any major Indian confrontations. The Mormon settlements at Ogden and Box Elder were constantly annoyed by Indians begging and bold incursions; meanwhile, the newly arrived farmers in Cache Valley encountered serious troubles from the aroused natives. Peter Maughan met with Bear Hunter, and both men sought to avoid trouble between the two peoples. With a large white population rapidly appropriating all the arable land in Cache Valley, it would be only a matter of time before an altercation of major proportions would generate a dramatic encounter between the settlers and the aboriginal population.

Traditional accounts of Utah Indian history have focused on the Walker and Black Hawk wars. Events of 1860 emphasize that a shift needs to be made to examine the escalation of hostilities in Nevada and southwestern Wyoming, especially incidents involving the

Northwestern Shoshoni of northern Utah. The two Indian wars are less significant than current histories would lead us to believe when compared to the Pyramid Lake War, attacks along the California Trail and on the mail line, and the later sanguinary massacre of Shoshoni at Bear River. The real Indian story clearly lies in these other theatres of action. The encounter at Bear River in 1863 between Connor's Volunteers and a village of Shoshoni was not an anomaly, not an atypical incident, but a vital part of Utah's history. It was tied to Mormon settlement and Indian policy and was a direct result of Indian-white hostility occurring throughout Shoshoni country in the vast expanse of Utah Territory. This new perspective also introduces elements that might refashion our thinking about Indian affairs west of South Pass in the years up to the end of the Civil War.

In assessing the importance of the Shoshoni wars in Utah as compared to the better-publicized Walker and Black Hawk wars, too often there has been a tendency to place events within the present boundaries of Utah. It needs to be reiterated that before 1861 Utah Territory encompassed all of present Nevada as well as Utah—a vast area populated by Shoshoni and Northern Paiute over which government and Mormon officials attempted to exercise some control. Subsequent boundary changes should not limit the vision of what really affected the region in these early years.

Another erroneous interpretation involves stereotyping the Shoshoni tribes as either skulking, helpless, and degraded Digger Indians, who were an oddity rather than a formidable adversary to white domination, or assuming they were all like Washakie's peaceful and cooperative Eastern Shoshoni. These two stereotypes dominate our view of the Shoshoni and cast them as ineffective opponents. Easily overlooked is the Shoshoni leader similar to Chief Pocatello who had an independent and reckless audacity that made him a dangerous and desperate adversary. While Pocatello lacked a comprehensive strategy, his young warriors looked to him for bold leadership comparable to that of chieftains in the Great Plains area. Accustomed to joining with the great Bannock chief, Tahgee, in buffalo hunting expeditions to Wyoming and Montana and in engaging in warfare with the Sioux, Pocatello and some of his fellow Shoshoni chieftains were a significant menace to Great Basin and Snake River travelers and settlers. This tendency to underrate the warrior qualities of the Shoshoni offers another explanation about why the Battle of Bear River has been vastly ignored. As will be shown, this engagement was a hard-fought encounter between desperate and skilled warriors and an equally resolute group of California troops.

The hostile and uncompromising attitude of Colonel Patrick E. Connor and his California Volunteers toward Indians probably stemmed partly from anger about the loss of white lives in the Pyramid Lake War. When the volunteers marched into Utah in the fall of 1862, they were looking for an opportunity to engage any Indians they could find in bloody conflict.

———————◆•◆◆•◆———————

EIGHT

The Overland Mail Line Comes Under Attack

As the year 1861 opened, the approaching Civil War began to more adversely influence Indian-white relations in the Great Basin and the Snake River area. Soon Camp Floyd would be dismantled as the troops were sent east to participate in the fratricidal contest. Troop withdrawal left a vacuum that was temporarily filled by Mormon militia units called upon to patrol the new telegraph and mail lines. The mobilization of some western volunteers in California did not proceed fast enough to provide the force necessary, and at the same time tensions were rising as white infiltration of the country strained Indian relations. The net result was another year of more conflict with white renegades interwoven with desperate native hunger and the growing tradition of trail warfare.

With the coming of the Civil War, the spirit of violent solutions was abroad in the land, and the Shoshoni increasingly reacted to the mounting numbers of whites pouring into Indian country. The warriors continued their guerrilla warfare as in years past, and it seemed that there was almost no place along the trails where tension did not break out into conflict.

The importance of emigrant travel at Fort Hall and beyond to Oregon and California in 1861 brought an appeal from Utah Superintendent of Indian Affairs Benjamin Davies that Henrie M. Chase be appointed a special agent among the Bannock and Shoshoni at Fort Hall. Chase had lived among these Indians near Portneuf Bridge for several years and reported to Davies on May 5, 1861, that the detachment of soldiers from Camp Floyd stationed near his home during the preceding summer "only served to increase the contempt of the Indians and influence them against the troops and people of the United

States." As he rightly pointed out, a resident agent might be able to stop the depredations of outlaw Indians from Utah Territory and the Snake River area who, since the Otter Massacre, "seem full of devilment and their appetites for blood & plunder appear to be sharpened." Both Chase and Davies recommended that a military post of two companies be established at Salmon Falls to protect emigrant travel. As it was, the nearest military encampments were at Walla Walla in Oregon Territory 600 miles away, at Fort Bridger 350 miles distant, and Camp Floyd 300 miles to the south. The Office of Indian Affairs failed to act on the suggestion.[1]

Even these distant posts were soon to be disrupted or abandoned as the outbreak of the Civil War divided the military in their loyalties to either the North or the South. Colonel Philip St. George Cooke assumed command of Camp Floyd on August 20, 1860. Cooke's Union sentiments were displayed when he renamed the post Fort Crittenden on February 6, 1861, after Senator John J. Crittenden of Kentucky, who was attempting to effect a compromise between the North and South. The last action of the troops in guarding the emigrant trails came with the dispatch of infantry and dragoons to Ruby Valley about thirty-five miles south of Elko on May 19, 1861, for one month of duty. Cooke received orders on June 7 or 8 to abandon the Utah encampment, and troops arrived back on June 19. Over one hundred soldiers had already resigned to join the Confederate forces. The remaining activities at Fort Crittenden during 1861 were devoted to selling off government equipment and marching the troops to the east. Utah Territory and eastern Oregon were left without the protection of any military force.[2]

To provide assistance to the Eastern Shoshoni and Bannock and to place two unofficial Indian agents among these two tribes, Superintendent Davies issued a license to Louis Robison and Joshua Terry on April 8 to trade in Green River County, Utah Territory. In July Washakie assembled his people at Bear Lake with the announced intention of making war on the Cheyenne who had killed his son and three subchiefs of the tribe. Washakie was seeking the assistance of his Bannock allies and had even declared peace with the Utes. The *Deseret News* editor, on July 10, 1861, warned emigrant parties they would be "considerably exposed" if a general Indian conflict should break out. The editor thought the Indians might destroy as many lives as the Northern and Southern armies in the Civil War then raging in the nation.

Farther west, Superintendent Davies held a grand council on an 1861 winter trip to Ruby Valley to satisfy the wants of about 800 Western Shoshoni, "Weber Snakes," a few Bannock, and some Paiute from Carson Valley. Davies described the tribes as being "very troublesome and dangerous and being numerous and brave are much feared." He distributed food and other supplies to these "very poor" Indians and carefully explained that the goods were provided by their "Great Captain at Washington" who was no Mormon but an American. He recommended to the commissioner of Indian affairs that the six-mile-square farm at Ruby be expanded into a reservation covering the entire valley.[3]

Within two months the Ruby Valley Indians became the responsibility of the new Territory of Nevada and were no longer of concern to Davies. The discovery of the Comstock Lode on June 11, 1859, had swelled the population of the area east of the Sierra Nevada so that pressure for a government separate from Mormon control in Utah had reached almost irrepressible proportions. The secession of the Southern states, which had formed the strongest opposition to the territorial status for Nevada, led to the formation of the territory on March 2, 1861.[4]

New Governor James W. Nye began to receive requests almost immediately from his constituents for arms to protect themselves from the natives. Prospectors and citizens in Humboldt County explained in July that the neighboring Indians were very angry about whites moving into their country and "the destruction of their grasses," plus other grievances. The petitioners asked for arms to protect themselves and soon organized a company of "Star Rangers."[5] Another citizen, James W. Hogan, reported an attack by either Bannock, Goose Creek, or Salt Lake Indians on a horse herd he was driving from the east. The assault took place in early August on Raft River at the Goose Creek Mountains near where the Shepherd massacre had occurred two years before. Hogan lost forty valuable horses and four mules and received a bad leg wound. He was sure that Mormons were involved. The governor ordered an investigation and just and proper action.[6]

Along the mail and Pony Express line between Salt Lake City and Carson Valley, responsibility for protection from Indian hostility was now divided between Nevada and Utah territories. On March 2, 1861, a law was enacted establishing a daily overland stagecoach mail and a semiweekly Pony Express over the central route to Sacramento.

The Central Overland California and Pike's Peak Express Company —or the "Clean Out of Cash and Poor Pay" company as its detractors called it—was to start coach service on July 1, 1861. At the same time the Western Union and Missouri Telegraph Company was continuing to build its telegraph line across the continent and finally connected the wires at Salt Lake City on October 24, 1861. The Pony Express was no longer needed, but during the early months of 1861 both the express riders and stagecoach operators, as well as the station agents, were subject to the hostility of neighboring Indians who seized every opportunity to acquire horses and food from the overland company.[7]

Evan M. Greene warned the Utah superintendent of Indian affairs on February 19, 1861, that the Shoshoni intended "to break up the mail stations" west of Great Salt Lake and kill the two agents at Deep Creek.[8] And Elijah Wilson reported his experience at Eight-Mile Station between Deep Creek and Schell Creek with two emigrant orphan brothers aged eleven and thirteen who had been left in the care of the agent there. The station keeper abandoned the post, and Wilson, only a boy himself, was caught with the other two for three days when Indians attacked the station. They were finally rescued by the arrival of some troops. This probably happened during the summer of 1861, although "Uncle Nick" Wilson could be very vague about dates.[9]

By October the Indians along the mail line were becoming desperate chiefly because the Overland firm had monopolized the grass to feed the company stock, depriving the Indians "of the seed which they have heretofore used as an article of food." The Utah superintendent wrote his superior on October 1 that he was leaving on a trip to provide for "their immediate wants."[10] Lieutenant E. M. Baker of Fort Churchill, visiting Ruby Valley in the same month, wrote that the Indians were without any provisions and explained that they usually lived during the winter on pine nuts and grass seeds. This year the pine nut crop had failed and "all, or nearly all, of their grass has been cut by the Stage Company or citizens living on the road." Baker said that unless the government provided them with food they would either starve to death or there would be another outbreak when the natives were driven to desperate measures.[11]

When James Duane Doty took over as Utah superintendent of Indian affairs late in 1861, he reported that the "very wild" Indians along the mail line were taking food from the mail company by force if it was not given freely by the station keepers. An assistant agent was shot and killed near Red Butte Station, and his wagon was looted and his mules driven off. Shoshoni were without doubt the perpetrators because they had just been refused food. The Indians threatened posts all along the line, insisting that the country belonged to them and that no treaty had ever been signed with the government. Doty sent agents to man posts in Ruby Valley and at Fort Bridger but complained that the government had placed nothing in his hands to give to the Indians.[12]

The month before, Doty's predecessor, Henry Martin, had also sent an urgent message to the commissioner requesting provisions for the Indians along the mail line.[13] It prompted an exchange between New York officials of the Overland Mail Company and the Office of Indian Affairs. The agents bombarded their New York office asking permission to feed the natives out of company stocks with the understanding that the government would reimburse the mail firm. A. J. Center, company treasurer, made the request of the commissioner of Indian affairs,[14] and when a prompt reply was not received, importuned United States Senator Milton S. Lathum for help, sending the senator copies of all correspondence and telegrams from the western agents of the company. These included a telegram from Agent T. Cook at Salt Lake City that "Indians by Hundreds at several stations, clamorous for food and threatening. They will steal or starve, will they starve?" Another missive from the agent at Fish Springs reported that 100 Indians camped near the station were demanding provisions or they would take them by force. He was instructed by the New York office to distribute 500 pounds of "chop feed" to the Indians but not all at one time.[15]

Roberts Creek Station was threatened on December 17 while Utah and Nevada officials tried to decide who had the responsibility to protect the post. Governor John W. Dawson of Utah finally wrote Governor Nye that Roberts Creek was in Nevada[16] but that the Utah superintendent of Indian affairs was nevertheless sending weekly rations of beef to the natives in Ruby Valley plus an agent and more supplies. Nye reported that the death of friendly Chief Shocup at Ruby and the succession to his office of Buck, "a troublesome Indian," was complicating matters.[17] Agent Warren Wasson reached the valley to have a talk with Buck and other Shoshoni chiefs. Wasson found the Indians "in destitute condition but quiet."[18]

For two years the Russell company had attempted to prove to the nation that mail could be delivered across the plains and mountains to the Pacific Coast "with certainty, celerity, and security." It had been a dramatic but costly experiment in terms of Indian hostility. It was reported that during the period the Pony Express was in operation, Indian attacks on the Overland Mail Company had caused the loss of 150 horses, seven stations, and sixteen men killed.[19]

Depredations on mail lines and emigrant parties in Utah Territory were partly the result of frequent changes in Indian service personnel who were not in the area for sufficient time to get acquainted with their duties. Superintendent Benjamin Davies came only long enough to be able to write on June 30, 1861, that his predecessors had allowed the reservations to deteriorate in ruin. He was followed by Henry Martin who served from August 6, 1861, to December. Agent A. Humphreys, in Utah for about two and a half years, discerned the chief problem: "owing to the frequent changes in the superintendency, there has not been any over one-third of the time."[20] Davies had recommended a reservation for the Northwestern Shoshoni either in Cache Valley or at Salmon River.[21] Humphreys thought that Cache Valley and other basins were already so settled that it would be impossible to establish the Indians in their former homelands.[22] In final desperation to try to subsist the natives, Humphreys "sold *all* the cattle, farming utensils, grain and furniture of the homes and office, to supply starving Indians with food" so that there was no public property left for the Indian Department in Utah.[23]

That was the situation when James Duane Doty arrived in December 1861 to take over the superintendency. Doty was an experienced congressman from Michigan and served his Utah job so successfully that he was appointed governor of the territory in June of 1863. He was a fortunate choice as superintendent of Indian affairs. Bancroft described his tenure in office: "During his residence in the territory he had made many friends and scarcely a single enemy, his intercourse with the citizens being always marked by the cordiality and freedom from constraint characteristic of western life and manners."[24] Doty found that no treaties had been signed with the Utah tribes to grant them compensation for their lands and that the appropriations had been so grudging as to leave the Indians starving. Before departing from Washington, D.C., for his western assign-

Governor James Duane Doty. Last photograph taken of Doty, ca. 1864.
Utah State Historical Society.

ment, the Post Office Department had asked him to check on the loyalty of the Overland Mail Company employees and ascertain the seriousness of the Indian attacks on the mail line. He also had requested the sum of $68,500 as an appropriation for the Indian service—an amount twice as large as the previous year.[25]

Superintendent Davies earlier in the year, and as the first of the three superintendents for 1861, had already discovered the principal cause of Indian depredations on the mail line in Utah when he visited the Gosiute near Deep Creek during the winter of 1860. He met them in the deep snow and found them "almost naked and too feeble from cold and hunger to drag" themselves along. When he asked why there were so few children among them, they replied that with the disappearance of game "they had nothing to feed them with; wherefore they *laid them by the stone*, which means that they had laid them on the ground to die and be eaten by the wolves." They begged Davies to teach them "to plow and make wheat for their suffering families."[26] By February 1861 the friendly Gosiute west of Grantsville were so hungry that they drove off eighteen or twenty head of cattle from the local herd. The angry citizens were able to recover nine of the animals but discovered that the natives had already slaughtered two during the rapid escape from the town. Some "strange" Indians, later identified as Shoshoni, had encouraged and participated in the raid. The white posse captured eleven of the Indians, released three who promised to retrieve the rest of the cattle, and eight others escaped. Chief Tabby of the Gosiute came in for a talk and agreed to try to return the stolen animals.[27] Evan M. Greene in reporting the incident to the *Deseret News* of February 13, 1861, wrote: "These Shoshones are so vicious, that the Gosh-Utes are afraid of them, and dare not attempt to drive them out of the land." Howard Egan of the mail line voiced the opinion that there was much dissatisfaction among the Gosiute because the various superintendents had made promises to them over the past three years that were still unfulfilled.[28]

North of Salt Lake City, Mormon Bishop Alvin Nichols of Brigham City wrote Superintendent Davies in mid-March 1861 that his people were having trouble with five bad Indians from friendly Chief Sagwitch's band of about ten lodges. Another of the tribe, whose lodge was separate from the others, frequently warned his white neighbors of plans to rob them, and as a result, the five malcontents had "a pique at him" and stole his horses, gun, blankets, and everything else he possessed. Nichols asked for help to relieve the man's suffering. The bishop also requested that something be done to stop the whiskey trade among the natives and to punish the Indian desperadoes who were stealing horses and cattle and killing work oxen, four of which had been slaughtered in the past two weeks. The begging Indians were a great burden to the community.[29] Much later in the year, a reporter of Brigham Young's trip to the northern settlements wrote the *Deseret News* on September 18, 1861 that the Indians at Box Elder were still disaffected.

The settlers and Northwestern Shoshoni in neighboring Cache Valley each suffered from the other's presence during 1861. Margaret McNiel Ballard, in a typical pioneer reaction, remembered how the Indians rode their horses into the houses, tramped the gardens "all to pieces," stole cattle and horses, and ate the supply of bread which her family always had on hand to feed the hungry natives so "they would be more friendly towards us."[30] Bishop Preston Thomas of Franklin wrote Brigham Young in late February that he was short almost a thousand bushels of grain for bread, and therefore "we shall be left very weak handed to carry on our works here & to defend ourselves against the Indians & nothing to give them when they come amongst us. . . ."[31] Recognizing that they could expect little food relief from the settlers, Bear Hunter and about twenty Shoshoni traveled to Salt Lake City on foot in late March seeking presents from Superintendent Davies. He supplied them with bacon, flour, shirts, hats, and cooking utensils, including a complete suit of "citizen's clothing" for the chief. The Indian leader informed Davies that upon his return to Cache Valley he intended to lead his people into the mountains to hunt and did not expect to return until the wheat harvest, "which will be a great blessing to the whites in the valley."[32]

From spring into July the Shoshoni of Cache remained friendly and peaceable.[33] By mid-July almost 1,500 Shoshoni were camped on Black's Fork (Blacksmith Fork? west of Hyrum), near the L.D.S. church farm. Maughan wrote, "They feel a little more stuborn than we would like to see"; Seth M. Blair was blunter about the Shoshoni, "who claim our fields Towns etc as their Land & want many presents to appease their cupidity   it seems hard that the people of God have not a place to build or plant that they can call their own." He added a self-fulfilling personal prophecy—"Yet a little season will give the

General Patrick Edward Connor, commander of the California Volunteers, ca. 1860s. *Utah State Historical Society*.

faithfull the Land of Zion. . . ." In a general council with Pe-ass wicks, Bear Hunter, Sagwitchs, and other chiefs, the Saints agreed to give the Indians sixty bushels of tithing wheat, 2,400 pounds of flour, four beef cattle, and five shirts for the five chiefs present. After the meeting, Maughan appointed three interpreters to watch the movements of the Indians, who agreed to leave as soon as they had eaten the donated food, a prospect "which we greatly desire," according to Blair.[34]

On their return to the valley in September, a group of Indians stole sixty horses from the settlers.[35] Bear Hunter decried the theft. He returned twenty-one head himself and saw to it that all but four young colts were brought in. Maughan expected that these would also be recovered, although he thought that a good many of the horses returned did not belong to people in the valley. He intended to try to find the right owners.[36]

The citizens of Utah and Nevada territories, the mail line, and the emigrant trains were left without any army protection after Fort Crittenden was abandoned. The secretary of war, on July 24, 1861, informed Governor John G. Downey of California that the government "accepts for three years one regiment of infantry and five companies of cavalry to guard the overland mail route from Carson Valley to Salt Lake and Fort Laramie."[37] Governor Downey wrote Patrick Edward Connor of Stockton, California, "Having confidence in your ability, and experience as a soldier, . . . I take pleasure in tendering to you the command of one of the five regiments called for by the . . . President. . . ."[38] The appointment of Connor to lead an expedition into Utah Territory emphasized the concern of President Abraham Lincoln and other Union leaders that California, with all its wealth, had to be kept tied to the North and that communications must be maintained between the East and the Pacific Coast. The enlistment of California volunteers to ensure the security of the mail and telegraph lines meant that Colonel Connor's role was critically important to the Union cause.

Connor was born in Kerry County, Ireland, on St. Patrick's Day, March 17, 1820. He emigrated with his parents at an early age to New York City but never forgot his Irish heritage. At the age of nineteen, on November 28, 1839, he enlisted in the regular army under his

Irish name of O'Connor and served for five years on the Iowa frontier until his honorable discharge as a private on November 28, 1844. He returned to New York where he engaged in the mercantile business until the new state of Texas beckoned in early 1846. When the Mexican War broke out, he joined a regiment of Texas volunteers on July 7, 1846, commanded by Colonel Albert Sidney Johnston and was given the rank of first lieutenant. At this time he changed his name from O'Connor. When the volunteer regiment was discharged, Connor reenlisted in the regular army on September 1, 1846. Attached to the command of General John E. Wool, he was promoted to captain on February 12, 1847, and participated in the Battle of Buena Vista. General Zachary Taylor's official account of the engagement noted, "Captain Conner's company of Texas Volunteers . . . fought bravely, its captain being wounded and two subalterns killed." Connor received a severe wound in the hand early in the fight but continued to direct his company throughout the day. It was reported that General Wool asked him, "Captain Connor, where are your men?" Pointing to the bodies of fifteen of his men lying on the field, Connor replied, "General. There!" and plunged on. With the main event over in the northern Mexico campaign and suffering from rheumatism, Connor resigned his commission on May 24, 1847, at Monterey. When gold was discovered in California, he left Texas and arrived in California January 22, 1850.[39]

In his first search for gold in the treasure state, Connor almost lost his life, an episode which nearly all of his biographers treat in some detail. He and three lieutenants from the United States Navy chartered the brig *Arabian* to found a settlement at the mouth of the Trinity River, not knowing that the stream did not flow into the Pacific Ocean. In attempting to land, using a whale boat, his party of eleven men met heavy surf; the boat overturned and only five survived to reach shore. Connor described the disaster to the *Sacramento Transcript* of April 20, 1850.

Connor then attempted to recoup his finances by cutting pilings at Humboldt Bay but could not sell them at San Francisco for even ten cents a foot when earlier the commodity had brought eighty cents a foot. His next adventure was as a member of twenty "California Rangers" organized under Harry Love and established by the state legislature to hunt down the famous bandit Joaquin Murietta. In July 1853 the rangers are said to have captured Murietta and received

$1,000 for killing him. One story has Connor as the "her" who shot and killed the desperado. Apparently tiring of such dangerous interludes, Connor sought greater peace and security by marrying Johanna Connor, a native of the same Irish county where he was born, and settling down in Stockton. He became a successful businessman, operating a surveying company, a gravel concern, the city waterworks, and finally taking a contract to build the foundation of the new state capitol at Sacramento, a venture from which he was released to enter the military service in 1861. His annual income by this time was over $8,000. He also held the job of postmaster for the city and captain of the Stockton Blues, as well as other commands in the state militia. During this period, three sons were born to the Connors, with only Maurice Joseph surviving. The Civil War found him to be a staunch Unionist among many Southerners in Stockton. Patrick Edward Connor was obviously a man of courage and adventurous spirit—shrewd, energetic, feisty, and independent and with natural talents for leadership and soldiering.[40]

Connor's regiment was recruited during September 1861 and went into camp on October 1 at Camp McDougall, three miles south of Stockton. A number of Stockton residents joined, including Dr. R. K. Reid, surgeon, and John A. Anderson, chaplain.[41] There were many sons of Erin and Saint Patrick. Their hometowns sounded like a roll call of the early gold rush: Fiddletown, Poverty Bar, Chinese Camp, Chili Gulch, Jenny Lind, Angel Camp, Mokelumne Hill, Don Pedro's Bar, and Camp Seco.[42] Agricultural Park in Stockton, renamed Camp Halleck, became the training camp for the ten companies, only seven of which finally followed Connor to Utah. The other three units were held in the Humboldt district until returned to Connor's forces in the summer of 1863. The colonel's commanding officer, Brigadier General G. Wright, ordered most of the regiment to Benicia Barracks on November 16 and decided to hold the troops there during the winter while distributing enough provisions to the Indians "who are in a starving condition along the route" to keep the mail from being interrupted. On December 6 Wright reviewed the six companies of the Third Infantry California Volunteers and the one company of the Second Volunteer Cavalry and found they were "in high order, well clothed, and presented a handsome appearance."[43] The following June 28, 1862, he made another inspection, noted their "fine appearance," and praised the "industry and untiring zeal and energy of Colonel Connor. . . . He has a regiment that the State may well be proud of."[44] The colonel and his troops seemed well prepared to patrol along the mail line to Salt Lake City when marching orders finally came for the seven companies of the "Utah Column" to leave Benicia Barracks on July 5, 1862.[45]

Contrary to General Wright's pious hope that the few provisions given the Shoshoni and Paiute would keep them quiet until Connor's troops reached the mail line in Nevada, Indian troubles continued during the first six months of 1862. As early as March 28, 1862, orders were given to prepare the California Volunteers for the march to Salt Lake City, but deep snows in the Sierra Nevada prevented the start until July. Wright expected that Connor would establish at least one intermediate post on the route, probably at Ruby Valley.[46]

The editor of the *Deseret News* watched the preparations of the volunteers for their movement to Utah and began a series of derisive reports about Connor and his military force that would continue throughout the year. He accused some of the merchants in his city on April 16 of being behind the troop movements as leeches trying to "get their fill of the nation's life-blood—treasury—pap. . . . The Indians want feeding—not fighting." He thought that reports of Indian depredations in Nevada were grossly exaggerated and that actually Chief Winnemucca of the Paiute "had equipped a hundred of his warriors with picks, pans and shovels and had gone north on a prospecting tour." The editor blamed the government for its failure to take care of the Indians in Utah Territory, which had resulted in the "onerous tax" exacted from the inhabitants of Utah to feed the natives. On the other hand, the *Sacramento Union* of April 4 was sure that the final destination of Connor's troops was "still further East" of Salt Lake City.

Meantime the Paiute and Shoshoni continued to steal cattle along the Humboldt during the winter of 1861–62 to avoid starvation. One citizen, J. W. Jacobs, wired Governor Nye of Nevada from Reese River on January 2 asking for a force of fifty men to help return some stolen cattle and promised he would "not kill any Indians if I can help it."[47] N. H. Mason reported the loss of thirty head of stock from his ranch on Walker River and asked for immediate assistance from the governor.[48] Agent John C. Burche of the Humboldt Agency distributed 6,000 pounds of provisions to the Indians during a two-month period from February 20 to late April and reported that the famished natives were "almost on the point of starvation" when he arrived. He found the Shoshoni to be "far less amicable, peaceable and honest than the Pah Utes and greatly more prone to stealing and mischief." He warned his superior, J. F. Lockhart, that white settlers were taking up the "Big Meadow" of the Humboldt and thus depriving the Indians of the edible roots necessary for existence.[49]

In a very revealing message about the difference between the point of view held by some military officers, Major Charles McDermit of Fort Churchill, a post located on the Carson River in western Nevada, appealed to Governor Nye for help to monitor the actions of a Captain Price who had instructions to act "as he may deem proper." The Indians were already excited because Price did not understand the natives and was unacquainted with their character. McDermit was afraid the captain might provoke a war and asked the governor to hurry to the post to stop Price from any kind of crazy action.[50]

Farther east along the mail line, Nye, in February 1862, deprecated fears that the stagecoaches would be attacked by Indians. He thought the ungrounded concerns of the station agents were partially a result of the pernicious system of feeding the neighboring Indians, who thus indolently failed to provide for their own winter's food supplies. When the governor received a report in late December 1861 that the Roberts Creek Station had been attacked, he sent a contingent of twenty-five soldiers under Captain Edwin A. Rowe. The troops arrived at Ruby Valley on December 27 to find that the only difficulty was a disagreement among the Indians themselves. While the soldiers remained at Ruby Valley, Indian Agent Warren Wasson visited Grub's Wells and Roberts Creek, where he found "fifty or sixty half starved Indians . . . in a most deplorable condition, subsisting principally upon the undigested barley obtained by washing the manure from the Overland Stables, in baskets, after the manner of separating gold from earth with a pan." Wasson advised that the chief threat to the mail line was from the Shoshoni White Knives and the Gosiute. He ended his late January letter with the news that he had just heard that the White Knives had stolen some cattle from Ruby Valley. He hoped the stock could be recovered "without a collision" occurring.[51]

When Captain Rowe's small force was ordered back to Fort Churchill on January 24, 1862,[52] the local citizens of Ruby Valley urged Agent Wasson to use his influence to keep the soldiers so they "would intimidate the natives & keep them down."[53] But apparently the troops left anyway, and within a few weeks, thirty-five Indians attacked Desert Creek on the Aurora Road and stole some horses.[54] At Reese River, other Indians from a band of "about 500" took twelve head of cattle.[55] H. Butterfield, of the Overland Mail Company, asked for a large number of troops to be stationed at Ruby Valley but was overruled by Frederick Cook, treasurer of the company, who said "he wants no more Soldiers out here."[56] Wasson agreed with Cook, writing on March 19 that the Indians were peaceable and that there would be no hostilities "unless the whites begin it."[57]

But depredations became so serious by late April that the postmaster general ordered all mail delivered by sea until interruptions on the Overland Mail Line ceased. The *Sacramento Union* of April 29, 1862, speculated that perhaps a few self-serving businessmen were exaggerating fears of Indian attacks to serve their own selfish purposes, but noted that orders to Colonel Connor to patrol the mail line meant that the government was acting in good faith after all. By June 7, the Salt Lake City correspondent of the *Union* was still asking when the overland mail might be resumed, noting that would-be stagecoach passengers had been waiting in the City of the Saints until they were "blue mouldy."

The successful threat of the Shoshoni that they would stop the "paper wagons" coincided with attacks on emigrant parties during June along the roads in the vicinity of Fort Hall. A party headed by two men named Smith and Kinkaid was assaulted between Raft River and Bear River near Fort Hall by some Bannock, and all but Smith and another man were killed. Smith was shot in the back by an arrow but finally reached a Bear River settlement with the arrow still protruding. Three other emigrant trains were attacked by Shoshoni near Soda Springs, with several people killed. Superintendent Doty of Utah Territory hoped that the secretary of war would try to hurry Connor's Volunteers along so they would reach the Utah settlements before winter.[58]

The attacks near Fort Hall and in western Nevada were nothing,

however, compared to the concentrated killings and burnings along
the mail line east of Salt Lake City to South Pass during the early
months of 1862. There an element was added to the equation of
Indian-white relations as Washakie's hold on his young warriors
slipped. The enticement of food and provisions at the convenient new
stage stations and the opportunity to gain honor in the age-old pursuit of horse theft were irresistible. A report of April 21 listed the killing of a dozen white men at the Devil's Gate Station.[59] The next day
J. E. Bromley of the Overland Mail Company wrote from Pacific
Springs that he would not run any more mail coaches over the line
until troops were sent to guard the road. He advised Joseph Holladay,
the brother of stagecoach king Ben Holladay, to hold all passengers,
as "we already have enough here that can't get through."[60] His decision was timely. On April 17 forty or fifty Indians had attacked two
stagecoaches carrying nine people about four miles west of Split Rock.
After a four-hour battle, the men were forced to abandon the
coaches, mules, and the mail and escaped with their lives. Six were
wounded, three quite seriously. Lem Flowers, suffering from two bad
wounds, wrote that it was impossible to continue the mail without
protection: "Everything taken from Three Crossings—Country full of
Indians." On April 19, twenty-four Indians, "either Snake or Arapahoes," struck the station at Green River and "killed the Station
Keeper, John Mallory, took 5 horses—all that was at the station—
destroyed all the harnesses, tore up all grain sacks, took off all
clothing whatever else they could carry."[61]

The *Sacramento Union* correspondent from Salt Lake City reported on April 28 that "rivers of blood and mountains of Indians
rush into *bona fide* existence and the end of the world is near at
hand. . . ."[62] But to those on the scene, there was no melodrama to
report. Four emigrants at Plante's Station wrote a proclamation to all
concerned informing travelers that depredations were occurring along
the mail line by either Indians or Mormons or both and that they
should unite in large companies before proceeding. One of the four
men, Tim Goodale, made an additional statement that emigrants
had looted the empty station buildings and the caches of harness at
Sweetwater Bridge. He also accused emigrants rather than Indians of
burning Wheeler Station at Devil's Gate.[63]

"Liberal," correspondent for the *Sacramento Union*, in a letter
published May 31, 1862, recapitulated the series of attacks made on

the eastern mail stations. In addition to the assaults involving Lem Flowers and John Mallory, the newsman listed a February attack on Split Rock Station in which two men were killed and fourteen mules taken. During the same night raid thirteen mules were stolen from Horse Creek Station thirty-five miles farther east. Other attacks on Split Rock, Rocky Ridge, and Dry Sandy stations resulted in a loss of twenty more mules, and another twenty-five horses and mules were driven off from Granger's Station. To add to the misery of Overland Mail Company officials, the roads east of Salt Lake City were bottomless pits of mud.

The incessant attacks on the eastern mail line prompted various government and Overland company officials to call for troops on a temporary basis until Connor's Volunteers could arrive from California to take over. Utah Superintendent of Indian Affairs James Doty wrote the Indian Office on March 24 asking for a military force to be stationed at Fort Hall because no travel would otherwise be safe.[64] On April 11, Utah Governor Frank Fuller and officials of the mail and telegraph companies responded by asking the secretary of war for a regiment of mounted rangers to be called into three months' service by Superintendent Doty to protect the mail line and the settlers of northern Utah who were being threatened and robbed by an insolent band of "2,000 Shoshones." Brigham Young took this as an obvious attempt to bypass the Utah militia, who, he indignantly wrote, "are ready and able . . . to take care of all the Indians, and are able and willing to protect the mail line if called upon to do so." He thought the 2,000 Shoshones under Washakie were "unusually quiet" and perfectly friendly.[65] The jurisdictional dispute was settled on April 25 when Governor Fuller called on General Daniel H. Wells of the Utah militia for twenty mounted rangers "for purposes of protection and defense of the United States mails . . . as well as the persons of passengers and all others connected with the line of the Overland Mail Company, east of Great Salt Lake City. . . ." Colonel Robert F. Burton, sheriff of Salt Lake County, was chosen to command the force, which included two sons of Brigham Young and two sons of Heber C. Kimball.[66]

The Burton Company left Salt Lake City April 26, 1862, and

returned on May 31, 1862. Arriving at Fort Bridger on May 4, the colonel found that all the stations west of Green River "look as though they had been deserted in a hurry." At Ice Spring Station he found twenty-six mail sacks cut open and the contents "scattered over the prairie." He was sure it was the work of white men. Assaults on the stations probably had been perpetrated by a band of about thirty "renegade Snakes & Bannacks from the north," although some of the group used good English and at least one spoke in German. On his trip he also observed the devastaton at Split Rock, learned of fifty head of stock taken from Plante's Station, saw how the paper mail had been "shamefully used" at Three Crossings, and heard from some mountaineers at Ham's Fork that they had lost thirty-five head of horses. When he finally met troops from the East sent out on an escort party, he returned his command to Salt Lake City. They had encountered no hostile Indians.[67]

Close on the heels of the dispatch of the Burton column, Army Adjutant General Lorenzo Thomas, under orders from President Abraham Lincoln and the secretary of war, telegraphed Brigham Young on April 28, 1862, to muster into service a company of cavalry for ninety days' enlistment to protect the mail line in and about Independence Rock on the Oregon Trail. It is interesting that the request was made to Brigham Young, not to Governor Fuller. Young quickly ordered General Wells to raise the company, which was put under the leadership of Captain Lot Smith, who, like Burton, had commanded Mormon troops when they harassed Johnston's Army during the Utah War. The 106 men of the Smith Company furnished at their own expense horses, bridles, saddles, and other equipment in keeping with normal militia practice in many states and territories.[68] Ben Holladay wired Brigham Young, "Many thanks for your prompt response to President Lincoln's request. As soon as the boys can give protection the mails shall be resumed."[69]

After a reminder from their Prophet and President to observe strict sobriety, to refrain from using profane language, and to hold evening prayers, Lot Smith's company left Salt Lake City May 1, 1862, and returned on August 14 without encountering any Indians responsible for the attacks. There are a number of diaries reporting the adventures of the troops as they patrolled the mail line. Private Joseph A. Fisher noted that "many of the Mail stations were still smouldering when we came upon them." The *Deseret News* of June 25, 1862, announced the cheering news of the appearance of the eastern mail even before the troops returned to Salt Lake City.

The troubles on the road to Fort Bridger and South Pass carried over to the Northwestern Shoshoni of Cache Valley during the first six months of 1862. Peter Maughan reported to Brigham Young on February 5 that the Indians had started killing cattle from the settlers' large herd. The Indians were under the control of a subchief named Pine, who "to my certain knowledge has been well treated by the Cache Valley brethren for the last two years. . . ." Maughan decided to send 150 Minute Men to guard the herd with instructions to try to hold a council with Chief "Sige-watch" (Sagwitch) who had always been friendly with the settlers. If those efforts failed and the Indians attacked, Dudley Merrill, in charge of the Minute Men, was told to "chastise in a way that will make them remember for years to come. . . ."[70]

Superintendent Doty visited the Indians of Cache Valley in late March and found the Northwestern bands in "a starving and destitute condition. No provision having been made for them, either as to clothing or provisions, by my predecessors, . . . they were enduring great suffering . . . with the prospect that they would rob the Mail Stations to sustain life. . . ." He exceeded his strained budget to buy wheat, flour, and clothing for the natives and recommended that they be placed on a reservation where they could cease to be beggars and could learn to become herdsmen. He wrote, "At present they are not satisfied with all that I have done for them, . . ." even though they had also been helped by the mail company and the local valley residents.[71] The *Deseret News* of June 11, 1862, applauded Doty's efforts and opined that troops would not be needed if the government would only give the superintendent sufficient funds. The editor believed the people would not be relieved from the "grievous tax" of having to feed the Indians until they were settled on farms where they could raise grain for themselves.[72]

By May 20, 1862, Seth Blair wrote that the Northwestern Shoshoni of Cache Valley were still "flocking in on us very fast [and] they are quite annoying & must be fed. . . ."[73] Six days later Maughan reported that the Indians were uneasy and feared that the Mormons would join the soldiers. Shoshoni from the Salmon River asked if the Saints "were willing to overlook the outbreak at that place in 1858.

. . ." Maughan reminded all of them that they had to stop stealing horses if they wished to retain Mormon friendship. Much to the dismay of the settlers, the Indians finally left the valley only after promising "to see us again at harvest. . . ."[74] Some of the Mormon church members in the Cache settlements were condemned by Mormon leaders for trading powder and horses to the Indians and in other ways promoting dissension among the natives. A church trial was held on June 21 at Logan in which five men were charged with gambling with neighboring Indians. G. G. Merrill, J. Merrill, and Mr. Price were "cut off. S. Collett to be re-baptized and R. Collett to leave the place" and have his case decided by civil authority since he was not a church member.[75]

Thus Indian-white relationships along Shoshoni trails in 1861 and early 1862 edged closer to the breaking point as most of the old factors continued to aggravate things and a number of new developments added further stress to the thin fabric of white restraint. The natives along the Humboldt and in the Gosiute area were especially deficient in food supplies and clothing and attempted to sustain life and warmth by attacking emigrant parties and stage stations. As usual, the tribes farther east were more self-sufficient, being closer to a supply of buffalo meat, but they, too, were now showing a decidedly hostile attitude toward all whites. The formation of the Nevada Territory brought the western Indians under closer supervision and decreased the strain on Utah authorities, although the constant shuffling of superintendents militated against any stable policy. A principal change in the pattern came with the sudden surge of Indian attacks on the mail stations east of Salt Lake City. Temporary militia assignments under Robert Burton and Lot Smith helped protect the roads until troops from California could be sent as a permanent force. The formation of the California Volunteers as a part of the Civil War effort to keep the transcontinental mail routes open brought hope to Utah settlers that Indian conflicts might be brought under control. The assignment of the veteran and experienced military officer Patrick Edward Connor, a man of action and resolution, as commander was an omen of change in the way federal military affairs would henceforth be conducted along the western trails. Connor would not be content with desultory patrols and occasional skirmishes.

By mid-year of 1862, the Shoshoni along the Overland Mail Line had sunk to a level of destitution unequaled before—a situation so desperate that the combined food supplies from the mail company, government officials, and the Mormon settlers could not satisfy the demand at a level that would sustain life for the Indians. Generalizations simply cannot sharpen a perception of their troubles. The full force of this decline can only be appreciated by a thorough description of the assaults that came as a result of Indian suffering. The stations were well stocked with food and horses and served as convenient corner grocery stores inviting starving natives to plunder them, especially in winter and early spring when other food sources were scarce. National attention was awakening to the need to protect the mail line as raids increased and Union officials worried about keeping communications open with California and the Pacific Coast.

From the point of view of wartime Washington, D.C., the answer to the deteriorating situation was to send a military force to eradicate the problem as quickly as possible, not to provide farms or new reservations for the Indians. The Mormon militia companies were stopgap measures until an imposing volunteer regiment could be mustered from California to meet the problem head-on. As Colonel Connor gathered his troops, they also dreamed of glory and adventure fighting the Rebels in Virginia. Disappointment at being kept in the deserts of the Great Basin became a factor in their attack at Bear River. The California Volunteers, by the summer of 1862, were poised like a sledgehammer in midair waiting for an inviting target upon which to fall.

The Mormon settlers of Cache Valley played their part. Tensions with neighboring Northwestern bands increased after the July 1860 killing of Chief Pagunap at Smithfield and the loss of two of the Saints at the hands of the revenge-seeking natives. Fighting seemed to be the rule during the next two years. Cache Valley residents mounted guard over their herds and fields and Chief Bear Hunter skillfully sought provisions for his people while negotiating with the Mormon leaders, but anger and frustration escalated on both sides as this impossible situation grew worse. The approach of the winter of 1862 brought with it signs that an irrepressible force of California soldiers might have an opportunity to smash a tribe of desperate Indians somewhere in the Great Basin. If the blow fell on the Shoshoni of

Cache Valley, it would be with the approbation of the fearful and angry Mormon farmers.

Brigham Young concurred with the general philosophy that Indian raids east along the communication line had to be controlled. He vigorously led out by committing Mormons to the general hostility and suppression-by-force policy when he seized the initiative in raising troops. It is true his strategy may have been to keep federal troops out of the picture, as it was later in the Black Hawk War, but the result was the same—Mormons were committed to the general spirit of the times and to an Indian policy of force. The former feed-rather-than-fight policy was given lip service in the settlements and still had a certain utility, but strains on it in 1861 and 1862 bespoke of a time when Mormons would contribute to the tragedy at Bear River by tacitly and actively participating in the military operation. The limitations of the feed-rather-than-fight policy can be seen again and again in the course of Mormon-Indian interaction. When push came to shove, Mormon settlers were capable of explosions of fury and appalling bloodlettings.

NINE

The California Volunteers Arrive

In the final months before the Bear River Massacre, several developments maintained the tempo of Indian-white conflict. Among these were administrative changes, new gold strikes in Idaho and Montana, poverty among the Indians, and repercussions from Indian violence along the trails and in the settlements and mining camps. New personalities also played a role in the continuing drama of Mormon dissension as Patrick Edward Connor and a new governor, Stephen Harding, tested Brigham Young. The final pieces leading to the massacre at Bear River slowly began to fall into place. In 1862 these particular incidents attracted little national notice, but to the participants—the starving Indians, the harassed Mormon settlers, overlanders, miners, the territories and states involved, and especially to Colonel Connor and the California Volunteers—they were crucial. Conflicts were converging to produce at Bear River one of the most horrible battles in American Indian history, but one which would remain relatively unknown.

The Mormon settlements and the California and Oregon coast metropolises brought a flow of civilization that impinged on the Shoshoni and the austere desert environment. The Trans-Mississippi experience and the westering process conspired with these elements to produce Indian dislocations. In significant ways, "overlanding" was receiving its first real test in terms of Indian relations. A second and admittedly more important scene in this process was played out on the Great Plains after the Civil War. No one was prepared to deal with the problems produced in 1860. Anglo-Americans wished the problems would go away, but the Indians had no place to go and the problems remained and intensified. Altruism, restraint, and the expedients used during earlier Indian frontiers were unequal to the desert magnitudes of the situation.

Supervision of the native tribes along the Snake River near Fort Boise in the last six months of 1862 had become more inefficient by placing these Indians under a new Washington superintendency in May 1861.[1] The new superintendency, in the territorial capital at Olympia, was even more distant from the Snake River area. The map used by the Washington superintendent in his annual report of 1862 showed a large vacant space with the word "Unexplored" south of the Salmon River, the words "Shoshonis and Snakes" just north of Snake River, and "Mountain Snakes" along the stream.[2] Oregon Superintendent J. M. Kirkpatrick, in his 1862 report, described the Bannock as a "mysterious people, living in rude lodges made of the willow brush. They know but little and are very improvident. . . ."[3] His colleague to the north, Superintendent C. H. Hale of Washington Territory, wrote in 1862 of the Snakes or Digger Indians "who infest the emigrant route. . . . Living amongst the sage brush, hiding in the canons, skulking behind rocks, they are seldom seen until they strike a blow." Hale presumed that the Snakes resided mostly in his territory.[4] Indian officials of Oregon and Washington knew less about the Shoshoni of the Snake River in 1862 than they had fifteen years earlier.

Volunteer General Benjamin Alvord sent Lieutenant Colonel Reuben F. Maury's command to guard the Oregon Trail near Salmon Falls in July 1862. Medorem Crawford of Oregon had already left in June with a force of seventy-five men to protect the last of the summer's emigration from Fort Hall to west of Fort Boise. Alvord ordered Maury to arrest and punish the Snake Indians who had murdered travelers in the fall of 1860.[5]

Superintendent Hale requested additional funds so he could set up an agency east of the Cascades[6] to control the "roving thievish and murderous bands who have frequently in times past imbued their hands in the blood of the unsuspecting emigrants, . . ."[7] but the money was not appropriated. Near the year's end, the *Walla Walla Statesman* of November 15, 1862, reported the melancholy news that Snake Indians had driven off the stock of a company of packers near Fort Boise. William Wilson reported to the newspaper that the Indians "manifest a decidedly inhospitable disposition toward the whites . . ." since the recent opening of the Boise mines. In the new gold district of the Beaverhead country in western Montana, the miners held a council with "about five hundred warriors" to insure peace. The natives expressed approval of the miners' search for gold and objected "only to having their lands taken up for permanent settlement." The white reporter stated that as soon as enough whites were in the area they would do as they pleased about Indian lands.[8]

The discovery of gold by John White on July 28, 1862, at Grasshopper Creek in the Beaverhead country led to an immense rush of miners from all over the West. The nearest supply point for the new camps was Salt Lake City, and soon the Montana Trail was crowded with freighters and parties of eager gold hunters hoping to make their fortunes in the diggings.[9] The sudden surge of northerly travel carried gold-seekers right through Northwestern Shoshoni homelands. Shoshoni and Bannock anger began erupting as early as midsummer of 1862 against south-north *and* east-west travel past Fort Hall.

The *Deseret News* of August 6, 1862, warned emigrant and mining parties that gold-digging operations in the Salmon River area would have "a great tendency to stir up the natives to war with those they consider intruders. . . ." Anticipating possible depredations by Shoshoni and Bannock, the commissioner of Indian affairs had instructed James Doty and his agent on July 22 to use a recent congressional appropriation of $20,000 to make a treaty with the "Shoshonees or Snake Indians." Doty was not to use the money in extinguishing title to Indian lands but was to distribute goods and annuities "suitable to their wants" to secure the safety of travelers over the Oregon, California, and Montana trails. In the event Doty could not gain the friendship of all the Shoshoni bands by treaty, he was to negotiate only with the tribe most dangerous to settlers and emigrants.[10]

With little likelihood that the scattered bands could be gathered together for a treaty conference, knowledgeable individuals looked ahead to a season of raids and killings. They were not mistaken. On July 18 Martin Moran was killed just west of Green River.[11] In the same general area, E. S. McComas reported, "This is where a great deal of depredations have been committed by the Indians & white Jayhawkers on the emigrants." He noted, on July 27, the grave of a man killed by Indians as well as a fight in which two more white men were badly wounded. McComas later saw the grave of G. W. Sanders near Raft River. Sanders had lost his horses to Indian raiders, and, in his efforts to retrieve them, died from exposure on July 27. On August 8 the McComas party met a company of about twelve Californians who had just had a fight with a band of Indians in which fourteen horses were shot and four men were wounded. The next day the McComas group found four white men killed and scalped "with indications of a hard fight."[12]

Perhaps the most remembered of the Snake River Indian attacks of 1862 were those that occurred on August 9 and 10 at Massacre Rocks west of present American Falls, Idaho. About 150 warriors first attacked the Smart train and then struck a company led by George W. Adams. Five white men were killed in the two assaults. The next morning Captain Kennedy of another train and thirty-five men attempted to retrieve property stolen from the two companies and engaged in a running fight with the Indians for three miles. Four more whites lost their lives. Captain Adams's daughter Elizabeth died of wounds two days after the attack, bringing the total number of emigrants killed to ten. It was charged that the Indian warriors were led by white men and were armed with good rifles. As Charles M. Harrison of the Smart company explained later, "not one of us had ever been called upon to defend our lives or property by the use of such weapons."[13]

Throughout the summer accounts poured in of many other Shoshoni attacks on emigrant parties near Fort Hall. Superintendent Doty was told by one traveler that he had seen the bodies of three white men beside two abandoned wagons at the junction of the Salt Lake and California trails.[14] On August 27, 1862, the *Deseret News* reported the killing and scalping of five men from a Denver company bound for the Salmon mines. The assailants looted the two wagons of groceries and "retired to their wick-i-ups." The same observer saw many dead cattle and horses lying around, indicating other attacks. The *Sacramento Union* of August 18, 1862, heard from its Salt Lake City correspondent about the discovery by the P. Lumas Company of three murdered emigrants on the California Trail south of the Snake River. One of the three was identified as a German, Carl Bartlett. Lumas and his five companions decided to give up trying to reach California and hurried to the safety of Salt Lake City instead of traveling along the Humboldt "where there was no immigration."

In his comprehensive journal, E. S. McComas listed several minor raids and depredations. On August 22 his company lost four cows to a raiding party and became so enraged at all Indians that when one wandered into camp wanting to trade three salmon, "some of us were in favor of shooting and some not." They finally let him leave in one piece. Four days later Indians stole a pony. At Catherine Creek the McComas emigrants found an encampment of 200 soldiers that looked like a town—tents were pitched, women washed and cooked, children played, and the men were engaged in sundry occupations.[15]

Medorem Crawford also reported a number of scattered attacks. On August 13 one military detachment discovered the body of an unknown man who had been shot in the head with a charge of buckshot. Charles Brown, a ferry operator at Fort Hall, was seriously wounded and stripped of all his clothes in an attack on August 24. He escaped by feigning death. A man named Phillips was taken prisoner near the Goose Creek Mountains and killed in "a most barbarous manner."[16] The editor of the *Deseret News* of September 10, 1862, reported that the Indians on the Snake River were very hostile to emigrants and mountaineers. The newspaperman did not know the reason. He warned the greedy gold-seekers who risked their lives to travel to the Salmon River that "all is not gold that glitters." The carnage along the trails near Fort Hall was so bad that thirty-two ferrymen and traders were said to be abandoning their posts and heading for Salt Lake City. The *News* underscored its warnings by relating the story of an attack on forty emigrants from Iowa who lost most of their cattle and horses and eleven wagons and had to endure two subsequent attacks in which four of their number were killed. The destitute and starving were saved by a rescue party of Mormon settlers from Cache Valley.[17]

James Doty listened to the tales of murder and assault and warned the commissioner of Indian affairs that there was at that time not a single agent from Fort Laramie to California, a distance of one thousand miles. He recommended that one be stationed at either Bear River, Soda Springs, or Fort Hall with a military post being established at the same place.[18] The commissioner finally decided to issue a proclamation to the public on September 19 warning all persons thinking of crossing the plains during the autumn months that many robberies and murders had been committed by the "numerous, powerful, and warlike" Bannock and Shoshoni and that their hostility made any journey over the western trails a perilous one.[19] Newspaper sources supported the announcement by reporting that renegade whites were involved with the Indians. The *Washington Statesman* of September 20, 1862, claimed that in the region of Fort Hall and Raft River in one instance alone, a band of Indians and white robbers had taken $15,000 from travelers.

A final large-scale engagement occurred on September 12 near Raft River when a party of fifteen well-armed men under Charles McBride and John Andrews, returning from California to the States, was ambushed by thirty-five or forty Indians after trying to purchase some beef from a herd of about 500 cattle owned by a supposedly friendly band of Shoshoni. In a fight that lasted most of the day, six of the whites were killed. That night the remaining nine men started for the Box Elder settlement and were saved from death after five days without food when they met an emigrant company.[20] Although Medorem Crawford wrote in his annual report for the year that only fifteen persons had been positively reported as killed in the Snake River attacks and that the accounts of massacres of emigrants by Indians had "been greatly exaggerated," the evidence now available indicates a much higher casualty rate.[21] Indeed the year 1862 turned out to be sanguinary as starving natives indulged in reckless and almost continuous sorties against unwary pilgrims and gold-miners along the trails.

Utah Superintendent of Indian Affairs James Duane Doty had been warned by a message from Little Soldier, chief of the Northwestern Shoshoni in the Weber area, on August 2, 1862, that the Indians north of Great Salt Lake planned an all-out war on travelers and settlers. He reported

> that the Shoshoni or snake Indians, and the Bannack Indians, inhabiting the northern part of this Territory and the Southern portion of Eastern Washington Territory, have united their forces for the purpose of making war upon, and committing depredations on the property of, the white people, settlers in this Territory, and the Emigrants to the Pacific coast by the Northern route. That for this purpose the Sho-sho-nee Indians have set aside Wash-i-kee, the great Chief of the Nation, because he is a man of peace and a friend to the whites, and have chosen in his place, as their leader, Pash-e-go, because he is a man of blood. That they are trying very hard to get the Cum-um-bahs, the Gos-Utes, and Sho-e-gars or Bannock Diggers, to join them. That they have already killed a number of Emigrants and committed many depreda-

tions on the property of the Settlers and Emigrants, stealing horses, cattle, &c.—That lately they have stolen and run off one hundred and fifty horses & mules at and about Ft. Bridger; a large number in the northern part of the Territory, and three head north of and within fifty miles of Great Salt Lake City. That they are now removing their families to the Salmon River country to get them out of danger—and that when the leaves turn red in the fall is the time they have agreed upon to assemble and when the leaves turn yellow and begin to fall the time they are to fall upon and exterminate all the settlers in the Territory. That all these war movements are instigated and led on by War-a-gi-ka, the Great Bannock prophet, in whom the Bannocks, and Sho-sho-nees have unbounded confidence and faith—who lives in the vicinity of Walla Walla, in Oregon, or Washington Territory. Little Soldier, very urgently warns the people of the great danger hanging over them and advises them to have their guns with them at all times, in the Kanyons and in their fields.[22]

Chief Washakie, however, was not "set aside" and remained friendly to whites, but, like many Indian headmen, he could not always control young hot heads, and some of his warriors appear to have been involved with the Fort Hall Indians and Northwestern Shoshoni in raids on the northern roads. Depredations continued due to government neglect of all the Northern Shoshoni tribes. While other Indians had treaties guaranteeing them presents of food and clothing each year, these "left-out" tribes were now throwing off restraint. The swiftest way for them to get the attention of men in authority was by attacking white citizens,[23] and it worked. The commissioner of Indian affairs appointed Doty, Luther Mann, and Henry Martin as a special commission to negotiate a treaty with the Northern Shoshoni.[24] Henry Martin bombarded Washington with demands for expense money and annuity goods so he could proceed to work with his two colleagues in signing treaties.[25] Nothing was accomplished during 1862. The secretary of the interior was finally forced to get involved and on January 13, 1863, made an "urgent" request to Congress for $50,000 for the Indians of Utah Territory to maintain their "goodwill."[26] Superintendent Doty wrote Governor James Nye in Nevada Territory asking his support in scheduling a meeting with the Shoshoni and Bannock to conclude treaties.[27] Affairs appeared to be coalescing so that council meetings and agreements between government officials and desperate and destitute Indians finally might occur in 1863.

James Doty reinforced his entreaties for more funds for Indian subsistence by emphasizing the necessity of keeping the mail line open. He wrote on July 30, 1862, "there has been no certainty or safety in the mails from this city Eastward. . . ." He also feared that the Gosiute and the Western Shoshoni were starving and that they too would begin to attack stagecoaches and stations. He had visited these western tribes to distribute presents and wrote:

> To say they are "destitute" but feeble describes their situation. They took the wheat . . . with the utmost avidity and with hearty thanks; and repeatedly I saw their children, lying on their bellies on the margins of the streams, cropping the young grass. I hope I shall receive the goods from the Dept. in time to clothe their nakedness before the snow falls and the winter commences.[28]

Two weeks after this letter, Doty reported that the Gosiute in Tooele and Rush valleys had declared their intention of robbing the mail line. They had already run off a number of cattle and horses from the Mormon settlements and had become so bold that "they enter the houses of farmers, and in an insolent manner demand food, and that meals shall be cooked for them."[29]

In his annual report for the year, Doty noted that he had distributed more presents to the Indians along the mail lines than to any other tribes in his district.[30] The Overland Mail Company helped by feeding the starving Gosiute and Western Shoshoni, an action "well appreciated by the Indians" according to Agent T. W. Hatch.[31] Frederick Cook, treasurer of the Overland Mail Company, tried to reassure his customers by dismissing any accounts of the mail being interrupted. This was on September 3, 1862, when he informed the *Sacramento Union* that mail delivery was on time with seventeen-day service from Placerville to the Missouri River.

———————————— ◆ ◆ ————————————

Throughout the early summer of 1862, many concerned with Indian affairs in Oregon, Nevada, and Utah waited impatiently for the snows in the Sierras to melt so that Colonel Connor's California Volunteers could march east. On June 25, 1862, the *Deseret News* anticipated their movement across the deserts of Nevada: "The Indians will of course be tremendously scared, and horse-thieves, gamblers, and other pests of community wondrously attracted by the gigantic demonstration." These statements by the Saints' leading newspaper were a far cry from heroic acclaim and did little to reassure Colonel Connor, who was already hostile and suspicious toward Mormon authorities. Connor finally left Stockton on July 12 with seven infantry companies (apparently companies C, D, and F were temporarily assigned to the Humboldt district). Almost 850 men, fifty wagons loaded with equipment and provisions, three ambulances, several carriages for officers' families, and a herd of several hundred cattle made an imposing procession for the Indian and white population, which usually saw only stagecoaches and small emigrant parties.[32] The column reached Fort Churchill just east of Carson City, Nevada, by August 3, and three days later Connor took command of the Military District of Utah. He warned all traitors to the Union that they would "receive the punishment they so richly deserved."[33]

Early in the expedition Connor faced discipline problems within his command with the freebooting Volunteers—a problem that was to recur at the Bear River Massacre. On August 11 Colonel Columbus Sims, commander of the Second Cavalry Troops, brought Captain Samuel P. Smith into Fort Churchill under guard after thirty men deserted on the march from California. Sims's other officers had threatened to leave him and proceed by themselves declaring that if the companies were left with Sims in command "there will not be thirty of them left in sixty days."[34] Within nine days, Sims was relieved of his command, and Major Edward McGarry was placed in charge of the cavalry.[35]

Although this may have been the most serious threat of wholesale desertion during the four years of Civil War service by the California Volunteers, the records do show a surprising number of men who just left for adventures elsewhere. Of the four cavalry companies and the one infantry company that fought at Bear River in January 1863, 21 percent, or 238 of the total enlistment of 1,121 men, deserted the ranks sometime during the four years of service. The figures vary from 13 percent, or 27 of the 212 soldiers in Company M, Second Cavalry, to a high of 30 percent, or 82 of the 277 men of Company H, Second Cavalry.[36] After reaching Salt Lake City, for example, Connor was forced to offer a reward of thirty dollars each for eleven deserters in the Deseret News of November 28, 1862.

As in most armies, Connor's subordinates varied in their leadership qualities and the discipline they imposed on their troops. Few matched the iron command of veteran Patrick Edward Connor, but Edward McGarry was soon acknowledged as second only to the colonel in the forcefulness and audacity with which he led his men. His soldiers hardly dared to risk his wrath, but eventually they mustered enough nerve to charge him with being drunk most of the time, even while on duty. In a written complaint from Camp Douglas on October 13, 1864,

> the men stated . . . that during the fall of 1862, while the regiment was on a march from Fort Churchill, Nevada, to Camp Douglas, Utah Territory, Colonel McGarry was "drunk" most of the time. They accused him of such nonsense as ordering Company K to dismount on the desert, lie down in the road and go to sleep, saying that he was leaving them to go out and fight Indians. He also threatened, according to the complaint, to shoot an enlisted man of Company K as an example to the other men. On another occasion he suggested tying Captain Smith, of the same company, behind a wagon. Colonel McGarry was at this time so under the influence of liquor, that after ordering his men to dismount and hold their horses, he lay down and slept until morning. The men held their mounts all night and did not reach camp until the following day at sunrise.[37]

Connor usually chose Major McGarry for the most difficult assignments despite this drinking.

By September 1, 1862, three companies of the Second Cavalry joined the Third Infantry and began construction of Fort Ruby.[38] Chaplain Anderson wrote the *San Francisco Bulletin* on September 24, 1862, and announced the deaths of three soldiers (two from typhoid fever), and expressed dismay about unhealthy conditions at the new post. He hoped that the Volunteers would be sent to Virginia to fight Rebels. This "patriotic desire to serve their country in shooting traitors instead of . . . freezing to death around sage brush fires . . ." partially accounted for the high incidence of desertions and was certainly shared by other members of the Third Infantry. Seven hundred soldiers subscribed $25,420 from their thirteen-dollar-a-month pay to the Union cause *and* proposed to General-in-Chief Henry W. Halleck that they would pay their own passage from San Francisco to Panama "for the privilege of going to the Potomac and agetting shot." The War Department refused their proposal, leaving them to serve out their enlistments in the "abomindable deserts" of Nevada and Utah, and this became a contributing factor in their strong desire to win glory by crushing the Indians.[39]

The first chance to gain military distinction in Indian engagements came soon. Reports arrived in mid-September about an attack on emigrants eight miles from Gravelly Ford on the Humboldt River. The commander at Fort Churchill wired Governor Nye that twenty-three emigrants had been killed and citizens along the lower Humboldt were asking for assistance.[40] General G. Wright promised the governor he would aid the residents,[41] but there weren't enough troops at Fort Churchill, and Connor was asked to punish the guilty parties. By this time the number killed had been reduced to twelve. The perpetrators, reportedly Shoshoni Indians perhaps helped by white men, had dumped the bodies into a cold spring to conceal their deed. One newspaper, the *Enterprise*, was quoted as saying that because "Col. Connor's boys have been spoiling for action" that it "would be a wise plan to let them vent a little of their pent up fighting spirit" on the Indians. The editor made the point that "as winter is the best season to operate against them, the matter should be attended to promptly. . . ."[42] He, of course, understood that by the time Connor could get his troops to Utah and into action against the Indians, the winter snows would prove to be an ally because the Shoshoni warriors would have less mobility.

Connor acted with dispatch. He issued orders to Major McGarry on September 29 to lead Companies H and K in an investigation of the Gravelly Ford attack. If friendly Indians delivered any tribe members implicated in the murders to McGarry, the major was to "immediately hang them, and leave their bodies thus exposed as an example of what evil-doers may expect while I command this district." McGarry was ordered to "destroy every male Indian whom you may encounter in the vicinity of the late massacres. This course may seem harsh and severe, but I desire that the order may be rigidly enforced, as I am satisfied that in the end it will prove the most merciful." The colonel was careful to note, "In no instance will you molest women and children."[43] Chaplain Anderson explained, "*No prisoners will be taken*. To young ladies in gas lit parlors such measures may seem harsh . . . [but] a rigorous and retributive retaliatory policy is the wisest."[44]

Connor then began to hold "pow-wows" with the neighboring Indians in Ruby Valley and offered various chiefs fifty dollars for each Indian implicated in the Gravelly Ford attack. Connor intended "to hang said live corpuses to a tree and leave them as a warning to other

Indians who have a penchant for murdering white men and ravishing emigrant girls."[45] Connor's sanguinary promises were enthusiastically reported by Chaplain Anderson.

In Major McGarry's formal report of his expedition he stated his companies reached Gravelly Ford on October 5 without having sighted any Indians. The soldiers did entice three Indians into camp who were shot by the guard when they ran away. McGarry wrote, "Fearing that they would escape, and not wishing to hazard the lives of my men in recapturing them alive, I ordered the guard to fire, and they were killed on the spot." Subsequently the command left on a scouting trip during which Captain Smith's troops captured fourteen or fifteen Indians. Nine were killed while attempting to escape by jumping into the river. Soon another six Indian men were taken prisoner. Two were released with the understanding that by evening they would bring into camp those who had taken part in the massacre or the other four prisoners would be killed. The next morning, true to his word, McGarry ordered the remaining four Indians shot. He released three Indian women and instructed them to tell their tribesmen that if they did not stop their attacks against emigrants he would return the next summer and "destroy them." The following day a detachment of troops under Lieutenants Darwin Chase and George D. Conrad killed eight more Indians who tried to avoid capture. McGarry's force thus had the "honor" of killing twenty-four Indians on this hunting expedition.[46] General Wright, in reporting McGarry's exploits, thought his action was "the only way to deal with those savages." Connor agreed "that the punishment was well merited . . . [and] the lesson taught them will have a salutary effect in checking future massacres on the route."[47] McGarry's ruthless, brutal, and indiscriminate killing was an ominous portent for the California Volunteers.

The *Deseret News* of November 19, 1862, was critical of the entire expedition. "It was but reasonable to suppose that all the natives found had been killed, whether innocent or guilty," noted the editor. Because McGarry could not "find trees large enough," he had not been able to carry out the colonel's orders to hang the twenty-four Indians and had been forced to shoot them. The *News* was convinced the Indians killed were innocent of any participation in the Gravelly Ford massacre and that the two natives sent out to bring in the murderers "had not time to do so before the hostages were shot." The editor preferred President Abraham Lincoln's more magnanimous decision not to permit the military to hang 300 Sioux for their massacre of 500 settlers in Minnesota. The president had instead said, "Hang some of the ringleaders only. . . ." The *News* offered the opinion that McGarry's ruthless action on orders from Connor would only incite the Indians to violence, particularly against the northern Mormon settlements.

The California Volunteers remained at Fort Ruby while Colonel Connor traveled to Salt Lake City during September to reconnoiter the road and choose a site for his permanent camp. On September 10, 1862, the *Deseret News* noted his arrival: "The Colonel took a stroll about town and looked around with an air of familiarity that indicated that after all Salt Lake City was something of a place, and might not be unpleasant notwithstanding its desert surrounding." Back at Fort Ruby Connor wrote his superior that the Mormons were a "community of traitors, murderers, fanatics, and whores," and that the federal officials were powerless to do anything about Brigham Young's despotic control Connor refused to settle his troops at Fort Crittenden and instead deliberately established Camp Douglas overlooking the city to keep a close watch on the Mormons as well as to police the mail lines.[48] From this point on he waged a cold war with Mormon authorities. Warning his commander that he fully expected Brigham Young's militia to attack him at any time, he made repeated requests for more troops.[49]

Connor and his Volunteers left Fort Ruby in late September and reached Salt Lake City on October 20. Six days later he declared Camp Douglas the headquarters of the Department of Utah. The *Deseret News* of October 22, 1862, welcomed the soldiers: "The troops looked . . . like a hardy set of fellows capable of performing any service that might be required." The *News* provided inadvertent evidence of what was expected when it continued, "Some of the horses seemed a little jaded, and not in as good condition as might be desired for an Indian campaign." The 850 men in the expedition settled down to prepare dugouts with tent roofs for winter quarters at the new camp on the benchlands three miles above Great Salt Lake City.[50]

While Connor and his soldiers and Brigham Young and his followers bristled at each other in Salt Lake Valley, Indian-white relations in Cache Valley fluctuated as both groups tried to accommodate

Fort Douglas from the north by C. R. Savage, photographer, ca. 1870s. *Utah State Historical Society.*

Camp Douglas soldier's quarters, 1864. *Utah State Historical Society.*

each other. These stopgap measures would ultimately prove insufficient for resolving the deep-seated tensions.

On August 7, 1862, Peter Maughan declared that everything was peaceable in the valley,[51] but settlers just across the mountains in Weber and Box Elder were suffering from the "thieving operations" of the natives.[52] A month later the *Deseret News* commented on September 10 that the Northwestern Shoshoni of Cache Valley were "inclined of late to be saucy and belligerent in their deportment, and have committed some depredations, and threaten to do more. They are reported to be unusually fond of beef, which, if they cannot get in one way, they will take in another. . . . They also . . . require from the inhabitants heavy contributions of flour." Brigham Young noted growing reluctance among his people in the northern valleys to maintain peace, but he still was insistent that his long-held policy of feeding the Indians be continued. James N. Jones of North Bend, just around the spur of the mountain from Cache Valley, acknowledged this in a letter to the Prophet. "I rec'd your letter an have given the Indians a beef critter as directed. . . ." Jones and his fellow Saints also delivered 205 bushels of wheat and 2,000 pounds of flour in addition "to what they get at our houses. . . ."[53] Despite these contributions, pioneer James Cantwell of Cache Valley recorded on September 27 "more horses stolen" and on two other occasions mentioned standing guard as a Minute Man because Bannock Indians were threatening to kill the Franklin settlers.[54]

Maughan discussed the troubles at length in a letter to President Young. A band of either Bannock or Shoshoni had stolen between thirty and forty horses from farmers and had gotten a twelve-hour start on the Minute Men who could only recover nine or ten of the animals. Maughan explained further:

> 6 friendly Indians (if I may be allowed the expression) went along with our men. . . . it does seem to me that the Indians on the North are determined to drive us to hostile measures. I suppose they have taken 100 horses in three weeks, . . . I have never seen them so bold and daring in the Brethrens houses insulting the woman etc and what still makes it worse is, that those that pretend to be friendly will harbour those scamps about their wickiups untill they get their plans laid for stealing. At the same time we have been given them tons of flour and Beef. . . .

The *Deseret News* feared that there would be other incursions into Cache Valley before winter set in.[55]

However, the main hostile action in the autumn of 1862 turned out to be a minor engagement between Chief Bear Hunter's band of Northwestern Shoshoni and Major Edward McGarry's cavalry troops. The origin of the fight was entwined with the Otter Massacre on the lower Snake River during the fall of 1860. As already noted, Alexis Van Orman, his wife, and one son had been murdered, while another son and the three daughters of the family were captured by Indians. The three girls had died of starvation leaving the boy, Reuben Van Orman, the only survivor. Strenuous efforts were made to rescue Reuben including missions sent out by Agent John Owen from his Flathead post,[56] a dispatch of three different military expeditions from Oregon, and at least one meeting between Utah Agent Benjamin Davies and Chief Sanpitch of the Northwestern Shoshoni. The Indian leader had announced that he knew that Bannock Indians were holding the four captive children in the Goose Creek Mountains and offered to aid in returning them to civilization.[57] Nothing came of this offer, but the Oregon military continued to run ads in territorial newspapers. One as late as July 15, 1862, in the *Portland Times* requested any information about the identity and location of the guilty Indians.

Zachias Van Orman, the children's uncle, initiated a personal mission to rescue them. In late 1862, Zachias learned from a relative who traveled to Oregon that he had seen a white boy living with a band of Indians in the Cache Valley area. Zachias arrived in Salt Lake City and asked Connor to help retrieve the ten-year-old Reuben. The colonel was happy to oblige and ordered Major McGarry to march to Cache Valley to meet Zachias Van Orman, who had gone ahead to try to locate Bear Hunter's camp.[58] Connor also sent an Indian named Jack to take word to the Cache Valley band that if they did not release the white boy immediately he "would wipe everyone of them out."[59]

McGarry arrived in Cache Valley on November 22, 1862, and was informed that about thirty or forty Indians were encamped near the town of Providence. Early morning of the next day he tried to surprise them by an attack. The Shoshoni, however, left in a hurry for a more defensible position in a canyon about a mile from the settlement. McGarry was able to capture one warrior trying to escape from the Indian camp. Bear Hunter and his men then rode out onto the bench between the mountains and the town and "made a war-like display, such as shouting, riding in a circle, and all sorts of antics known only to their race." The major accepted the challenge, divided his forces into three attacking units, and ordered the soldiers "to kill every Indian they could see." After about two hours of fighting, Chief Bear Hunter appeared on a hill with a flag of truce, which McGarry mistook for another war-like demonstration until an interested white spectator, Lee Dees,[60] volunteered to talk to Bear Hunter. Dees then informed the major that the chief "did not want to fight anymore," claiming "long friendship with the whites and always desiring peace." McGarry ordered a cease-fire, and Bear Hunter and about twenty of his warriors came in and surrendered.[61]

McGarry then discovered that the white boy had left the Indian camp several days before, so he told Bear Hunter that he would hold him and four of his men hostage until the boy was brought in. Three members of the band returned with Reuben Van Orman the next day, and McGarry released the chief and his warriors. Although in his official account of the battle McGarry claimed to have killed three of the Shoshoni, other accounts agreed with the *Deseret News* report that the results were "federal loss, none—Red skins the same." McGarry was pleased to report to Connor that he had accomplished his mission "without the loss or scratch of man or horse."[62]

The ten-year-old boy was now safe with white people at Camp Douglas, where he spent the next winter, but there was doubt that he was really Reuben Van Orman. Indian Tom and other Shoshoni gave positive and reliable information that the boy was the half-breed son of a French mountaineer and a sister of Chief Washakie. Although he had yellow hair and blue eyes, he could not speak any English and was a full member of the Northwestern Shoshoni nation.[63] He had become a pawn in the war game being played out between the California Volunteers and the Cache Valley Shoshoni.

The day after the fight at Providence, Bear Hunter and his band came into the settlement "and abused the people for not helping them to retain the boy, . . . declaring that the settlers were cowards and dared not fight. . . ."[64] In one account Bear Hunter announced he would ambush the next group of soldiers he met and dared them to travel north for a battle. The Indians' hostile demonstration against the citizens for feeding and sheltering the soldiers resulted in seventy Minute Men being sent from Logan. After a talk they gave the natives two beeves and a large quantity of flour, as the "best and cheapest policy," with the citizens of Logan supplying the provisions.[65]

The Northwestern Shoshoni, angered when the California Volunteers took Wakashie's nephew, soon became further enraged with McGarry. Colonel Connor ordered the major to lead 100 cavalrymen to Bear River Ferry west of Brigham City where a large Indian encampment was supposedly holding stolen emigrant stock. The troops left Camp Douglas in the greatest secrecy the evening of December 4. They marched all through the next night and arrived at Empey's Bear River Ferry at dawn prepared "to give them [Indians] a little taste of the fighting qualities of the Volunteers. . . ." Somehow the Indians had learned of the departure of the soldiers and cut the ferry rope. The troops recovered a scow and crossed the river, although they were forced to leave their horses behind. The Indian camp lay in full view on a hill beyond the adjacent Malad River. Four unwary Indians were captured and made prisoner, and McGarry sent a message to the Shoshoni stating that if the stock was not delivered by noon the next day, he would shoot the captives. The chiefs responded by picking up the whole camp and moving north to Cache Valley. McGarry ordered the hostages tied by their hands to the ferry rope and executed. Fifty-one shots were fired before all expired, and the bodies were then "tumbled into the river."[66]

The *Deseret News* was critical about the marksmanship of the executioners. At one point the *News* editor asked why the troops had missed a golden opportunity for attack, forgetting that the cavalrymen were unhorsed at the time.[67] The *News* article also mentioned that "the killing of the four prisoners may have a salutary effect upon the natives in that region, but it is feared that it will tend to make them more hostile and vindictive."[68] The *Sacramento Union*, however, came to McGarry's defense at once: "Now here is another nice opportunity for certain papers to become lachrymose and howl piteously over the just vengeance which has fallen upon these human fiends who have too long infested these regions and perpetrated their deeds of cruelty with perfect impunity." The editor attacked newspapers that defended the rights of the natives and pointed out in support of these arguments that one of the Indians executed was wearing pants stolen from an emigrant the previous season.[69] Subsequently the editor singled out the *Deseret News* as one of the newspapers that had made "unfavorable mention" of McGarry's expedition.[70]

Anticipating a replay of the indecisive efforts of the military in earlier times, the Shoshoni reacted to the killing of their comrades with hostility. On December 24 they stole over twenty head of horses from Box Elder and Cache Valley farms. The *Deseret News* of December 31, 1862, stated that the Indians had settled on a course of revenge and that they were "mad, and determined to do as much injury as possible to the white race. . . . " The *Sacramento Union*, on the other hand, cited the approval of Connor's superiors for the tactics he was employing and noted Connor "means to give the redskins all they deserve—if he can catch them, . . . and the first approach of Spring will see the California volunteers on the march in every direction to clean out the Indians."[71]

Many settlers in Utah as well as travelers along the western trails were pleased to see Connor's troops located in Salt Lake City after the incessant Indian attacks near Fort Hall and along the Humboldt during the last six months of 1862. While Oregon and Washington authorities had sent out military escorts for emigrant parties, there had still been serious attacks at Massacre Rocks on the Smart, Adams, and Kennedy trains, which led the commissioner of Indian affairs to issue a proclamation on September 19 warning all travelers of perils along the roads. Superintendent Doty proposed a congressional appropriation to treat with the Shoshoni, but months slipped away before he could call a council with Washakie and other tribes.

Connor was forced to wait for winter snows to melt in the Sierra Nevada to move his troops east. In early July he marched across Nevada and established Fort Ruby. A month later the Volunteers moved to Salt Lake City to establish Camp Douglas overlooking the Mormon capital. While in Nevada, McGarry's ruthless expedition to punish Indians caught near the site of the Gravelly Ford murders telegraphed a message to the Indians of Utah and Nevada that was repeated later on in his trips north to Cache Valley and Bear River Ferry. The Northwestern Shoshoni were incited to retaliate as a result of McGarry's violence, especially when he killed the four hostages. The Cache Valley settlers were apprehensive about an increase in attacks from neighboring Indians, while Connor's troops, indignant at being denied an opportunity of going to Virginia to shoot Confederate Rebels, became determined to seize other occasions to gain military glory in offensives against the Indians. The increased travel along the Montana Trail directly through Shoshoni homelands only meant more conflict.

Historians have failed to take much notice of the Indian raids along the Snake River and attacks by the California Volunteers under McGarry's leadership in the closing months of 1862. Even at the time, little attention was paid to these incidents because the Civil War captured the attention of the nation. As separate occurrences, these events have importance for western history, but, when placed together, they form a mosaic of discord. The failure of writers about the West to recognize the pattern of Indian hostility and army retaliation that led to the final engagement at Bear River also stems partly from a Mormon tendency to perceive themselves as being isolated from the rest of the nation and its citizens. The movements of army troops and counterattacks by Indian tribes were largely removed from the Saints' preoccupation with establishing the Kingdom of God on earth and surviving in their desert environment. Indian attacks that resulted in the deaths of individual Mormons or losses of stock were certainly keenly felt, but when the army moved in the Saints tended merely to look on as bystanders. Tacitly, if not overtly, the Mormons were accomplices in the encounter with Chief Bear Hunter's people about to occur on January 29, 1863.

———— •◆ ◆•————

TEN

From Battle to Massacre

In late 1862 and early 1863 events precipitating the battle at Bear River began to coalesce against the backdrop of military life at Camp Douglas. The California Volunteers were firmly ensconced and Connor kept his troops in shape by ordering drills twice a day. As Corporal Hiram G. Tuttle confided to his diary on January 5, 1863, "Drill and dress parade today. Nothing more but nearly hell."[1] Connor also took steps to keep the noxious whiskey establishments from nestling up against the soldiers' quarters by extending the post boundaries—a step he hoped would change the number of "without leave of absence" incidents.[2] But drills and dress parades could not calm the Volunteers' discontent. They were dissatisfied with camp life and longed for action to win a little glory and bring Connor "what he merits, and what the troops long for—that Brigadier's commission. . . ."[3]

In a letter on December 20, 1862, Connor declared that the energetic and aggressive actions of his troops had secured the mail line from Ruby Valley to Ham's Fork. Some soldiers had been sent to Fort Bridger to squash an Indian attack supposedly instigated by Mormons, and, as usual, Connor blamed the Mormons for supplying the Indians and purchasing stolen emigrant equipment from them. The Mormons adamantly responded that unscrupulous traders were responsible for dealing in stolen emigrant goods.[4] Agent Luther Mann and other agents again warned the Indian Office in Washington, D.C., that unless Congress voted money the Indians would continue to make trouble.[5] But these occurrences were insignificant compared to events stemming from increased travel across Northwestern Shoshoni territory as miners journeyed to Grasshopper Creek and the Beaverhead mines.

On January 14, 1863, A. H. Conover, operator of an express service between Salt Lake City and Montana, arrived with news that expressmen George Clayton and Henry Bean had been murdered on the Cache Valley road. Conover reported that the Shoshoni were determined "to avenge the blood of their comrades" killed by McGarry's soldiers, at Bear River Ferry and that the "spiteful" Indians intended to "kill every white man they should meet with on the north side of Bear River, till they should be fully avenged. . . ." The *Deseret News* wanted measures taken to "dispose them to peace."[6]

In another incident on January 5, 1863, ten men coming south from the mines were reported killed by Indian raiders.[7] The next day a party of eight men traveling to Salt Lake City by a new route through Cache Valley missed the main ford near Franklin and ended up on Bear River opposite the village of Richmond. Leaving the others, three of the travelers went to Richmond for help and returned to discover that the Indians had driven off all the stock and robbed the wagons, "behaving very uncourteously to the five men. . . ." The group induced the Indians to return part of the stock and moved three wagons to the east bank of the river. The Indians then gathered on the west side and fired across the river killing John Henry Smith of Walla Walla, Washington Territory.[8] The survivors raced for safety to Richmond, and Mormon Bishop Marriner W. Merrill sent out a party of four men to rescue Smith's body for burial in the city cemetery.[9]

When William Bevins, one of the miners, arrived in Salt Lake City, he signed an affidavit before Chief Justice John F. Kinney describing Smith's murder. Kinney immediately issued a warrant for the arrest of Chiefs Bear Hunter, Sanpitch, and Sagwitch of the Northwestern bands and ordered territorial marshal Isaac L. Gibbs to seek assistance from Connor for a military force to "effect the arrest of the guilty Indians," as the *Sacramento Union* put it.[10] The colonel had already decided to make an expedition north to chastise the Cache Valley Indians after receiving news of the attacks. He informed the marshal that "my arrangements for our expedition against the Indians were made, and that it was not my intention to take any prisoners, but that he could accompany me." Gibbs did so and later was commended by Connor for his aid in caring for the wounded soldiers. Connor made it clear that legal documents had nothing to do with his decision: "Being satisfied that they [the Indians] were part of the same band who had been murdering emigrants on the overland mail route for the past fifteen years and [were] the principal actors and leaders in the horrid massacre of the past summer, I determined, although the weather was unfavorable to an expedition, to chastize them if possible."[11] Connor was also responding to a general order that had been issued by the Department of the Pacific on April 7, 1862, spelling out the action military leaders in the West were to take against hostile natives: "Every Indian captured in this district during the present war who has been engaged in hostilities against whites, present or absent, will be hanged on the spot, women and children in all cases being spared."[12]

While Connor was making his plans, Chief Sanpitch was in Salt Lake City asking Brigham Young for help in reestablishing peace with the Indians on the northern frontier. "Liberal," a correspondent for the *Sacramento Union*, understood that the Prophet had told Sanpitch the Mormon people had suffered enough from the Shoshoni of Cache Valley and that if more blood were spilled the Mormons might just "pitch in" and help the troops.[13]

Fearing that the Shoshoni in their camp on Bear River might leave and deprive the Volunteers of a chance for a little "Indian killing,"[14] Connor determined that secrecy about his troop movements would be necessary so the Indians wouldn't move before the soldiers arrived. Connor had always considered winter the best time to attack an Indian village because the warriors would be settled and encumbered with their wives and children. As Mormon leader George A. Smith watched the highly mysterious army preparations proceeding at Camp Douglas and heard Connor's intention to "exterminate" the Indians who had been killing emigrants, he predicted that the expedition would "result in catching some friendly Indians, murdering them, and letting the guilty scamps remain undisturbed in their mountain haunts."[15] At the soldiers' quarters, Corporal Tuttle confided to his diary on January 19, "Received orders to be ready to march at any moment."[16]

Instructions to move came on January 21, 1863. Captain Samuel W. Hoyt of Company K, Third Infantry Regiment, was ordered to leave the next day in command of sixty-nine Volunteers. Fifteen baggage wagons carrying a twenty-day supply of rations and two howitzers with a supply of 100 shells were sent with him.[17] The troops marched out of camp "in a heavy snowstorm" with the ostensible and widely proclaimed mission to protect wagon trains hauling grain from Cache Valley.[18] Connor's next move was to dispatch 220 men of Companies A, H, K, and M, Second Cavalry, under his personal command on January 24. They were to march by night to a rendezvous with the infantry and cavalry forces and join a combined attack upon arrival at Bear River. As the *San Francisco Bulletin* of February 9, 1863, expressed it, Connor's plan of action to deceive the Indians into thinking that only a small force was being sent against them which might appear "to outsiders a queer mode of whipping red-skins. . . ." The editor was convinced that the tactic would prevent the Indians from "skedaddling to the mountains, . . ." and that "fear is the only motive they respect. . . ." The *Sacramento Union* of February 7, 1863, agreed that the Shoshoni would probably be "utterly 'used up' " by Connor while the *Deseret News* of January 28, 1863, chimed in that "with ordinary good luck the volunteers will 'wipe them out.'. . ."

Captain Hoyt's detachment marched placidly along giving the Shoshoni time to learn that this was just another army patrol coming to escort a wagon train. The command traveled thirteen miles the first day, another twenty-five the next to the Weber River, and then eighteen miles to Willard. They made another march of fourteen miles and, the following day, one of twenty-five miles to Mendon where they "laid over" a day to await the arrival of the cavalry units. On January 28, as Corporal Tuttle recounted, "Left camp 12 at night, went 34 miles to Franklin and camped."[19]

In his Special Order No. 11, dated January 24, to the companies of the Second Cavalry, Colonel Connor very carefully specified what arms and rations should be taken as well as ammunition. Captain Daniel McLean of Company H, with Lieutenant G. D. Conrad and fifty-five men, were to be "fully equipped for active service, with forty (40) rounds of Carbine ammunition and thirty (30) rounds of Pistol ammunition, per man . . . for duty in the field." Captain George F. Price and Lieutenant C. D. Clark of Company M with their fifty-five men were to have forty rounds of rifle ammunition and thirty rounds of pistol ammunition for each soldier. Lieutenant Darwin Chase of Company K and his sixty-five men were issued forty rounds of rifle and thirty rounds of pistol ammunition per man. Finally, Lieutenant John Quinn of Company A and his forty-five men received forty rounds of carbine and thirty rounds of pistol ammunition for each dragoon. With almost 16,000 rounds of ammunition, the California Volunteers did not have to worry about running out of shots. The orders concluded, "Each man will take with him the rations drawn and on hand for the balance of this month. Three days rations to be cooked and carried with his Haversacks. The least number of cooking utensils will be taken."[20] Two officer visitors to Camp Douglas accompanied the expediton—Major Patrick A. Gallagher from Ruby Valley and Captain David J. Berry.

The Shoshoni warriors, secure in their camp at Bear River and unaware of the intentions of the hard-charging troops, were obviously not as well supplied with arms and ammunition as the soldiers. The troops were so heavily loaded with ammunition that it was not surprising that Charles E. Middleton of Ogden could find "a catridge box full of catridges" in the road on January 28.[21] During the engagement the Shoshoni were so short of ammunition that old men and women had to mold bullets in the middle of the fight.[22] At least one trooper was wounded by arrows, evidence that not every warrior even had a rifle.[23]

Despite the armaments carried by Connor's troops, the colonel complained after the fight at Bear River about the Whitney rifles in use by two of his cavalry units "a very unwieldy arm and quite unsuited to cavalry service."[24] The other troopers could have been armed with either Burnside, Maynard, or Sharps carbines. Many volunteer regiments were issued the Burnside weapon during the Civil War, and the California Volunteers may have had this gun. The Sharps carbine "was not the best-liked cavalry weapon in the army." There is no indication about the type of pistol used by the California Volunteers from among three in common issue: the 1858 Remington, .44 caliber; the Colt Model 1860, .44 caliber; or the .36 caliber Colt navy Model 1851.[25] Connor had also requested some new pistols in his letter of February 26, 1863, noting that the ones in service in his outfit were "out of repair, and some totally unserviceable," which was not surprising after their heavy use at Bear River the month before.[26]

The march to Franklin was a bitter experience for riflemen and cavalrymen, with weather so cold that whiskey rations froze in the canteens. The snow varied from one foot on the Salt Lake Valley floor to four feet on the divide between Brigham City and Cache Valley, and the infantry had a difficult task getting their wagons and howitzers through. The cavalry units rode sixty-eight miles the first night arriving at Brigham City with feet frozen in the stirrups and "whiskers and moustache . . . so chained together by ice that opening the mouth became most difficult. . . ."[27] Of the approximately 275 officers and men, including "Dutch Joe" and five other irregulars who went along, about 75 were lost to the command because of frozen feet.[28] Some had to be left at Brigham City. Fighting Indians in midwinter at below zero temperatures was an unusual experience in United States military history, but Connor never wavered.

Colonel Connor was fortunate in being able to recruit the famed Mormon scout Orrin Porter Rockwell as his guide for the sum of $5 a day.[29] Rockwell was aware of Shoshoni boasts that they would "thrash the soldiers" at the first opportunity and informed the colonel in advance that the Indians were awaiting any attack by the Volunteers and had "thrown up intrenchments" at their camp. It was reported, with evident exaggeration, that there were as many as 600 warriors behind the breastworks and manning the rifle pits to defend the seventy-five lodges of their people.[30] Jim Gamble, a miner from the Grasshopper mines, had spoken to some Cache Valley Shoshoni on his way to Salt Lake City and reported the Indians had told him that they had nothing against the settlers but meant to continue to take revenge on white travelers for the injustices done them by McGarry's troops.[31]

When Company K of the Third Infantry and the four companies of the Second Cavalry bivouacked at Mendon on January 27, Connor issued very careful orders for the rest of the journey. The infantry marched into Franklin at about 5:00 P.M. on January 28. Just before the soldiers came in sight, William Hull was ordered by Bishop Preston Thomas to sack nine bushels of wheat for three Indians from Bear Hunter's band who had been sent by the chief for another installment on the tribute the Mormon pioneers were used to paying. Hull later recalled, "We had two of the three horses loaded, having put three bushels on each horse . . . when I looked up and saw the Soldiers approaching from the south. I said to the Indian boys, 'Here comes the *Toquashes* [Indian name for soldiers] maybe, you will all be killed.' They answered 'maybe Toquashes be killed too,' but not waiting for the third horse to be loaded, they quickly jumped upon their horses and led the three horses away, disappearing in the distance." Alexander Stalker noted in a letter to Peter Maughan that Bear Hunter himself had visited the settlement and "traded for some bread stuff."[32] The chief was therefore quite aware of the presence of the infantry but probably did not know about the four cavalry units that arrived in Franklin at midnight. The cavalry "fraternized with the infantry" as both units prepared for the assault on the Indian camp the next morning.[33]

To ensure the infantry and cavalry would arrive at the same time at the Indian encampment on Bear River twelve miles away, Connor ordered Captain Hoyt to start at 1:00 A.M. with the wagon train, howitzers, and infantry. Hoyt, however, was delayed while trying to find a local guide who could direct the troops to the ford leading to the Indian camp.[34] Two brothers, Edmond and Joseph S. Nelson, of Franklin, were finally "counselled" by local Mormon leaders to accompany the troops,[35] but the infantry did not start until just after 3:00 A.M. Connor and the cavalry left an hour later and passed Hoyt's company at a point about four miles from the river. The infantrymen struggled to move the heavy wagons and howitzers through the snow and wished they could have traded their wagons for the sleighs knowledgeable Mormon settlers used for winter transportation in Cache Valley. The howitzers never did reach the scene of battle and remained stuck in a snowdrift six miles back. Their presence would have saved the Volunteers many casualties but would possibly have made the carnage among the Indians even more devastating.[36]

When Major McGarry and the first cavalry units reached the bluffs overlooking Bear River at 6:00 A.M., just as dawn was breaking, they could see smoke rising from early fires lighted at the Indian camp across the stream. The Bear River here meanders through a level flood plain that is a little less then a mile wide, and the river at this point makes a sharp turn to the west deviating from its usual north-south course. The river runs between bluffs two hundred feet high, and the bluffs on the south side are so steep that it would be almost impossible to get a wagon down them; they would even be difficult for men on horseback to negotiate. In winter the river is a rather swift-flowing stream about 175 feet wide and 3 or 4 feet deep. Beaver Creek (ever after called Battle Creek) lies across the river at its western bend. It flows southwest through a small valley to the edge of the western bluffs where it turns abruptly west and flows almost parallel to Bear but also provided an excellent defensive position behind the steep

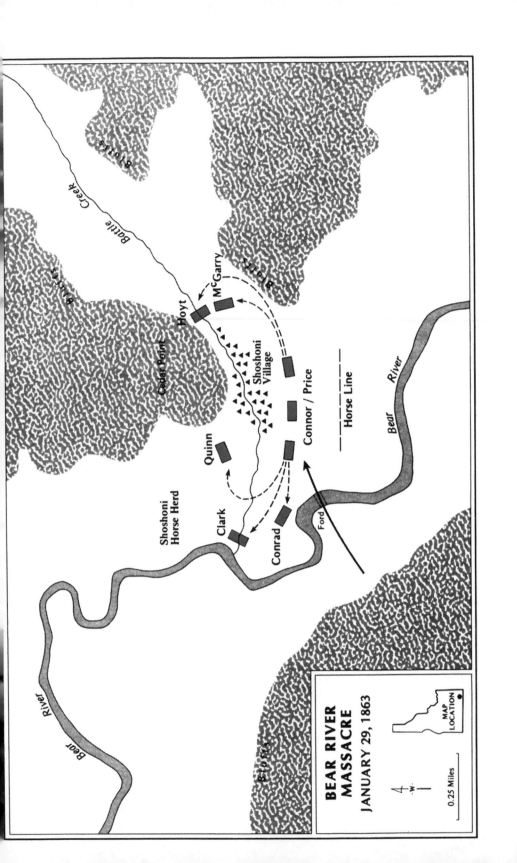

BEAR RIVER
MASSACRE
JANUARY 29, 1863

Horse Line

Shoshoni Horse Herd

Shoshoni Village

Cedar Point

Battle Creek

Bluffs

Bluffs

Bear River

Bear River

Bear River

Ford

McGarry

Hoyt

Quinn

Clark

Conrad

Connor / Price

MAP LOCATION

0.25 Miles

River for a little under a mile before turning south to empty into the river. Cedar Point, a sharp headland, juts out close to Battle Creek where the stream enters the main valley. At its south end, the creek flows close to what is called today Wayland Hot Springs, one of the reasons the Shoshoni had chosen the site for a winter camp. A flat tableland about three-tenths of a mile wide lies between the river and Battle Creek, although old-time residents believe the river used to flow much closer to the creek before a flood changed its course.[37]

The only newspaper correspondent actually present at the battle reported for the *San Francisco Bulletin*. He described the Battle Creek ravine as being six to twelve feet deep and thirty to forty feet wide with an almost vertical bank on the east side. The Indians had cut three exits through this side so they could ride their horses in and out of camp. News writers mistakenly described rifle pits and entrenchments which the Indians had supposedly dug into the side of the bank to provide cover as they awaited the attack. Later observations revealed that these minor excavations were really just steps cut into the bank to afford easy access out of the ravine. Connor wrote, in his official report, that "under the embankments they had constructed artificial covers of willows thickly woven together, from behind which they could fire without being observed."[38] The river ford that the Nelson brothers were to pinpoint for Connor was located just above the mouth of Battle Creek. A dense overgrowth of willows, some twenty feet tall, covered the bed of Battle Creek and extended up and over the west bank across level ground to the steep bluffs stretching south from Cedar Point.

The Indian encampment was nestled along the bed of Battle Creek beginning south of Cedar Point where the ravine widened out to about seventy feet. Most of the seventy-five lodges were located here, although some extended toward the south where part of the Indian horse herd was tethered next to a large meadow that provided excellent grazing. Estimating an average of six persons for each tipi, there were probably about 450 Shoshoni men, women, and children in the camp. The base of each lodge was built up with stones and earth to keep the dwelling warm. The hot springs at the south edge of the encampment offered more warmth, and the Indians would be very reluctant to leave their snug quarters, "a miniature Sebastopol," unless an extreme crisis occurred. The camp was chosen for comfort, banks of the ravine with escape routes at the north by way of Battle Creek valley or at the south through the mouth of the creek.[39]

To the less than two hundred warriors roused from warm beds by early riser Chief Sagwitch the sight of an equal number of troops gathered in the frosty dawn across the river, while disconcerting, did not dim their confidence in the security of their position behind the banks of Beaver Creek. There was the expectation that the army leaders would follow the usual pattern of demanding that the Indians surrender those guilty of the recent murders or, at most, take some hostages until a parley could resolve any problems between the two forces.[40] The Shoshoni, with War Chief Bear Hunter in command, failed to realize the intentions of the daring and implacable military commander now facing them.[41] The bands of Bear Hunter and Sagwitch who occupied the village could have used the strength of Chief Pocatello. Pocatello and his followers apparently had left camp the day before, but the Cache Valley Shoshoni were not overly concerned.[42] There were no Bannock in the camp, as later reported by some writers; this was to be a wholly Northwestern Shoshoni operation.[43]

Connor was so afraid that his quarry might escape that he ordered Major McGarry to cross the river "and surround before attackting" the Indians while he remained in the rear for a few minutes to order the infantry to speed up its advance. With Companies K and M in the lead, the cavalrymen started across the ford in water so deep that nearly every man got his feet wet. Private John R. Lee later described the crossing: "That was a bad looking river, half frozen over and swift. The horses did not want to go in it. Two old boys got throwed by their horses."[44] On the west bank the troopers found open ground about four or five hundred yards from the ravine from whence about fifty warriors "sallied out . . . and with fiendish malignity waived the scalps of white women and challenged the troops to battle. . . ." This was Connor's description. The accompanying newspaper correspondent wrote: "Here redskins were evidently full of good humor and eager for the fray. One of the chiefs was galloping up and down the bench in front of his warriors, haranguing them and dangling his spear on which was hung a female scalp in the face of the troops, while many of the warriors sang out: 'Fours right, fours left, Come on, you California sons of b—s.' . . ."[45]

This was too much for the combative McGarry. He calculated that it was impossible for him to surround the large camp with his small force because of the difficult terrain, so he ordered his troops to advance a short distance and then to dismount and form a line with Company M on the right and K on the left. Every fourth soldier served as a horse holder, which reduced the number of men who now attacked across the open ground. The Indians fired the first volley wounding one trooper and then quickly retired to their hidden positions behind the east bank of Battle Creek. While the officers remained mounted, the soldiers were ordered to take whatever cover they could from the murderous fire pouring out of the willow-lined bank of the ravine. Companies A and H joined the firing line at about this time. Lieutenant Chase had dressed as a dandy and was an inviting target with his gaily caparisoned horse and uniform. He was struck twice but continued directing his men for about twenty minutes before retiring. Shortly after, Captain McLean was also hit twice and lost his horse. From seven to fourteen troopers were killed and perhaps twenty wounded in this first half-hour exchange. "Men [were] falling fast and thick, . . . " and five horses were killed. McGarry was forced to order a retreat to a point out of reach of the Indian fire, but neither he nor his men meant to give up the battle. The Shoshoni warriors, safe behind their screened trench, dominated the exchange, offering only elusive targets as they bobbed up for quick shots before sinking down behind their protected cover along the high bank of Battle Creek.

By this time Connor was on the scene. Leaving a line of holding fire in front of the Indians, he ordered McGarry to take twenty men to attempt a flanking movement on the Shoshoni left by leading the troopers up and around the north bluffs to the head of Battle Creek ravine. Company K, Third Infantry, had by this time reached the battle and, eager to join the fray, plunged into the icy river but found it impossible to cross the swift stream. Many of the infantrymen suffered terribly when their clothing immediately froze to their bodies. Connor ordered some of the horse holders to take their mounts and ferry the infantry across the river. The foot soldiers joined McGarry's men and the combined force of about seventy-five men attacked down the ravine covering both sides and the creek bed. To complete the bottling-up process, Lieutenant Clark was ordered to move the remainder of Company K, Second Cavalry, in a holding attack against the Indian right flank. Clark was to control any escape attempts at the mouth of Battle Creek by placing some men astride the creek bed. Finally, Lieutenant Quinn was dispatched west across Battle Creek to attack north and east against the Indian village and cut off any escape to the west over the bluffs.

When McGarry's troops began moving down the ravine with enfilading fire, this was the signal for all four military units to attack the Indian camp simultaneously. For the remaining two hours the battle became hand-to-hand and man-to-man fighting as the troopers advanced from lodge to lodge against the "dogged obstinacy" of the Shoshoni warriors. Indeed, the Indians had no choice while the soldiers "settled themselves down to the work before them, as a dray horse would set himself to pull his load up hill." In the fierce contest at his holding position immediately opposite the Indian camp, Captain Price lost eight men either killed or mortally wounded. Later the troopers counted the bodies of forty-eight Indians in one pile as a result of the effective "execution" by Price's troopers.

The slaughter of Indian warriors was immeasurably aided by the pistols and the generous supply of ammunition. The soldiers used their small arms in the hand-to-hand encounters, and Mormon Alexander Stalker later reported the troops "found their revolvers of incalculable value. . . ."[46] Some of the officers, at least, were two-gun men. One eyewitness report noted that "Capt. McLean had a pistol shot out of his right hand . . . and while drawing another with the left received a bullet in the groin. . . ." The close fighting in the dense willow thickets was later described by the purple-prose newsman who accompanied the expedition as a "vomiting volcano," punctuated by "the snakish whistle of the bullets. . . ."[47]

Colonel Connor and the two visiting soldiers, Major Gallagher and Captain Berry, were with Price's troops when the remaining Indian warriors finally broke from what had become a trap in the bed of Battle Creek. "A wild yell from the troops" alerted Connor, who sent Lieutenant Conrad and a detachment to regain their mounts from the horse line and to cut off the Indians racing for Bear River. Lieutenant Quinn joined the pursuit with his mounted troopers who helped drive the warriors into the willow-lined river banks. Further hand-to-hand struggles took place in which Lieutenant Quinn had a horse shot from under him, Gallagher and Berry were seriously wounded, and "one of the men close by Colonel Connor was shot from his horse." The officers dismounted and joined their men in the close warfare raging up and down the riverbank when they discovered they were targets for Indian fire. No orders were given, but each man chose an Indian antagonist and fought to the finish. When some of the Indians attempted to swim across the river, riflemen standing on shore picked them off. They either were swept downstream to find refuge under the ice or a watery grave. A few escaped by clambering up the west bluffs above Battle Creek.

By ten o'clock, after four hours of fighting, with the first hour of battle being in predawn darkness, the massacre was over. Surgeon Reid had established an aid station near the horse line, but the fighting was so intense and at such close quarters that the wounded men had been left where they fell. The cold was severe and many of the soldiers fought with frozen feet and "with fingers so frozen that they could not tell they had a cartridge in their hands unless they looked for it there." There were a number of miraculous escapes. Captain Price received a ball on his left side that fortunately struck a package of pistol cartridges in his pocket. The captain stopped for a second expecting to fall, but discovered no blood and "felt much relieved in his feelings." The *San Francisco Bulletin* reporter accompanying the expedition described the scene on the battlefield: "The carnage presented in the ravine was horrible. Warrior piled on warrior, horses mangled and wounded in every conceivable form, with here and there a squaw and papoose, who had been accidentally killed. . . ."[48]

Throughout the engagement, most of the Indian women apparently sought shelter for themselves and their children wherever they could. Connor had always warned his troops against shooting Indian women and children,[49] but in the constant shower of bullets many were gunned down. The soldiers probably made little attempt to discriminate when their own lives were at stake. One observer insisted that "as soon as the squaws and children ascertained that the soldiers did not desire to kill them, they came out of the ravine and quietly walked to our rear. The same writer noted that three women and two children were accidentally killed.[50] The *New York Times* correspondent, reporting the battle from other accounts, thought ten women had been killed;[51] the Indian "Matigan" (Matigund) informed Samuel Roskelley that up to thirty women were killed "and many children";[52] James H. Martineau of the Cache Valley settlers reported ninety women and children killed;[53] observer William Hull was of the opinion that about 265 women and children had been killed.[54] The single eyewitness reporter approached the problem from another perspective and announced that 120 women and children had survived the bloodbath,[55] while Connor listed 160 as captives after the battle.[56] It seems probable that a large number of Indian women and children were dead on the field after the close-quarters fighting in the confined and densely grown area of the engagement. Connor's estimate of the number of surviving women and children may be the most accurate.

The colonel also estimated that his force of slightly less than 200 men had engaged 300 Indian warriors at Bear River, but the latter figure seems inflated by at least 100.[57] Furthermore, while his soldiers were mostly young, physically fit, and vigorous men, at least some of the so-called warriors would have been elderly, and perhaps a few were crippled by disease or accident. The available evidence about the number of Indian men who escaped is surprisingly consistent. Nearly all close observers reported that about twenty got away.[58] Four young warriors rode off on four army horses while the soldiers were picking up their wounded.[59] Chief Sagwitch also escaped when he "tumbled into the River and floated down under some brush and lay there till night, and after dark he and some more warriors . . . took off two of the soldiers horses and some of their own ponies and went north." He survived the holocaust with only a wound in his hand. His twelve-year-old son, Yeager Timbimboo, also survived by playing dead on the battlefield. A soldier discovered that the youth was alive but refused to shoot him.[60] Subchief Lehi (spelled Leight by Connor) lost his life, as did Chief Bear Hunter. For some reason the story was circulated after the engagement that Bear Hunter was killed while molding bullets by a campfire. As war chief, it seems doubtful he would have been engaged in this activity in the midst of a firefight.[61] For a total casualty figure, Connor reported, "We found 224 bodies on the field, . . .";[62] his subordinate, Colonel George S. Evans of the Second Cavalry, recorded that "we succeeded in almost annihilating the band; having killed some two hundred and seventy-five—224 bodies were found on the field and as many as fifty fell in the river. . . ."[63] From the Indian point of view, Moroni Timbimboo, grandson of Chief Sagwitch relied on Indian tradition when he told an interviewer "there ain't no 200 Indians killed. There were less than that."[64] But writing to the commissioner of Indian affairs just eighteen days after the fight, Agent James Doty, as one of the most responsible figures involved in the entire course of Indian affairs in Utah Territory reported: "The Indians state that there were 255 men, women and children killed in the late engagement on Bear river."[65] The newspaper correspondents usually adopted Connor's estimate of Indian deaths, although the eyewitness *San Francisco Bulletin* correspondent listed the number as between 225 and 267. The *Deseret News* thought 250 to 300 was a proper guess, and the *Union Vedette*, four years after the event, announced that 278 had been killed on the field and 25 were killed while trying to swim the river.[66]

Dismissing the reminiscences of old settlers like 75-year-old Richard J. M. Bee, who recalled that 1,200 Indians and 200 soldiers had been killed and 1,500 horses captured, close observers from Franklin and other towns in Cache Valley also estimated the Indian deaths.[67] John D. Dowdle and Wilford Woodruff apparently accepted Connor's figure, entering the number 225 in their journals.[68] Henry Ballard reported "about 200" Indians killed.[69] Another Mormon pioneer, William G. Nelson of Franklin, visited the battlefield the day following the massacre. Called by Porter Rockwell on orders from Colonel Connor, Nelson, William Head, James Packer, Isaac Packer, and others were asked to take sleighs to the river to pick up wounded soldiers. Nelson asked Connor for permission to visit the battlefield and was granted it if he promised to touch nothing. He and a friend, Ephraim Ellsworth, saw where "14 soldiers and 5 of their horses had fallen in the snow." They counted 76 dead Indians in the creek bed but apparently were so sickened by the sight that they did not proceed farther.[70]

Four other Cache Valley residents contributed their accounts of the Indian battle casualties. Samuel Roskelley talked with the Indian "Matigund" on February 8, 1863. Matigund said about 60 warriors were killed and another 30 wounded, "some of which will die." Adding this to the total of 30 Indian women he had reported as dead, Matigund's figure was 90 or somewhat more.[71] Alexander Stalker in his letter of January 30, 1863, gave 175 as the most reliable estimate.[72] The man who seems to have established the highest count of Indian dead was the usually accurate Martineau, author of a military history of Cache Valley. He indicated that precisely 368 Indians had been killed but identified his source only as "an eyewitness from Franklin," and furthermore, he wrote his description twenty years after the event.[73] Also raising a question is the fact that Martineau, just nine days after the battle, reported to his church leaders that from 200 to 250 were killed, a figure which is closer to the incident and probably closer to the facts.[74] Careful and accurate Peter Maughan wrote Brigham Young on February 4, 1863, that Israel J. Clark had just returned from an inspection of the battlefield and "as near as we can find out there were about 120 Indians killed and about 90 Squaws & children, several have counted them to about that number."[75] Clark's total thus came to 210 killed.

Weighing the evidence from these sources and aware that proximity in place and time count heavily in such evaluations, it seems evident that at least three estimates are reliable. Agent Doty talked with Northwestern Shoshoni leaders shortly after the engagement, and surely they had reasonable knowledge of the number slain. Their figure of 255 can be compared with the 210 reported by Peter Maughan, who did not include an estimate of perhaps as many as 25 or 30 who lost their lives in Bear River. And while it has been somewhat fashionable to discount the enumeration made by Connor's troopers, there was no real reason for the victorious commander either to build up or decrease the actual number. On April 12, 1863, the clerk who was writing Brigham Young's Manuscript History, a day-to-day account of Young's activities, noted that "Col. Connor and his men destroyed some 250 men, women and children of the Indians. . . ." Thus, a reasonable estimate of Indian dead from the engagement at Bear River would be 250. It should be noted, however, that Connor did not differentiate among the casualties by sex or age. His detachment to survey the battlefield may not have done so, and perhaps also he had no desire to be labeled as a "squaw killer."

The mopping up operations by his troops resulted in a lot of booty, which "more than paid all the expenses of the expedition," as the *Union Vedette* reporter nicely put it. The salvage operators were gratified to learn that many of the wagon covers they retrieved bore the names of emigrant owners. Blankets, combs, looking glasses, and cooking utensils gave evidence of having been stolen from wagon trains. The soldiers also recovered over 1,000 bushels of wheat and flour, potatoes, beef, and "live chickens stolen from the settlements." The reporter added, "a portion of the food was left for the women and children. . . ." The troopers also gathered in about 175 horses and used some as infantry mounts for the return to Camp

Douglas. As a last gesture, the victors "appropriated to themselves as trophies of the war buffalo robes, gewgaws, beads, pipes, tomahawks, knives, arrows, and all such things."[76]

In addition to taking nearly all Indian property, after the battle some soldiers spent the rest of the day in more reprehensible activities. Soldiers reported to Alexander Stalker that wounded Indians who were so incapacitated they could not move "were killed by being hit in the head with an axe."[77] James Martineau wrote of one instance in which a soldier found a dead woman clutching a little infant still alive. The soldier "in mercy to the babe, killed it."[78] Martineau also recorded more barbarity: "Several squaws were killed because they would not submit quietly to be ravished, and other squaws were ravished in the agony of death."[79] "Matigund" told Samuel Roskelley "the way the Soldiers used the Squaws after the battle was shameful. . . ."[80] In confirmation of these atrocities, Peter Maughan reported to Brigham Young that about twenty strange Indians had come into Franklin and that "all are familiar with the conduct of the troops towards the Squaws etc. . . ."[81] In another letter, Maughan wrote: "Bro Israel J Clark has just returned from visiting the Battlefield and give the most sickening accounts of the inhuman acts of the Soldiers, as related to him by the squaws that still remain on the ground. . . . They killed the wounded by Knocking them in the head with an axe and then commenced to ravish the Squaws which was done to the very height of brutality   they affirm that some were used in the act of dying from their wounds. The above reports are substantiated by others that were present at the time." Maughan stated that the Indian women were afraid to come into the settlements because the soldiers might return.[82] Most of the survivors traveled to the head of Marsh Creek several miles north where Chief Sagwitch had set up a temporary camp after his escape from the conflict.[83]

The morning after the fight, Bishop Preston Thomas sent some of the men from Franklin to the battlefield to offer assistance to Indian survivors. Matthew P. Fifield found one Shoshoni mother hiding in a "willowy copse" and holding her baby out of the water to save its life. Fifield took her to a campfire and helped get her dry clothes.[84] Two women and three children were taken into Franklin where the settlers cared for them. The two women eventually rejoined their tribe, but two little boys were taken into the homes of William Hull and Edwin

Nielson. One died at the age of four and the other at nineteen. Hull also adopted the third child, a little girl, who grew up to marry a white man, Heber Riley, and to raise a large family.[85]

The bodies of the Shoshoni lay where they had fallen on the field, prey to wolves and magpies. In the fall of 1863, Captain James L. Fisk, on his expedition to the Rocky Mountains, visited the scene and recorded, "Many of the skeletons of the Indians yet remained on the ground, their bones scattered by the wolves."[86] A *Deseret News* reporter, five years after the event, also saw the site and revealed one Mormon view of the defeat of the Indians by writing, "The bleached skeletons of scores of noble red men still ornament the grounds." He expressed regret that Pocatello and his "gang" had not been annihilated in the engagement.[87]

The Mormon settlers of Cache Valley expressed their gratitude for "the movement of Col. Connor as an intervention of the Almighty, . . ." by placing this statement of approval in the official minutes of the Logan Ward.[88] Peter Maughan added a final epitaph for the slain Northwestern Shoshoni, reporting to Brigham Young:

> I feel my skirts clear of their blood. They rejected the way of life and salvation which have been pointed out to them from time to time (especially for the last two years) and thus have perished relying on their own strength and wisdom.
>
> We have pretty good reason to believe that if they had gained the Victory over the Soldiers their intention was to take our Herd and drive it right to the Salmon River Country for their own special benefit.[89]

There was a mixture of piety and pragmatism in his words.

After the mopping up operations, Connor ordered the bodies of the fourteen soldiers killed during the engagement moved south across the river to a camp set up by Lieutenant Honeyman at the base of the bluffs. By nightfall the men were assembled around fires fed by the tentpoles taken from the burned tipis, and the wounded were housed in tents. Because about seventy-five of the soldiers had frozen feet, only twenty-five were fit enough to stand guard that night. Connor dispatched a messenger to Camp Douglas with news of the "victory" and with instructions to Lieutenant Colonel Evans to send a relief expedition to meet the returning troops. With the help of Porter Rockwell, arrangements were made to bring eighteen sleds and teams from Franklin and Richmond to transport the dead and wounded back to Camp Douglas. They and their Mormon drivers arrived at the soldiers' camp at daybreak on Friday January 30.[90] At the end of the march to Camp Douglas, the military authorities paid the teamsters $42 for the trip plus provisions for their journey home.[91] The *Sacramento Union* reporter approved of the actions of the Mormon guide: "Porter Rockwell . . . is given great praise for the manner he exerted himself in behalf of the soldiers, causing the inhabitants to furnish sheets and contribute such delicacies as the wounded required."[92] It is interesting that Colonel Connor blasted the Mormon settlers for not helping him on the march to Franklin but failed to acknowledge the Saints assistance on the return trip to Camp Douglas.[93]

The battered expedition spent the night of January 30 at Franklin where the able-bodied men camped in the local Mormon tithing yard.[94] Mary Ann Hull remembered how the wounded were cared for. "We fixed up the meeting house with beds and everyone in town were solicited for cloth to make bandages for the wounded. The suffering was terrible. We could hear nothing but moans all night." She added, "Pay was not thought of in those days."[95] Riding on the eight-foot sleds built with two solid runners "gave a very hard and choppy ride," which only added to the agony of the wounded.[96]

At Logan on the night of January 31 the citizens took in the soldiers—as many as fifteen for each household. They provided beds, furnished supper and breakfast, and even got up a few parties for those able to attend.[97] Margaret Ballard sent bread, butter, and eggs for the troopers camped on the Mormon "Tabernacle Square."[98] The next day the troops battled snowdrifts in the pass between Wellsville and Brigham City but had to give up and return to Wellsville for the night. Bishop Maughan gathered men and teams the following morning and beat a path over the mountains to Brigham City where the exhausted soldiers spent the night of February 2.

The expedition set up camp at Ogden where a Dr. Williamson and a Dr. Walcott Steele from Dayton, Nevada, helped Dr. Reid care for the wounded. Parson Anderson also showed up to offer spiritual guidance.[99] Lieutenant Chase was so weak that he had been left at Brigham City but was taken on the next day to Farmington where he died. Chase had once been a member of the Mormon church and for a time had served a short jail sentence in Missouri with Apostle Parley P. Pratt.[100] When he was picked up at the battlefield by William

Nelson, Chase begged Nelson and another Mormon Elder, Fileman Merrill, to perform the religious rite of administering to him to relieve his pain. Nelson answered, "I said I thought it would be the wrong thing to do, so he was not administered to."[101]

The historical secretary of the Church of Jesus Christ of Latter-day Saints wrote on February 4, 1863, "Col. Connor and his horseman passed the office for Camp Douglas about 5:00 P.M."[102] The colonel brought with him fifty-four or seventy or seventy-five frostbitten men, depending on which source is read.[103] Another man had died at Farmington, so there were now sixteen bodies to be interred. A funeral for the sixteen servicemen was held on February 5; Lieutenant Chase was buried the next day. The last death occurred on March 24, 1863, when Private William H. Lake finally succumbed to his wounds.[104] The church secretary commented, "The Soldiers that were buried were mostly Catholics."[105] The total number who died as a result of the action amounted to twenty-two enlisted men and the one officer, Lieutenant Chase. Within the next five months, even more soldiers were discharged as a result of disabilities stemming from wounds received in the battle. As the list in Appendix A reveals, "The Indians evidently aimed at the belt, as most of the killed and wounded were hit in the lungs or other parts of the trunk."[106] Connor reported on February 26, 1863, that he still had ninety men sick in quarters and twenty-two in the hospital, while four had toes amputated and two lost a finger each.[107]

After the melancholy burial of his dead, Connor complimented his troops and informed his superiors about the battle.[108] He gathered his soldiers in a dress parade on February 6 to praise their courage and endurance during the engagement against the Indians.[109] The soldiers were also honored in other ways. Among the many poems that clogged the columns of frontier newspapers was one entitled an "Anniversary Log" by E. P. Kingston. It appeared on February 1, 1864, in the *Union Vedette* and had one verse that read:

> Ten o'clock; the fight is over! Four long hours of
>   Blood and death;
> Four long hours of savage conflict—firm lips and
>   bated breath.
> Where shall now the great "Bear Hunter"—where
>   shall "Lehigh" now be found.
> There! with nearly thrice an hundred, dead upon
>   the battle ground.

There, the foe who knew no pity—who ne'er
   checked his wrath to save,
Shall have snow flakes for his cerements,
   and the ice-drift for his grave!

There were no eulogies for the native side.

In his formal report of the encounter, the colonel singled out Majors McGarry and Gallagher and Surgeon Reid for their "skill, gallantry and bravery. . . ."[110] Brigadier General G. Wright, commanding the Department of the Pacific, announced the "signal victory" by Connor's troops[111] and commended their "heroic conduct . . . in that terrible combat. . . ."[112] Not to be outdone in rhetorical flourishes, California Governor Leland Stanford added his encomiums.[113] On March 29 General-in-Chief H. W. Halleck praised Connor's "splended victory" at Bear River and granted him the longed-for brigadier general's commission.[114]

In spite of this, all was not commendatory. General Connor came under criticism for losing twenty-three men at Bear River after Captain S. P. Smith led an attack on some Gosiute in May 1863 and killed fifty-three of the Indians with no casualties. A newspaperman reported, "The men render great praise to Captain Smith for his bravery and gallant conduct during these desperate engagements, and regret that he could not have been at the Bear River fight, where he undoubtedly would have mitigated the great loss of life and the number wounded for the small number engaged."[115]

The Cache Valley settlers were satisfied that Connor's aggressive tactics in the battle with the Northwest Shoshoni meant that they would "never again attempt a fair stand-up fight,"[116] and that the engagement had "put a quietus on the Indians."[117] Isaac Sorensen was a little more cautious: "This put an end or mostly so to Indian depredations in Cache Valley. . . ."[118] Samuel Roskelley reported a different result. The Indians told him they were so angry with the soldiers that they intended to steal all the horses they could and would "kill every white man they could find. . . ."[119] The *New York Times* chimed in with a common eastern point of view, wondering if Connor's extermination of the Shoshoni might not prove a "dear-bought one," and expressed the thought that conciliation was sometimes better than a fight.[120] The *Portland Oregonian* used the incident at Bear River to charge that while California had contributed

Colonel Connor returns with Orrin Porter Rockwell after Battle of Bear River, artist unknown. *Fort Douglas Officers' Club.*

seven regiments to the Civil War, Oregon had sent only seven companies and asked its patriotic citizens to emulate the California Volunteers by enlisting more troops for the Union cause.[121]

———————————•◆ ◆•———————————

For fifteen years the Northwestern Shoshoni watched aggressive Mormon pioneers usurp their lands and the large cattle herds destroy the grass seeds that constituted their basic food supply. The natives were compelled to compete with white hunters for dwindling amounts of wild game. The Indians could only choose between begging from their prosperous farm neighbors or raiding well-provisioned emigrant wagons or mail stations, depending on how desperate they were for food and clothing. Furthermore, the introduction of white culture had brought with it a desire among the Indians for white clothing, tools, guns, etc., and emigrant parties offered tempting targets. White incursions reached a breaking point when parties of miners began to trek across Shoshoni homelands to get to the gold mines in Montana.

A new and threatening element was added when United States regular troops established Camp Floyd. The Indians were more familiar with being fed by the Mormons than with fighting, and they were initially unprepared for encounters with soldiers. Attempts to negotiate with the Indians using parleys, truces, and treaties accustomed tribal leaders to expect these solutions. Connor's Volunteers had very different goals that reflected the prevalent mood of violence and bloodshed gripping America. The Volunteers were adventurers spoiling for a fight and longing for glory. Although disciplined by their colonel, they could go too far in the midst of battle if their commanders turned their backs and gave them tacit permission especially if the enemies were ignoble "savages." The record of the Volunteers at Gravelly Ford, Cache Valley, and Bear River Ferry demonstrated their ruthless attitude toward the natives. A reporter from the *Sacramento Union* pointed out on May 30, 1863, that the Volunteers had killed 375 Indians since their arrival in Utah Territory with a loss of only two officers and twenty-two men (twenty-three of these came from the Bear River encounter).

Connor's intention to take no prisoners at Bear River and his efforts to keep his expedition secret to maintain the element of surprise set the stage for bloodletting. His attack on a camp where there were women and children ensured the deaths of many who were not even combatants, and, as noted, his official report carefully listed only 224 casualties without any reference to age or sex.

The first hour of the engagement had all the elements of a battle. The Indians were entrenched and prepared for the attack, the troops suffered their greatest casualties in assaulting their foe across open ground, and the soldiers continued at a disadvantage until orders were given to flank the Indian position from the end of the ravine. As the combined infantry and cavalry units advanced down the defile with a devastating enfilading fire, and as other troops were dispatched to command the western bluffs in the rear of the Indian camp and to seal off any escape route at the mouth of the ravine, the next two hours of the fight developed into a massacre. Outgunned, the Indian men, women, and children fell in heaps before the Volunteers. In fact, the close-quarters combat in the thick willows with the several shots each soldier had from his pistol and his store of thirty cartridges meant that the Indians could not compete in the individual duels that took place. The last hour of the four-hour fight degenerated into a brutal slaughter as the soldiers went around with axes or other handy weapons beating wounded Indians in the head to end their suffering "in mercy." For the Northwestern bands the tragedy was of immense proportions—at first a battle, then a massacre, and finally a wholesale slaughter. Accepting Don Russell's analysis of "How Many Indians Were Killed?", as mentioned in the Introduction to this book, the massacre at Bear River was evidently the first major Indian massacre in the Trans-Mississippi West. There were smaller affairs, but Connor's killing of 250 Northwestern Shoshoni ranks as the most bloodthirsty of the five incidents examined by Russell.

While most Indian massacres in the American West depend on the perspective of white reporters and officials for their telling, the sanguinary killing at Bear River has been reconstructed from traditional accounts passed down from generation to generation. Mae T. Parry, granddaughter of Chief Sagwitch, published an Indian portrayal of the "Massacre at Boa Ogoi" in 1976 (Appendix B). Even though it depends on oral transmission of facts from over a hundred years ago, Mae T. Parry vividly recreates the memories and emotions of the survivors of the massacre.[122]

ELEVEN

The Last Years of
the Shoshoni Frontier

Connor's efforts to punish the Northern Shoshoni and subdue them proved ineffective. The surviving Northwestern bands, enraged at the slaughter of their neighbors, friends, and relatives, mounted new hostilities against the Mormon settlers whom they perceived as accomplices of the military. For six months after the massacre, Mormon leaders in Cache Valley had a difficult time protecting homes and livestock. Indian raiding parties were very careful to avoid General Connor's troops, and, as news of the deaths speedily traveled through Shoshoni country, chiefs such as Pocatello kept out of Connor's way. Superintendent Doty was slowly able to convince the tribes that the government was sincere about offering agreements to end the warfare, and the bands of warriors gradually settled down and began to come in for talks. Five treaties were negotiated by Doty in 1863. These and the distribution of presents, with the promise of annual gifts, brought peace to the Great Basin and Snake River areas after twenty-five years. One of the longest periods of Indian warfare in American history began to wind down after 1863. The Shoshoni frontier was receding before the advance of civilization and the armed power of the government.

The sword unsheathed by General Connor also failed to bring peace to the trails west of South Pass. At Boise River, where 15,000 miners were busily trying to make their fortunes, the Shoshoni bands struck back at white interlopers. In late February and throughout March of 1863, reports to the *Washington Statesman* at Walla Walla indicated almost constant hostility between the miners and the neighboring Indians. In retaliation for the loss of some stock, a party of packers killed two Indians;[1] another group of miners retrieved thirty-six stolen horses after killing one Indian and wounding another;[2] and one newspaper correspondent exaggeratedly claimed that the Shoshoni had already robbed pack trains of almost 500 animals.[3] When two men were killed on the Snake River in mid-March, their companions and other miners adopted the motto, "Kill every Snake Indian on sight." The miners demanded protection from the military,[4] and petitions from suffering miners asking for help poured into the office of Governor W. H. Wallace of Idaho Territory.[5]

The perennial troubles with emigrants traversing the Oregon Trail added to the apprehensions of more permanent settlers in the Boise region. Seventeen-year-old Mrs. A. A. Cooper recorded how her train of frightened travelers expected to be massacred at any moment. After several scares the party actually met four Indians who came to sell fish. "Some were for slaying these four Indians right away. . . ." but good sense prevailed and they were allowed to depart in peace.[6]

Oregon Indian Superintendent J. W. Huntington, in a long letter to the commissioner of Indian affairs on June 1, 1863, revealed the usual ignorance of his office about the Snake River Shoshoni. However, he insisted that part of the $20,000 congressional appropriation of July 2, 1862, be used to treat with the Snake Indians. Huntington felt that an all-out war with the Snake River Shoshoni was inevitable and regretted, as did General Benjamin Alvord, that Oregon troops could not be sent to the area until midsummer.[7]

Alvord finally appointed Colonel Reuben F. Maury to command an expedition against the Snake Indians. In August Maury reported that most of the Shoshoni along the Snake River had traveled to Fort Hall to make a treaty with General Connor, although some of the more hostile warriors were still south of Salmon Falls. At the falls one of Maury's detachments met about 200 Shoshoni who were so destitute and defenseless that the troops "could not, with any regard for humanity, assault them." Maury met Captain Modorem Crawford's military escort near Ross Fork on August 17 and was told by Crawford that there had been no difficulty with the emigration this far on the journey to Oregon. The Indians at Fort Hall looked forward to treaty negotiations with Connor realizing that "any other policy . . . would lead to extermination." The Shoshoni along the Snake River "expressed great desire for peace and a willingness to do anything or go anywhere they might be directed," but by late fall they were still waiting for Connor and his peace council.[8] It did not arrive until the following spring, and conflict for the Shoshoni of the Boise region did not cease until they moved to the Fort Hall Reservation in early 1869.[9]

* * *

Despite their lack of legal responsibility for the Shoshoni and Bannock at Fort Hall, Utah Indian agents continued surveillance of these tribes and attempted to provide presents for them. Agent F. M. Hatch complained in February 1863 that the few goods allotted to Utah usually were given to the Indians who visited Salt Lake City frequently, whereas those two or three hundred miles away received very little.[10] Superintendent Doty also had a gripe since the $20,000 appropriation to be used for negotiating treaties had not arrived in December 1862 as promised. This left the Indians believing "that the President has cast them off, and does not intend to give them any more presents."[11] When the money was finally sent for treaty negotiations, the commissioner left its distribution to Doty's discretion, warning that the money should be used as economically as possible.[12] James Duane Doty was so successful as superintendent of Indian affairs that, in June, he was made governor of the Territory of Utah, a position which would enhance his role as peacemaker with the tribes.[13]

Doty seized an opportunity to check up on the Shoshoni and Bannock at Fort Hall by accompanying General Connor on his trip to Soda Springs in the late spring of 1863. The general wanted to follow up on his victory at Bear River by imposing his will on the Indians near the junction of the new Montana Trail with the Oregon and California trails. He planned to garrison a post in the area to guard emigrant parties traveling to the coast and groups headed for the Beaverhead mines. His other purpose was to help found an anti-Mormon settlement next to the new post. During the winter at Camp Douglas he had assisted and protected a group of dissenters from the church, the Morrisites, who feared persecution from the Saints.[14]

On May 5 Captain David Black and Company H, Third Infantry, California Volunteers, left Camp Douglas for Soda Springs accompanied by 160 Morrisites. The following day Connor left with Company H, Second Cavalry, under the command of Lieutenant Cyrus D. Clark, hoping to surprise the remnants of the hostile bands he had engaged at Bear River in January by making two secret night marches beyond Brigham City. He encountered only two lodges of friendly Shoshoni in Portneuf Valley and "passed on without molesting these Indians." At Snake River Ferry, near Fort Hall, he and Superintendent Doty held their council with about 300 Shoshoni. The general explained his troops were being stationed in the area to protect both good Indians and white people but would "visit the most summary punishment, even to extermination" on any Indians who attacked emigrants or settlers. He was told that Pocatello, "the great chief of the hostile Shoshoni," was on the lower Snake River, that Sagwitch was in Cache Valley, and that Sanpitch was farther east. Connor then sent Lieutenant Clark and twenty-five men to reconnoiter a new road from the Blackfoot River. On May 20 the infantry arrived at Soda Springs with the anti-Mormon settlers, and Camp Connor was officially established three days later. The town was located just west of the military camp. After six days at the new post, Connor left for Camp Douglas, arriving there May 30.[15]

In the report to his commander about the trip to Soda Springs and the establishment of Camp Connor, the general also noted that later he had left Salt Lake City on June 3 for Fort Bridger where he talked with about 700 of the Eastern Shoshoni who "are tired of fighting and want to be at peace. . . . The fight of last winter is telling on them." They gave up 150 stolen horses and mules. Connor sent a detachment of troops after two small hostile bands numbering about 100 warriors whom he hoped to "destroy" soon. With this exception and uncertain knowledge about conditions at the Boise mines, he considered the Indian troubles in his district "very near an end."[16]

After his meeting with the Eastern Shoshoni under Chief Washakie in early June,[17] Connor, with Doty, then prepared for negotiations with the tribe to conclude a formal treaty of peace. The Salt Lake City correspondent for the *Sacramento Union* explained the circumstances behind the preparations. Washakie had always been friendly to the whites. "He never seeks presents—he never begs—but will allow his men to receive presents," but they would not presume to do so in his presence. If he ever decided to go to war with the whites, he would first "send in his 'papers,'" recommendations given him by military and other government officials. According to the reporter, the chief was now a bitter enemy of the Mormons and those "Mormon Indians" who hung around the Utah settlements. The Cache Valley Shoshoni, having been deceived by the Mormons who had helped the soldiers at Bear River, now were "on the war path against the Saints."[18] Superintendent Doty carefully explained to the commissioner of Indian affairs that he was proceeding to the treaty council under the original orders of July 22, 1862, and that the commissioner should realize that Washakie's tribe constituted only one-third of all the Shoshoni. It would be necessary to travel to several points and conclude several treaties in order to achieve peace with all the Shoshoni bands.[19]

The treaty with the Eastern Shoshoni, finalized on July 2, 1863, contained the following provisions: Article 1 reestablished friendly relations; Article 2 required the Indians to help maintain safety for travelers along the trails and to deliver to proper officials of the United States any offenders who committed depredations on emigrants and settlers; Article 3 maintained the right to continue telegraph, stage, and, later, railroad routes through Shoshoni territory; Article 4 outlined the boundaries of Washakie's tribe, which included the Wind River Mountains; Article 5 established that the Eastern Shoshoni were to receive an annuity payment of $10,000 a year for twenty years; Article 6 acknowledged that the tribe had received $6,000 in presents at the time of the signing of the treaty; and Article 7 added a qualification that the Shoshoni could not claim any more land than they had held while their country was under Mexican law. The treaty was ratified by the United States Senate on March 7, 1864.[20]

General Connor's peaceful forays into Shoshoni country at Fort Hall and Fort Bridger were quite different from his experiences in Utah territory, where serious troubles with the Ute Indians brought sharp clashes with the California Volunteers. The continued expansion of Mormon settlements and the fact that the Utes were not involved in the Bear River affair meant that friction was likely to persist in central Utah. Trouble started when Lieutenant Anthony Ethier and twenty-five men were sent on an Indian-hunting expedition to Skull Valley, west of Great Salt Lake. Ethier did not sight any natives until he neared Cedar Fort. There he found about 100 peaceful Northern Shoshoni or "Weber Utes," under Little Soldier with their chiefs "riding the war circle." After being fired on he attacked the Indian position twice and wounded one Indian but was forced to withdraw to guard his horses, which were in danger of capture. He moved his men to Fort Crittenden and sent word to Connor that the Mormons in the neighborhood had not only not helped him guard his animals but were actually talking treacherously to the Indians in "plain sight of me."[21]

The general responded to Ethier's message by dispatching Captain George F. Price and fifty-one men to Fort Crittenden as reinforcements. The combined force then spent three days tracking the fleeing Little Soldier Shoshoni band to Spanish Fork, where, on the evening of April 4, some Ute Indians were discovered at the mouth of Spanish Fork Canyon.

The California Volunteers now attempted to repeat with the Ute the extermination they had administered on Bear Hunter's Shoshoni at Bear River. Over the next eleven days they engaged in three skirmishes with the Ute during which a Ute warrior was killed as the result of an attack by the troops in Spanish Fork Canyon. On April 12, in what turned out to be a comic opera affair, a small howitzer detachment defended itself against 100 attacking Ute in the Mormon town of Pleasant Grove and drove off the warriors after killing four of their own mules with a misdirected shot. In a final and more serious affair of April 15, a large body of the Volunteers under Lieutenant Colonel George S. Evans, assaulted about 200 Ute in Spanish Fork Canyon and succeeded in killing thirty of the Indians with the loss of one, Lieutenant F. A. Peel, the only other casualty of the California Volunteers in Utah besides the twenty-three killed at Bear River. One hundred and seventy-one of the Volunteers were engaged in the battle.[22] Superintendent Doty was certain that if he had received his $20,000 appropriation the previous December, as promised, the difficulties with the Ute and with Little Soldier's Shoshoni band could have been avoided.[23]

General Connor finally undertook to secure peace with Little Soldier by sending William Hickman as a government agent to persuade the chief to come to Camp Douglas for a talk. Little Soldier was understandably distrustful of any council with the Volunteers and refused to budge from his mountain retreat twenty-five miles west of Salt Lake City until Hickman had delivered some presents of blankets "to convince them that he was not talking 'forked,' and trying to entrap them." Even then, the chief only consented to send one of his trusted lieutenants, Weber Jim, to meet with General Connor. On June 24 Connor and Weber Jim concluded a treaty of peace, or "satisfactory understanding," as the general expressed it. There was no formal, written document, only a verbal agreement. With Little

Soldier finally convinced of Connor's sincerity, the chief surrendered all the government stock held by his band and came in to confer with the general and Doty.[24] Other presents were delivered to the band at a cost of $3,700 to the Utah superintendency.[25] The *Deseret News* of July 1, 1863, expressed the hope that the troops would now no longer "fight inoffensive Indians" like Little Soldiers's band.

———————————————◆◆◆◆————————————————

Of all Indian difficulties faced by the military and Doty's office in 1863, the first priority was protecting the Overland Mail Company stations. Delayed appropriation of the $20,000 for treaties exposed the Indians along the mail line to great hardship and left them with only one alternative—to rob the stations for food supplies. The Overland Mail Company claimed it had spent $12,000 subsidizing the natives along the route the year before (more than the amount supplied by the government), but could no longer afford to do so.[26]

The prospect of starvation and the ruthless tactics of the California Volunteers angered the natives west of Salt Lake City, and they began a series of attacks on the mail stations. Word reached the city on March 22 that the stage driver and a passenger had been killed at Deep Creek. The very next day news arrived that two men had been killed and scalped at Eight-Mile Creek and that all the hay at the station had been burned.[27]

Connor immediately ordered Major Gallagher, in charge of Fort Ruby, to capture and punish the perpetrators. Gallagher was sure he could keep the road open and safe—"My whole aim has been the detection and punishment of the Indians who have been committing depredations on the Overland Mail Line. . . ." Major Gallagher and General Connor were frustrated, however, by the hit-and-run guerrilla tactics and the Indians' refusal to challenge Connor's troops in open battle.[28]

Assaults on the mail stations continued. On March 26 about a dozen Indians attacked Willow Station but were driven off. The warriors then struck Boyd's Station.[29] The next week the stage was set upon near Schell Creek Station and one of the horses killed, but the driver escaped by increasing "the speed of his horses. . . ." Six Indians were driven away from Faust's Station when they tried to drive off stock.[30] In early May Captain Samuel P. Smith went "Indian hunting" and annihilated a band of fifty-three Gosiute who were "supposed to be the ones that committed depredations on the overland route." No one was sure, but there were now fewer natives to worry about.[31] Captain Smith was an especially ferocious Indian killer and was rewarded for his butcheries by being promoted to major on May 9, 1865.

The savagery of the Indian attacks was emphasized when the stage was riddled with bullets and the driver and a stage company employee were killed and mutilated at Point of the Mountain, twenty-five miles south of Salt Lake City. A few days later at the same spot a second coach was assailed and two more men were murdered.[32] Phebe Westwood, a non-Mormon resident of Fort Crittenden, who saw the scalps of two of the victims, was exasperated with the Mormon people because they still showed friendship to Indians. She exploded in a letter to a friend, "The Bishop down there treated the Indians with Tobacco, and ordered the people to feed them, and it made me so mad that I pitched into them, and told them what I thought of them, and then I felt better."[33]

In a sharp exchange of hostility along the mail line in 1863, Captain Smith in mid-June killed ten Indians at Government Springs. Then, during the first of August, he "discovered a nest of Gosh-Utes" about twenty miles north of Schell Creek Station and killed twelve of them, "only two escaping."[34] Smith's relentless Indian hunting was revenged by Chief Peah-namp, whose wife and child were among those killed by Smith and his troops.[35] Peah-namp and his warriors assaulted Canyon Station, and the stationkeeper, William Riley, was shot and then thrown onto the woodpile, which was set afire. Four soldiers in the barn were either killed outright or while trying to escape on horseback. The last was caught, and "as he was so bald on the top of his head, and a good growth of whiskers on his chin, they scalped that and left him where he fell." The warriors then burned all the buildings.[36] The *Deseret News* of July 15, 1863, stated that things had gotten undeniably worse along the mail line since the Volunteers had been stationed on the route. The editor thought the soldiers' habit of nailing the scalps of Indian victims to station walls only assured more attacks.

General Connor assuaged his frustration at not being able to stem the Indian onslaughts by assuring his superiors that despite having to patrol 800 miles of road, there was no danger to travelers or stagecoaches.[37] By August 1863 that was more accurate than it had been earlier in the spring and summer. Connor stated that Mormons disguised as Indians were instigating most of the difficulties and asked for two cannon and two field guns with battery wagons and caissons to meet this threat of the subversive Saints.[38]

The *Deseret News* writer also heard that General Connor had given orders to "shoot all Indians . . . whether friends or enemies, without distinction" but could not believe he was "thus void of humanity."[39] Four years after the events of 1863, a New York writer by the name of Mark Twain was not so sure that this forgotten general of the West could not have given such a command:

> I am waiting patiently to hear that they have ordered General Connor out to polish off those Indians, but the news never comes. He has shown that he knows how to fight the kind of Indians that God made, but I suppose the humanitarians want somebody to fight the Indians that J. Fennimore Cooper made. There is just where the mistake is. The Cooper Indians are dead—died with their creator. The kind that are left are of altogether a different breed, and cannot be successfully fought with poetry, and sentiment, and soft soap, and magnanimity.[40]

Connor's determination to bring all "bad" Indians to justice can especially be seen with reference to Chief Pocatello. After the encounter at Bear River, the colonel had reported that Pocatello and Sanpitch "with their bands of murderers" were still at large but that he hoped "to be able to kill or capture them before spring."[41] There were reports of expeditions against Pocatello and of Connor's desire to find him.[42] On July 6, however, Governor Doty excitedly wired the commissioner of Indian affairs for instructions because Pocatello had sent word that he "wished to treat for peace."[43] More definite news came from Mormon Bishop Alvin Nichols of Brigham City—Pocatello was so in favor of a council of peace that he was willing to give ten horses to prove his sincerity and would grant guarantees for the safety of travelers through his country. He was afraid to come to Salt Lake City though, where the soldiers, not knowing the nature of his mission, might kill him.[44] Connor also heard from Pocatello. In one message, the chief, "begging for peace," and asking for a conference, "says he is tired of war, and has been effectually driven from the Territory with a small remnant of his once powerful band."[45] Pocatello offered again to treat on Connor's terms and proposed a meeting with the general at Brigham City on July 30.[46]

Before the council could be set up, however, other Northwestern Shoshoni in Cache Valley initiated more attacks. The slaughter at Bear River aroused a spirit of revenge instead of leaving the Indians cowering. As Alexander Stalker reported of a meeting with Sagwitch, "He said he saw Mormons help the soldiers to fight and that he will use all the influence he has with other Indians to Steal from us."[47] A Cache Valley correspondent to the *Deseret News*, writing on March 22, reported the theft of a horse by a son of Sagwitch and warned that Indians in from the north "say they will fight the troops should they dare to show themselves in their country."[48]

The first overt action by Cache Valley Shoshoni occurred on May 1 when three of the Indians came upon Andrew Morrison and William Howell loading wood in Cub River Canyon above Franklin. Morrison attempted to talk to the warriors but was told that "the white man had killed Indians at Battle Creek and now they are going to kill every white man they could." Morrison was immediately struck by two arrows in the chest while Howell ran for his life to the town three miles away. A rescue party found Morrison still alive, although one of the arrowheads was so close to his heart that the town physician was afraid to remove it and just stuffed some cotton into the open wound. Morrison survived another twenty-seven years carrying the Indian souvenir. The Minute Men were not able to find the three Shoshoni.[49]

The day after the assault, Sagwitch's band drove off a herd of horses from Millville twenty-five miles to the south. Captain Franklin Weaver and fifteen Minute Men left immediately to recover the animals and were able to capture Sagwitch, his two sons, a brother-in-law, a woman, and three children. The horses were nowhere in sight. Taking one man hostage, the militia tried to force the return of the horses but was unsuccessful. John Fish Wright reported that "a son of Sagwitch accused his father of being a coward, and grabbed his bow and arrow and tried to shoot Weaver, but I being near him grabbed the arrow as he was letting it fly, the men drew their pistols and would have shot him had not Weaver ordered them not to fire."[50] A couple of weeks later, Indians stole more horses and cattle and a posse of sixteen men unsuccessfully searched the nearby mountains.[51]

A more serious matter took place on May 9 when members of the Sagwitch band approached two boys in Box Elder Canyon, drove off four horses and an ox, and attempted to steal an entire herd of cattle. A relief party roused by the boys discovered the Indians had killed, mutilated, and stripped William Thorp who was mining coal in the canyon. Thorp left a widow and ten children.[52]

The raids continued. Indians drove off about a hundred head of horses from neighboring Ogden Valley and two horses from the Bannack City Express Company herd. J. C. Wright, who reported these incidents, was certain the Shoshoni intended to "satiate their bloodthirsty propensities and traditions of revenge for their defeat . . . in the battle last winter. . . ." For once, the settlers who went in pursuit successfully retrieved 108 of the animals.[53]

In a very strong letter on May 9, Ezra Taft Benson and Peter Maughan demanded satisfaction from the Indians. The two Mormon leaders wrote that the Shoshoni

> now threaten to steal some of the Mormon women . . . their intentions . . . is to not only steal but kill us. . . . the hostile Indians are the remains of the Bands that were in the fight at Bear River last winter and they say they intend having their pay out of the Mormon as they are afraid to tackle the soldiers   . . . and while they are doing these things they are eating the very flour that has been donated to them by the brethren. . . . we do not wish to kill except we are justified. . . . it seems to us that the ball is fairly open for they have forced it upon us. The Brethren feel tired of bearing their insults and it has been with much persuasion that we have thus far restrained them from wiping them out of existance.[54]

Peter Maughan elaborated on the Indian troubles in Cache Valley in a letter to Brigham Young on May 23:

> We have had some excitement among the Indians. . . . They have stole a great many Horses and tried to Kill the Brethren at various times to take horses by force. they have shot at men and boys several times within a week past, but have not succeeded in hurting any one. they are skulking in the brush all over the Valley in small squads 3 or 4 together, watching for a good chance. We sent Sige-a-watch after some horses about two weeks since. he has returned with four and had to steal them to get them away. he reports a great many of our horses at Sanpitches Camp East of Bear River Lake and says that those are the Indians that are doing us the damage as a retaliation for the Mormons helping the Soldiers at Bear River last winter. here I am compelled to admit that they have reason to feel bad. . . . Wash-a-kee is friendly and has an influential Indian traveling in the Mountains teaching his brethren to send the

Mormon horses home and then behave themselves. We expect large Bands in here soon to trade Buffalo skins and other traps in their line of business. We are instructing the Brethren to give them a full proof of our honesty by dealing liberally and thus establish that confidence and friendship that the signs of the times demand. . . . Conor is expected in Logan today or tomorrow with his Cavalry. . . . There were 11 soldiers there all the time I was there. they manifested the most filthy and disgusting code of Civilization I have ever heard."

It seemed obvious to Saint and Indian official alike that some kind of treaty arrangements should be negotiated to provide subsistence to the wandering bands of Northwestern Shoshoni and to bring an end to their depredations.

Governor Doty finally met with the chiefs of nine bands of the Northwestern group of Shoshoni at Brigham City on July 30, 1863, and concluded the Treaty of Box Elder. The leaders present were Pocatello, Toomontso, Sanpitch, Tosowitz, Yahnoway, Weerahsoop, Pahragoosahd, Tahkwetoonah, and Omrshee.[56] Sagwitch was detained because he was made a prisoner by a detachment of California Volunteers. Doty sent a messenger to the troop commander asking that no violence be committed against him and that he be released to attend the treaty negotiations. Despite the plea, the following night some "fiend" shot Sagwitch in the chest inflicting a serious wound from which he, nevertheless, later recovered. The officer in charge of the troops said the perpetrator of the attack could not be found.[57]

There were five articles in the Treaty of Box Elder. Article 1 established friendly relations between the Shoshoni and the United States; Article 2 included the provisions of the Treaty of Fort Bridger to which the assembled chiefs agreed; Article 3 provided for an annuity of $5,000 and $2,000 in presents at the time of the signing of the agreements; Article 4 defined the boundaries of the country "claimed by Pokatello, for himself and his people," the country between the Portneuf Mountains on the east and Raft River on the west; and Article 5, added as a later amendment by Congress, stated the Shoshoni could claim no more land than that which they had occupied formerly under Mexican law.[58] This amendment necessitated another meeting with the tribes to get their assent which Doty was able to accomplish in a council of November 13, 1863, again at Box Elder. There were four or five hundred Indians in attendance who "joyfully participated" in the annuity goods provided by the treaty. Only five lodges of a group from the Goose Creek Mountains refused to sign the document. Doty hoped to visit them later to encourage them in approving the agreement. The supposed remnants of Bear Hunter's band participated—just seven individuals who had survived the massacre at Bear River.[59] The *Deseret News* August 5, 1863, hoped that the peace terms would prevent any recurrence of the robberies, plundering, and tragic scenes that had taken place in the northern Utah settlements over the past decade.

From this time and for the next several years, the Northwestern bands gathered each fall on the lower Bear River near Brigham City to receive their annuity presents of blankets, clothing, and food and to talk to the superintendent of Indian affairs for Utah about mutual problems. The establishment of the Fort Hall Indian Reservation by 1869 offered them a home to which they were encouraged to go, and by late 1875 nearly all of them were living at Fort Hall. There was one exception. About 200 had joined the Mormon church by 1875, and this group accepted the help of the Mormons to establish themselves on farms at the Washakie colony in Malad Valley. Today these people have left Washakie to become a part of the white culture, whereas the descendants of the other Northwestern Shoshoni still live on the Fort Hall Reservation. It is ironic that the almost 2,000 Northwestern Indians who once roamed Cache and Weber valleys and along the northern shores of Great Salt Lake have been lost to Utah history and now reside in "Idaho."

Chief Pocatello continued to receive the most attention from officials and newspaper writers after the treaty of peace. On July 28, 1864, Peter Maughan was pleased to write that a public dinner had just been prepared for 200 Shoshoni during which the Indians' "old Bishop . . . made the tears to flow from some of the Brethren that were present, . . . [and] Pokatello took dinner at my house. . . ."[60] The chief had one more run-in with General Connor, who arrested him in early November 1864 on complaint of Ben Holladay, the owner of the Northern Stage Line. Holladay learned that the alleged offenses were inconsequential and requested Connor to turn the Indian leader over to Utah Indian Superintendent O. H. Irish, who immediately released him. The Shoshoni band, when they heard that Connor intended to hang Pocatello, had gone to the mountains to prepare for war, which Irish was able to forestall.[61] An expenditure of $2,000 for presents for Pocatello and his people had "a most salutary effect" and brought peace once again to the Box Elder and Cache Valley areas.[62]

———————————•◆ ◆•———————————

Governor Doty and General Connor now turned their attention to securing agreements with the Western Shoshoni of Nevada, the Gosiute, and the Fort Hall Shoshoni and Bannock. Arrangements were made so that Governor Nye of Nevada could participate in a council finally held at Fort Ruby on October 1 to treat with the Western Shoshoni.[63] As Nye later pointed out, these Indians had "never received much attention from the government. . . ." The conferees agreed, first, that the boundary between Utah and Nevada territories should run through a valley about fifty miles east of Ruby Valley, and this would define each governor's responsibilities for the Indian inhabitants of the region.[64] The two main tribes represented at the negotiations were the Tosowitch, or White Knives, and the Unkoahs. Nye estimated that these bands totaled about 2,500 individuals.[65]

The provisions of the Treaty at Ruby Valley finally agreed upon were similar to those for the Eastern and Northwestern Shoshoni. Article 1 established peace and friendship between the contracting parties; Article 2 assured the safety of routes of travel and provided for mail stations and military posts; Article 3 permitted the operation of telegraph, stage, and railroad lines through the area; Article 4 allowed mineral exploration and for the use of timber; Article 5 outlined the boundaries of Western Shoshoni lands; Article 6 set the stage for an eventual reservation to be established for the wandering bands; Article 7 granted the Indians an annuity of $5,000 for a period of twenty years; and Article 8 acknowledged $5,000 in presents distributed during the negotiations. Twelve chiefs, led by Te-moak, signed the treaty.[66] Today, the Western Shoshoni are still scattered in isolated colonies throughout northeastern and central Nevada, although some did consent to move to the Duck Valley Reservation when it was established.

About 350 of the Shoshoni Gosiute bands west of Great Salt Lake met with Governor Doty in Tooele Valley on October 12, 1863. He noted in his formal report that another 100 from Ibapah, Schell Creek, and "the Desert" would have been present "but for their fear of the soldiers. . . ." These apprehensions were valid—the governor noted that over a hundred Gosiute had been killed by Connor's troops during the past year and "the survivors beg for peace." Another 200, not present at the council, ranged along the southern border of their territory. All were to participate in the treaty benefits.[67] The eight articles of the Treaty of Tooele Valley were almost identical to the provisions of the Ruby Valley agreement except that the Gosiute, being fewer in number, were to receive an annuity of only $1,000 for twenty years and $1,000 at the time of the treaty signing. Doty thought the annuity should be increased to $2,000 if the Gosiute were to become farmers.[68] Article 8 contained the qualifying amendment about making claims to lands beyond what had existed under Mexican law. Chief Tabby and three other leaders attached their marks to the document.[69] The descendants of these Gosiute are farmers and ranchers today at Ibapah in western Utah.

The final Shoshoni agreement was made at Soda Springs on October 14, 1863, between Doty and Connor and about 150 Bannock under their leaders Toso-kwauberaht, the principal chief (also known as Le Grand Coquin), Tahgee, and Matigund. Doty estimated the Bannock at 1,000 people. Chief Tendoy of the Lemhi Shoshoni sent word that he could not attend the conference to represent his 1,500 tribal members because they were all away on the annual buffalo hunt in Montana. But Tendoy assured the government officials that he and his followers assented to the treaty and wished to continue their friendly relations with the United States. The Fort Hall Shoshoni no doubt had representatives in attendance, although Doty did not name any chiefs. The governor estimated the total number of Indians who joined in the Treaty of Soda Springs at 8,650, an exaggeraged figure. The actual number would have been closer to 5,000.

The Shoshoni and Bannock agreed to the terms offered to the other Shoshoni groups with one exception. The tribes promised to maintain safe routes of travel between Salt Lake City and the Beaverhead and Boise mining areas. The Indians received presents worth $3,000 and were promised an annuity of $20,000 for twenty years. The boundaries of their country extended from the lower Humboldt and Salmon Falls on the west to the Wind River Mountains on the east.[70]

On March 7, 1864, all five treaties negotiated by Doty and Connor between July 1 and October 14, 1863, were ratified by the United States Senate, along with the amendment concerning interest in the

Indian lands under Mexican law. four of the Shoshoni groups met in council a second time with Doty and his representative to grant approval of the Mexican amendment. The government officials, however, were never able to assemble the more mobile and independent Fort Hall and Lemhi Shoshoni and Bannock a second time to get their assent to the provision about claims under Mexican law. The inclusion of this amendment was unfortunate for two reasons. Indian homelands lying north of the forty-second parallel were outside Mexican territory and had never been subject to Mexican law so this term was meaningless, and without approving this amendment, the Fort Hall and Lemhi Shoshoni and Bannock were forced to wait another five years before the Treaty of Fort Bridger of July 3, 1868, granted them government recongnition, annuity goods, and a home at Fort Hall. As for the approximately 600 Boise and Bruneau Shoshoni, they had an even more difficult time as hostilities continued with the miners and settlers in the Boise region. For this reason, they were the first Indians to be moved to the new reservation at Fort Hall in the spring of 1869.[71]

The Shoshoni agreements of 1863 made the western trails peaceable and quiet. The commissioner of Indian affairs noted that "these Indians have long been a scourge to the citizens of Utah and Nevada, and a terror to the emigrants and travellers over the routes leading through those territories."[72] With peace finally achieved, Governors Nye and Doty, the various Indians agents under them, and General Connor and his officers were satisfied about the cessation of hostilities.[73] The general was sure that the peace secured "from the Snake River on the North to the lower Settlements of Utah, and from the Rocky Mountains of the East to Reese River on the West, . . . " was due to the "indomitable bravery, activity and willingly endured hardships of the California Column under my command. . . . The Indians, one and all, . . . are Evidently Seriously inclined to peace in the future, and after the Severe Experiences of last Winter, Spring and Summer, will hesitate long ere they again provoke hostilities."[74] Governor Doty agreed that peace had come because of the "presence and efficiency of the United States Troops, and the signal defeat of Bear Hunter and his allies. . . ."[75] The commissioner of Indian affairs was also impressed that the Indians had sought peace because

Washakie on horseback. *Smithsonian Institution*.

Snake Indians. *Smithsonian Institution*.

the California Volunteers had given the Indians "a wholesome idea of the power of the white man. . . ."[76]

After two years exercising this power over the tribes of Utah, Idaho, and Nevada, there were the beginnings of a reaction. Superintendent Irish of Utah complained to the commissioner, "If the Military Authorities will allow me to manage these Indians without any further interference, I am satisfied that by a judicious use of the appropriations made I can maintain peace."[77] At about the same time, on November 23, 1863, because army units were becoming too free in their indiscriminate killing of Indian captives, the Military Department of the Pacific was forced to issue a general order to all officers barring them from "executing any Indian prisoners on any pretext whatever. . . ." The military could hold Indian prisoners under guard but had to turn them over to civil authorities for trial and punishment. Indians were "amenable to the civil law equally with whites. . . ."[78]

While the ruthless destruction of Shoshoni Indians by the California Volunteers no doubt helped persuade survivors to come to the bargaining table, the promise of a permanent relationship with the government and the distribution of annuity goods were the major factors in bringing peace to the Great Basin and the Snake River plains. As Governor Nye put it, "They are now anxiously expecting presents. . . ."[79] The Indians were understandably uneasy as they watched thousands of miners pour into their country and destroy the native food crops. Agent John C. Burche of Nevada Territory was particularly expressive as he described the destitution of the Indians of his district whose subsistence had now almost completely vanished.

> The game of the mountains and valleys is being frightened away by the appearance of the white man in the wild region, and the continued crack of his unerring rifle. The pine-nut trees are rapidly being cut down and used for building purposes or fuel. The bunch-grasses, the seed of which formerly supplied the Indians with one of their chief articles of food, and which abounds in the Humboldt country, now fails to yield even the most scanty harvest, owing to its being eaten off as fast as it sprouts by the vast amount of stock which has been brought to the country by the settlers and drovers.[80]

The commissioner added a similar assessment of the condition of the Shoshoni:

The scarcity of game in these territories, and the occupation of the most fertile portions thereof by our settlements, have reduced these Indians to a state of extreme destitution, and for several years past they have been almost literally compelled to resort to plunder in order to obtain the necessaries of life. It is not to be expected that a wild and war-like people will tamely submit to the occupation of their country by another race, and to starvation as a consequence thereof.[81]

Both Governor Doty and Superintendent Irish strongly urged establishing reservations for the Indians of Utah, but, as noted, the Northwestern Shoshoni were forced to wait for a reserve at Fort Hall, Idaho, before they could find a home.[82] To help sustain at least one Northwestern band, Irish made arrangements for a chief and his fifteen lodges of people to herd stock in the "northern portion of the Territory. . . ." The Indians received provisions from the Mormon farmers for the winter's employment.[83]

The transition from a food-gathering, nomadic lifeway to a settled existence as herdsmen or farmers and recipients of annual presents from the government had been a long process for the Shoshoni of the Oregon, California, and Montana trails. The terrible tragedy at Bear River was followed by several months of angry retaliation in Cache Valley and along the mail route to the west. But the unceasing pressure from Connor's troops and the indefatigable exertions of Governor Doty led to the series of treaties that, for the first time, gave the Shoshoni hope that some means were at hand to keep them from starvation. Gifts of food, clothing, and utensils when treaties were signed were the first assurances of assistance. The promise of an annual distribution of provisions was also evidence of help, a commitment that the various chiefs were determined to maintain by keeping their followers at peace. Only minor troubles punctuated the next few relatively quiet years in Shoshoni country until in the late 1870s when the inadequacies of reservation life provoked several western tribes into a series of wars, including the Bannock War of 1878.

From 1840 to 1864 Americans coursed the Oregon and California trails and the Overland Mail Line through country peopled by Shoshoni Indians. Near Fort Bridger travelers first met Washakie's friendly Eastern Shoshoni; then the Fort Hall Shoshoni and their neighbors, the Bannock; and finally, on the Oregon Trail, the Boise and Bruneau Shoshoni. On the road to California, emigrants passed along the edge of Gosiute Shoshoni country and through Western Shoshoni and then Paiute areas to the Carson Valley. The Indians of central interest to this story, the Northwestern Shoshoni of northern Utah, haunted the area at the junction of the Oregon and California trails near the Goose Creek Mountains, but chiefly interacted with Mormon settlers who occupied Indian homelands in Cache and Weber valleys and along the eastern and northern shores of Great Salt Lake.

With such a variety of Shoshoni peoples, speaking the same language and having similar lifestyles, it is understandable that early travelers and settlers, as well as government officials and military officers, had difficulty identifying the Indians who raided camps, settlements, and cattle and horse herds. The modern researcher, too, can often only guess at which Shoshoni band was involved in a particular event.

From 1840 to 1845, there was peaceful coexistence along the western trails between Shoshoni and emigrant, but more and more travelers caused the destruction of traditional Indian food supplies, and some natives struck back. Nefarious traders, bandit groups disguised as Indians, and irresponsible emigrants who took shots at Shoshoni as though they were wild game generated retaliation from a confused and frightened native population. There was a rising incidence of Indian attacks in the late 1840s and during the entire decade of the 1850s, finally culminating in a series of massacres during 1859 and 1860. The Otter Massacre on the lower Snake River was the most brutal. From 1860 until mid-1863, the Overland Mail Line stations offered tempting targets to destitute Indians. Although attacks on emigrant parties aroused the indignation of westerners, it was the interruption of mail service that caused the most national anger, especially among newspaper editors.

Mormon pioneers settling Salt Lake Valley in 1847 introduced a new note in Indian-white relations. Brigham Young chose to keep peace with neighboring Indians by feeding them, and this led to many charges over the years that the Saints were in league with the Shoshoni and were instigating attacks on travelers. The Mountain Meadows Massacre of 1857 clinched these arguments for some, but others realized that the Saints suffered from Indian attacks as much as non-Mormon settlers and travelers. Brigham Young acted as superintendent of Indian affairs for Utah Territory during a seven-year period (1850–57) and due to proximity was forced to accept responsibility for the Shoshoni and Bannock in the Fort Hall area as well. Young also supervised the Gosiute and Western Shoshoni bands all the way to the Sierra Nevada, a truly Brobdingnagian task, which Congress failed to support with adequate appropriations.

The Utah War stripped Young of his positions as governor and superintendent of Indian affairs and brought Johnston's Army to Camp Floyd south of Salt Lake City. For almost three years this large expedition remained in the territory and patrolled the western roads and engaged in sorties against hostile natives. The Shoshoni learned how ruthless United States troops could be but also learned how to use hit-and-run tactics to frustrate military efforts. The most publicized forays by the troops were those directed at Northwestern Shoshoni bands in the Box Elder and Cache valleys where Mormon farmers, by 1859–60, had taken over some of the choicest sections of Northwestern homelands thus precipitating a new and critical time. The Shoshoni here were particularly incensed by the Mormon refusal to acknowledge Indian land ownership and to offer payment for acres appropriated. This grievance, plus the mounting destitution of the Indians as their traditional food supplies disappeared, led to a major confrontation with military detachments from California.

Troop units from Oregon Territory were also involved in patrolling the Oregon Trail from Boise to Fort Hall, but, like the Camp Floyd contingents, they had difficulty pinning down and capturing Shoshoni marauders. Army and citizen soldiers from Fort Churchill and the Carson Valley area attempted to guard the lower Humboldt road so that it appeared to observers far removed from the scene that the western trails were under careful supervision by the military. The attacks on emigrant trains, attended sometimes by brutality and savage torture and mutilation, aroused extreme hostility toward all Indians, but they were not as numerous, considered against the backdrop of twenty-five years of travel by thousands of emigrants, as some believed. Rumors and fears tended to exaggerate numbers of people killed and wounded; the fictional story of the so-called Almo Massacre of 295 people is the most ludicrous example. It was easy to overlook the number of Indians killed in hostile actions—few were interested in recording Indian losses, only the number of whites killed.

With the rising number of attacks on emigrant trains, and particularly the assaults on the mail stations west of Salt Lake City, between 1860–62 new military units were assigned to Utah Territory. The Civil War brought abandonment of Camp Floyd, and regular army troops returned east, leaving western roads unprotected. To fill the gap, Colonel Patrick Edward Connor and his California Volunteers were dispatched to Salt Lake City where, late in 1862, they founded Camp Douglas and proceeded on a number of Indian-killing expeditions to secure the roads and settlements and to satisfy their hunger for glory. The killing of Indians at Gravelly Ford and elsewhere in Nevada demonstrated their determination to wipe out recalcitrant Indians. When word came in January of 1863 of the murders of some miners in Cache Valley, Connor seized the opportunity to revenge the deaths by a winter attack on Chief Bear Hunter's tribe at Battle Creek. The resulting massacre of about 250 Indian men, women, and children made Connor a brigadier general and convinced the Indians of the Great Basin and the Snake River plains that they should not attempt a stand-up fight again with the California soldiers. It did not mean the Shoshoni ceased their guerrilla warfare. To the contrary, attacks continued through midsummer of 1863 against the Mormon settlers who had aided Connor to revenge the Shoshoni deaths.

The importance of the Bear River Massacre has been largely lost to American history because it happened during the Civil War when an obscure engagement with the Indians in far-off Utah became a minor incident compared to battles on the eastern front. If Connor's attack on Bear Hunter's village had occurred later, in the 1870s along with the Custer Massacre and army massacres of Indians, Connor might not be the West's forgotten general, and information about the slaughter of 250 Northwestern Shoshoni might not be relegated to a small and little noticed monument near Battle Creek in southern Idaho. The story of Connor's destruction of a peaceful village of Shoshoni on January 29, 1863, has few parallels in American western history for rapine and human atrocity. It is perhaps time for Utah historians to revise their bias toward Mormon history to include the Indian troubles in the northern counties and especially the Bear River Massacre so that these events receive more prominence in local studies. It is perhaps also time for national historians to review Indian wars of later years in light of early white-Indian interactions west of South Pass.

In retrospect, the annihilation of the Northwestern Shoshoni at

Bear River seems an unnecessary and extremely cruel action. Superintendent James Duane Doty, under orders from the Indian Office in Washington that were almost a year old, was already planning a series of treaties, which he finally negotiated during 1863 and which brought peace to Shoshoni country. There is no doubt that Connor's "victory" at Bear River and subsequent expeditions to Soda Springs and elsewhere helped convince the tribes that treaties were the best course, but such agreements had been sought for years and the Indians were pleased finally to get some assurance of protection and annuities from the government. Several more years of waiting passed before reservations were established as permanent homes for the Shoshoni of the Great Basin and Idaho, bringing to a final end the nomadic lifeway the Indians had known for centuries before white colonization of the Trans-Mississippi West.

Casualties from the Battle of Bear River

Second Cavalry—Company A
Killed—James W. Baldwin, private, through the cheek
George German, private, above the heart
Wounded—John Welch, private, arrow in each lung, dangerously
John William Wall, private, shot in right arm, dangerously
William H. Lake, private, shot in the mouth, badly
William Jay, private, index finger shot off, slightly
James Montgomery, private, right lung, dangerously

Company H
Killed—Charles L. Hollowell, private, center of chest
John K. Briggs, private, through the chest
Wounded—Bartel C. Hutchinson, private, right arm, badly
Frank A. Farley, private, right side, badly
Hugh Connor, private, left eye, dangerously
James Logue, right elbow, badly
Michael O'Brien, private, left lung, dangerously
Patrick Frawley, private, right shoulder and spine, dangerously
Philip Schaub, private, left lung, dangerously
Joseph A. Clowes, private, right shoulder, slightly
John Franklin, private, right hip and neck, dangerously
James Cantillon, sergeant, left lung, dangerously
Thompson Ridge, private, right arm, slightly

Company K
Killed—Christian Smith, bugler, center of chest, right to left
Shelbourne C. Reed, private, through the head
Adolphus Rowe, private, through both lungs
Lewis Anderson, private, through the heart
Henry W. Trempf, private, through both lungs
Wounded—Morris Illig, private, right shoulder, badly
Alonzo A.P.V. McCoy, private, navel, slightly

Benjamin Landis, corporal, right shoulder, dangerously
Robert Hargrave, private, thigh, badly
William M. Slocum, private, right lung, dangerously
John S. Lee, private, right arm and hip, badly
Albert N. Parker, private, left arm, badly
Eugene J. Brady, private, nose and face, dangerously
Nathaniel Kinsley, private, right side and arm, dangerously
Sylvanius S. Longley, private, neck, badly
John Dailey, 1st sergeant, left breast and shoulder, dangerously
Patrick H. Kelly, corporal, abdomen, slightly

Company M

Killed—George C. Cox, private, through both lungs
George W. Horton, private, through the heart
Asa F. Howard, wagoner, through the heart
Wounded—Anthony Stevens, sergeant, chest and shoulder, dangerously
Philip Humbert, private, top of head, slightly
Adolph Hupfner, bugler, right arm, slightly
John Stevens, private, top of head, slightly
Joshua Leggett, private, left shoulder, dangerously
Thaddeus Barcafer, private, right shoulder, dangerously
Reuben Miller, private, right shoulder, dangerously
E. C. Chase, private, right shoulder, badly
James H. *or* Joseph (?) Forbes, private, hand and arm, badly
Leander W. Hughes, corporal, nose and right side, badly
Levi D. Hughes, private, right leg, badly
William M. Davis, private, right lung, died at Ogden, February 3, 1863
William H. Hood, private, left hand and groin, badly
Lorin Robbins, sergeant, right side, badly

Third Infantry—Company K

Killed—John A. Baker, private, through heart and stomach
Samuel J. W. Thomas, private, through the chest
Wounded—Adoniram J. Austin, 1st sergeant, right eye, dangerously
Ebenezer C. Hoyt, sergeant, left lung, dangerously
John Hensley, private, right leg, badly
Thomas B. Walker, private, left side, badly

Officers Wounded

Major Peter A. Gallagher, Third Infantry, left arm, badly
Captain Daniel McLean, Company H, Second Cavalry, left thigh and right arm, dangerously
Lieutenant Darwin Chase, Company K, Second Cavalry, left lung, dangerously
Lieutenant David E. Berry, Company A, Second Cavalry, right shoulder, dangerously

Officers and Men in Hospital with
Frosted Feet, Second Cavalry

Company A—Corporals Adolph Spraggle and Moses Duval
  Privates George K. Swan, John D. Marker, S. Shomadan, Roger M. McNulty, and James P. McCue
Company H—Sergeant John W. Kilgore
  Privates George Fisher, John W. Stultz, Augustus Landgraf, John H. Allman, Thomas Bradley, Theron R. Gaston, Andrew J. Lockhard, Harvey Smith, James M. Norton, William A. Stier, William M. Maher, William W. Goodell, William C. Walton, Edward J. Casano, Harry A. McDonald
Company K—Sergeant William M. Beach
  Corporals William L. White, James R. Hunt
  Privates John Lincoln, David Burns, Daley S. Ausley, Matthew Atmore, Frederick W. Becker, Joseph *or* Nathaniel Chapman (?), John G. Hertle, Samuel L. Caldwell, C. Howe, Joseph Hill, George Johnson, Arthur Mitchell, James McKown, Alonzo R. Palmer, Charles Wilson, and David Barton
Company M—Sergeant John Cullen
  Corporals Alfred P. Hewitt and William M. Steel
  Privates William W. Collins, Andrew J. Case, James Dyer, John McGonigle, and Daniel Griffin

Third Infantry

Company K—Sergeants Cornelius J. Herron and Charles F. Williams
  Corporals J. H. Zollman, John Wingate, and W. A. Bennett
  Privates William St. John, Algeray Ramsdell, James E. Epperson, Arthur F. H. Randall, William H. Farnham, John Borland, Giles W. Ticknor, A. Rensho, Barton B. Bigelow, J. Anderson, James Urquhart, Francis L. Bourasso, Frank W. Branch, Aldis L. Bailey, William Carlton, Daniel Donoghue, Charles H. Godbold, John Haywood, Charles W. Heath, John Manning, William G. Way, and Joseph German

Recapitulation

Died—Second Cavalry

Lieutenant Darwin Chase, Company K, February 4, 1863, at Farmington, U.T.
Private William M. Davis, Company M, February 3, 1863, at Ogden, U.T.
Sergeant James Cantillon, Company H, February 4, 1863, at Camp Douglas, U.T.
Private William M. Slocum, Company K, February 5, 1863, at Camp Douglas, U.T.

Sergeant Anthony Stevens, Company M, February 6, 1863, at Camp Douglas, U.T.

Private Michael O'Brien, Company H, February 7, 1863, at Camp Douglas, U.T.

Private John W. Wall, Company A, February 8, 1863, at Camp Douglas, U.T.

Corporal Patrick Frawley, Company H, February 9, 1863, at Camp Douglas, U.T.

Private William H. Lake, Company A, March 24, 1863, at Camp Douglas, U.T.*

Discharged for Reasons of Disability
Second Cavalry—Company A

James Montgomery, private, "Discharged Camp Douglas, U.T., June 29, 1863, for disability caused by wounds received at battle of Bear River, U.T., January 29, 1863"

Company H

John Franklin, private, "Discharged at Camp Douglas, U.T., May 27, 1863, by reason of diability—wounded in the side at battle of Bear River, U.T., Jan. 29, 1863"

Company K

Benjamin Landis, corporal—"Discharged at Camp Douglas, U.T., May 28, 1863, for disability caused from wounds received in the battle of Bear River, Jan. 29, 1863"

Walter B. Welton, corporal—"Discharged at Camp Douglas, U.T., May 28, 1863, for disability caused from wounds received in the battle of Bear River, Jan. 29, 1863"

Morris Illig, private—"Discharged Aug. 15, 1863, by reason of disability caused by wounds received in the battle of Bear River, Jan. 29, 1863"

Albert N. Parker, private—"Discharged at Camp Douglas, May 28, 1863, by reason of disability caused from wounds received in the battle of Bear River, Jan. 29, 1863"

---

*Richard H. Orton, comp., *Records of California Men in the War of Rebellion, 1861 to 1867*, pp. 178-79, 200-208, 257-66, 274-83, 293-303, 589-94; National Archives, "California. Regt'l Order Book, 2d Cavalry, Adjutant General's Office"; National Archives, "California. 2nd Cav. Regtl Reports Indian Scouts, etc., April 29/62 to Dec. 15/63, Casualties," pp. 14-15. Original Report submitted by Robert K. Reid, Surgeon Third Infantry California Volunteers. Official copy sent to G. Wright, Brigadier General, Commanding United States Army.

Company M

William H. Hood, private—"Discharged at Fort Bridger, Wy. T., June 22, 1863, for disability caused by wound received in battle of Bear River, U.T., Jan. 29, 1863"*

---

*Orton, *Records*, pp. 206, 262, 276, 280–81, 298.

Massacre at Boa Ogoi

(Mae T. Parry is a granddaughter of Chief Sagwitch, who fought in the Bear River Massacre at the conflict on Battle Creek.)
Copyright © 1976 by Mae T. Parry

The Shoshone Indians were a large nation of Indians and they lived and traveled over a large territory. The Eastern Shoshones, under Chief Washakie, lived in the Wyoming area. Chief Washakie was known as their head chief. He was known all over the western country as one of the most intelligent and able Indian chiefs.

Chief Washakie had several sub-chiefs under his leadership. The sub-chiefs had between three hundred to four hundred Indians in their bands. Chief Pocatello had the Fort Hall area Shoshones. The Northwestern Shoshones traveled under the leadership of Chief Sagwitch Timbimboo and Chief Bear Hunter. These two leaders saw the entry of President Brigham Young into the Salt Lake valley. They knew from the actions of the pioneers that they wanted to be friends, so they welcomed the pioneers and their leaders into the Shoshone country.

The Northwestern Shoshones traveled with the changing seasons. They looked upon the earth not just as a place to live, but they called the earth their mother. She was the provider of their livelihood. The mountains, streams and plains stood forever they said, but the seasons walked around annually. All things in nature were fixed for the Indian. In the early fall the Northwesterns moved into the general area of Salmon, Idaho, to fish. After the fishing was over and the fish had been prepared for winter use, they moved into Wyoming to hunt buffalo, elk, moose and antelope. It was very important to get the big game for it meant food, clothing and shelter to them. In the spring and summer most of their time was spent traveling about Utah. Here they gathered seeds, berries, roots and also hunted smaller game. In late October a move was made into western Utah and parts of Nevada for the gathering of pine nuts. Most of the food was gathered and dried for their winter camping site, an area near Franklin, Idaho. Little did they realize that in 1863 this area would be a blood bath for them.

The river northwest of Franklin was a natural place for the Indians to go every winter.

The land along the Bear River had a natural depression and thousands of willows and brush covered the area. This was also an ideal winter spot for the Northwestern Shoshones because of the natural hot springs that was around this area. They were sheltered from the winter blizzards by the willows and brush. Their teepees were warm and they were content. Franklin was also centrally located in the Shoshone country. Another of their wintering areas was around Promontory, Utah, because the winters were milder and the water was plentiful there.

The Northwestern Shoshones gathered in the Franklin area for meetings and winter sports as well as for summer fun. They took part in foot races, horse races, hockey, dancing and just general all-around fun. In the winter they used dried deer hides for sleighs. In the summer the children would dig make-believe fox holes along the banks of the Bear River and play Indians at war. Over the years the holes got larger as the children dug deeper. They would also sit in the dug outs and fish in the Bear River. (White history has it that these holes were rifle pits dug out quickly by the Indians as Connor was descending upon them. This was nearly impossible within an hour's time because the ground was frozen with ice and snow.) The Indians from the Eastern Shoshone band and Chief Pocatello's band always came and joined in the fun. They competed against each other for prizes.

A few weeks before the massacre of January 29, 1863, the Shoshones all gathered together near Bear River, at the Indian camping ground, and held what is referred to as the Warm Dance. This certain dance was to bring in the warm weather and drive out the cold. If Colonel Patrick E. Connor had only known the ways of the Red Man, he would have been able to kill thousands of Indians instead of hundreds. If the settlers had only known the nature and customs of the Indians, they would have sent for Col. Connor and his men the first week of January.

As the Northwestern Shoshones were settling down from the visiting and reminiscing, a few Indian trouble makers decided to go and steal some horses and cattle. They went into a nearby farmer's corral, drove the animals out, and headed north. Along the way they killed the cattle and ate them. The three men involved were One-Eyed Tom, Zee coo chee (Chipmunk) and Qua ha da do coo wat (Lean or Skinny Antelope). About the same time some miners and Indians got into a fight and the miners were killed. These Indians were not from the Northwestern Shoshone group but had come from Chief Pocatello's band. The miners' horses and belongings were taken into their part of the country. The third incident the Indians believe led to the massacre was another fight between some white boys and some Indians, in which two white boys and two Indian boys were killed. Again, they were not Northwestern Shoshones involved in this incident. Because they were Indians, everything was blamed on them.

Because of these three incidents, most of the Indians were getting restless. They could feel that trouble was going to start soon. The people around Franklin were starting to call the Indians "stealing savages" and "beggars." They did not understand that the Indians were also human with feelings like every one else. Several Indians were becoming bitter and defensive and were starting to feel that what was theirs was being taken away little by little. Their seat that extended from coast to coast was being invaded by the Whites and they felt that shortly there would be no place to pitch their teepees. They were starting to feel like prisoners in their own country. Many began to feel like trapped animals who would fight for their lives up to the end.

On the night of January 27, 1863, one of the older men by the name of Tin dup, foresaw the calamity which was about to take place. In his dream he saw his people being killed by the pony soldiers. He told the Indians of his dream and told them to move out of the area. "Do it now, tonight!," he said. Some families believed Tin dup's dream and moved, thus sparing their lives.

In the meantime a white friend of the Indians came to the camp and told them that the settlers of Cache Valley had made plans to get rid of the Northwestern Shoshones and that they had sent an appeal to Colonel Connor to come and settle the Indian affairs once and for all. Because of this, the Indians knew for days that Col. Connor was going to come after them. They did not know however, that the Colonel would fire first and not ask any questions.

Chief Sagwitch, being an early riser, got up just as usual on the morning of January 29, 1863. He left his teepee and stood outside surveying the area around the camp. The hills to the east of their camp were covered with a steaming mist. The mist crept lower down the hill and all of a sudden Chief Sagwitch realized what was happening. The soldiers from Camp Douglas from Salt Lake City had arrived. The Chief was not surprised. He started calling to the sleeping Indians. They quickly gathered their bows and arrows, tomahawks and a few rifles. Some of the Indians were so excited that they gathered up whatever was in sight to fight with. Some picked up their woven willow winnow pans and baskets and stuck their rifles through them. It appeared as though they had shields for protection.

Chief Sagwitch shouted to his people not to shoot first. He thought that perhaps this military man was a just and wise man. He thought that the Colonel would ask for the guilty men, whom he would have immediately turned over to the soldiers. He felt that the rest of them would be saved by doing this. He told his people to be brave and calm. Many of the Indians ran toward the river and dropped into the snow. They knew that they were not all guilty but they had no choice but to fight for their lives if attacked. Some had dropped into the holes the children had dug along the river bank. Never did the grown men realize that they would be using the children's play foxholes to await real military soldiers.

Without so much as asking the Indians for the guilty party, the Colonel and his men began to fire on the Indians. But what was an arrow compared to the muskets of the army. The Indians were being slaughtered like wild rabbits. Indian men, women, children and babies were being slaughtered left and right. No butcher could have murdered any better than Colonel Connor and his vicious California volunteers. Most of the action took place along the river banks and among the willows.

The massacre started early in the morning, according to the Indians, and lasted all day. The Bear River that was frozen solid a few moments before was now starting to flow. The Northwestern Shoshones were jumping into the river and trying to escape by swimming across the river. The blazing white snow was now brilliant red with blood. The willow trees that were used for protection were now bent down as if in defeat. The old dry leaves which had been clinging to the willows were now flying through the air like whizzing bullets.

Ray Diamond, a nephew of Chief Sagwitch, was successful in his escape attempt. He swam across the river and found shelter away from the battle. He lived to be over one hundred years old. He told and re-told the massacre of the Battle of Bear River to the younger generations until the time he died. Many Indian women also jumped into the river and swam with babies upon their backs. Most of them died. One Indian lady, Anzee chee, was being chased by the soldiers. She jumped into the river and went under an overhanging bank. By keeping her head up under the bank she was saved. She watched the battle from her hiding place at the same trying to nurse the shoulder and breast wounds she received. Anzee chee carried the scars from her wounds for the rest of her life. She would show them to the young Indian children as she told of the massacre of their people. She also told of throwing her own small baby into the river where the child drowned and floated down the river with the other dead bodies and bloody red ice. Another man swam with his buffalo robe upon his back. The soldiers shot and shot at him but their bullets could not penetrate the buffalo robe.

The Indians which were still alive were calling to their chief to escape so he could be saved. Chief Sagwitch escaped with a wound in his hand, after having two horses shot from under him. Another Indian escaped by holding onto the tail of the horse Chief Sagwitch rode across the Bear River.

The very cruelest and meanest killing was that of Chief Bear Hunter. Perhaps it was the cruelest death in the White-Indian struggle. Knowing that he was one of the leaders, the soldiers shot Bear Hunter; they whipped him, kicked him and tried several means of torture on him. Through all of this the old chief did not utter a word, as crying and carrying on was the sign of a coward. Because he would not die or cry for mercy, the soldiers became very angry. One of the military men took his rifle, stepped to a burning campfire and heated his bayonet until it was glowing red. He then ran the burning hot metal through the chief's ears. Chief Bear Hunter went to his maker a man of honor. He left a wife and children behind.

Yeager Timbimboo or Da boo zee (cotton tail rabbit) a son of Chief Sagwitch, was about twelve years old and remembered the fight very well. He re-told the story several times a year and re-lived the scene in his memory. He told his story over the years to friends, relatives and grandchildren until the story became imprinted upon their minds. The grandchildren memorized the story and could repeat it by heart. Yeager Timbimboo told of feeling excited as any young boy would have during the fighting. He felt as if he was flying around. He dashed in and out among the whizzing bullets but was not hit. He heard cries of pain and saw death all around him. The little Indian boy kept running around until he came upon a little grass teepee that was so full of people that it was actually moving along the ground. Inside the grass hut Da boo zee found his grandmother, Que he gup. She suggested they go outside and lie among the dead. She feared the soldiers were going to set the teepee on fire any moment. The boy obeyed and pretended to be dead. "Keep your eyes closed at all times," his grandmother whispered, "Maybe in this way our lives may be saved." Yeager Timbimboo and his grandmother lay on the freezing battlefield all day. At the end of the day the soldiers were moving among the Indians in search of the wounded to put them out of their misery. Yeager, being a curious boy, wanted to watch the fighting once more. This nearly cost him his life. A soldier came upon him and saw that he was alive and looking around. The military man stood over Yeager, his gun pointing at the young boy's head ready to fire. The soldier stared at the boy and the boy at the soldier. The second time the soldier raised his rifle the little boy knew his time to die was near. The soldier then lowered his gun and a moment later raised it again. For some reason he could not complete his task. He took his rifle down and walked away. What went through this soldier's mind will never be known. Perhaps a power beyond our comprehension stopped this soldier from killing young Yeager so that the story of this massacre could be written. Yeager Timbimboo got the scolding of his young life. His grandmother reminded him that he was supposed to remain motionless at all times, keep his eyes closed and play dead. He had disobeyed and this had nearly cost him his life.

Soquitch (Lot of Buffalo) Timbimboo, at this time was a grown man. He was the oldest of Chief Sagwitch's children. He remembered many things about the massacre. He escaped on a horse with his girl friend behind him. Again bullets were flying in their direction as they tried to escape to the hills. One of the bullets found its mark and the Indian girl fell off the horse. She was dead. Soquitch kept going and reached safety. He dismounted from his horse and sat down by an old cedar tree which was concealed by some brushes. He proceeded to watch what the white settlers and Colonel Connor called the Battle of Bear River. To this young man this was the cruelest turn of events he had ever witnessed. The Little Indian camp was vanishing right before his eyes. Toward evening the field of massacre was silent, except for the cries of the wounded soldiers being carried away. The Northwestern Shoshones who had escaped watched as the wagons left the camp. As they drove off, the wagon wheels made a very mournful sound as they squeaked along the snow. Blood drippings could be seen along the trail they left. The Indians had done some damage to the military with the little they had. The Indians fought mostly by hand.

By nightfall the Indians who had escaped were cold, wet and hungry. There was no food to be found, for the soldiers had done a good job of scattering their food on the ground and setting fire to it. All of the teepees were burnt to the ground except one. The lone standing teepee looked as if it were made of net. This was the teepee of Chief Sagwitch and his family.

After the soldiers had left, Chief Sagwitch made his way to his teepee. He opened the flap and found his wife lying there dead, beside her was an infant daughter who was still alive. Sagwitch ordered some others that had come with him to take the baby girl from her mother, put her into her cradle board (kono) and hang her on the branch of a nearby tree. He hoped that some kind hearted settler would pick up the infant girl and raise her. He knew that without nourishment from her mother the baby girl would die anyway. His orders were carried out.

The Indians could not believe what had just taken place. Sagwitch was a very stunned and shocked man, stricken and sad at heart. He stood idly and mournfully gazed at the scene. He was remembering that just the day before their camp had been a happy place. He remembered the many seasons the Northwestern Shoshones had spent in and around Battle Creek on the Bear River. He sighed and turned away. Dead Indian bodies were everywhere. The Indians realized they could not hold proper funeral services for their dead, so many were thrown into the still flowing Bear River. A water burial was better than having animals eat their bodies. At this time old Chief Sagwitch realized that there were two different worlds in which different people lived. One group was greedy and wanted everything. The other group only wanted to live and travel around their land as before. One group made their wishes and dreams come true by making themselves the conqueror and the other almost became a vanishing American.

As darkness fell upon the camp a large fire was seen at a distance and a voice was heard to say, "If there are any more survivors, come over to my camp fire and get dry and warm." The Indians that were able to walk hurriedly went to the raging fire. They were tattered and torn in body and in mind. Almost every one of them had suffered one or more wounds. Each man, woman and child was in a dazed condition. Their eyes were sunken and glazed; their faces looked hollow. They were just starting to realize what had taken place. An old medicine man moved among the wounded and sick trying to heal them without much success. Their stories of escape were sad indeed. One Northwestern Shoshone chief had escaped and another chief had suffered one of the cruelest deaths in American history.

A little Indian boy by the name of Bishop (Red clay), told of his survival. He had chosen to remain in the little wheat grass teepee that was moving along the frozen ground. When he came out of the teepee he was scared and cold and he wandered around in a dazed condition until he was found by a relative. In his cold little hand he carried a bowl of frozen pine nut gravy. Food was so precious to this little boy of six years that he clung to this bowl all day. His father told him that his mother was dead and his baby sister was left hanging in her kono in hopes that someone would pick her up. The little boy could not utter a word or cry. His grief was too much. He was frozen and in deep shock.

A few years after the massacre at Bear River, Chief Sagwitch's people begged him and his cousin Ejupie (Coyote) Moemberg to go and ask President Brigham Young for assistance as they were starving to death. While they were gone, an uncle that was left in charge, sold Little Bishop to a Mormon family for a Mormon quilt, bag of beans, sheep and a sack of flour. The Mormons raised him and gave him the name of Frank Timbimboo Warner. He was sent to school and quickly learned the English language among other things. He graduated from the old Brigham Young College in Logan and taught penmanship and reading to farm families. He drove his horse and buggy from farm to farm, town to town, up and down the Cache Valley. This man was converted to the Latter-Day Saint Church and served two missions to Vermont. How proud his people were of his accomplishments. Proudest of all were the children of old Chief Sagwitch. Their father's dream had come true. The Chief always knew that if an Indian child was taught young he could really make something of himself.

Word of the Battle of Bear River spread quickly to other Indians. Some Northwestern Shoshones living near Brigham City, Utah, heard the story. Two women decided to ride to Promontory, Utah, and tell the news to some other Northwestern members. They had gone into mourning for their dead friends and relatives. Poe be hup Moemberg and her friends cut their long braids and slashed their arms and legs. This was the custom after someone's death. Crying and wailing as loud as they could, the two women rode fast to Promontory and told of the massacre.

A few days after the battle, because Chief Sagwitch was a great man of honor, he sent his oldest son Soquitch, a cousin Hyrum Wo go saw, and Ray Diamond to bring back the horses which were stolen before the battle. They rode into the Pocatello area and returned the horses, but the cattle had been killed and eaten. These three men returned the horses to the settlers.

The Indians that survived the battle said that the soldiers stole their buffalo robes and anything else they could take for souvenirs. They took such things as pelts of small animals to trade with traveling white men who were seeking gold. They took such things as tomahawks, stone axes, willow baskets, Indian head dresses, bows and arrows and much more. Perhaps somewhere at Camp Fort Douglas is stored a great collection of Northwestern Shoshone artifacts.

The morning after the massacre, the few Indians that remained looked at their destroyed village in horror and disbelief. They now saw things they had not noticed the night before. The ground was covered in various colors, red from blood, black from the fires of their teepees and food, and brown from the many seeds and nuts which had been scattered. There were also blue and purple areas made up of their dried berries. They noticed pieces of the teepee poles which the soldiers had burned to keep themselves warm. After looking at the depressing scene, the Indians decided to move to Promontory where the remainder of the Northwestern Shoshones were wintering.

Approximately thirteen people remembered and told various experiences of the massacre. They were:

Chief Sagwitch Timbimboo
Soquitch Timbimboo
Yeager (Da boo zee) Timbimboo

Ray Diamond
Peter Ottogary
Hyrum Wo go saw
Bishop (Frank Timbimboo Warner)
Tin dup and family
Chief Bear Hunter's widow
Twenge Timbimboo (Soquitch's wife, married after battle)
Anzie or Anzie chee
Tecka me da key
Mo jo guitch

The massacre at Bear River added to the extermination of the Northwestern Shoshone Indians. To the Northwestern Shoshone Indians, Colonel Patrick E. Connor was not a great Indian fighter nor a great hero. He was not fair in his dealings with the Indians. He shot first and did not give the Indians a chance to explain. To the Northwestern Shoshone Indians he was an unjust man and a coward. For years after the attack Indians were heard to say that Colonel Connor was the meanest and the most cruel man they had ever seen or met. Perhaps his motto was, "The only good Indian is a dead Indian." The U.S. Army under Colonel Patrick E. Connor had humiliated the Northwestern Shoshones. All Col. Connor wanted was promotion after promotion and that is what he got—Brigadier General Patrick E. Connor.

The American Indian believing he was a proud race was humbled and put to shame. But like all growing things, he sprang up from the humiliation. He did not hang his head down but he still looked up and forward.

Today a monument stands near Battle Creek. The plaque should read:

> The Massacre of Bear River was fought in this vicinity January 29, 1863. Colonel P. E. Connor and his California volunteers from Camp Douglas, Utah, all but annihilated the Northwestern Shoshone Tribe. Chief Sagwitch Timbimboo escaped the massacre. Chief Bear Hunter was tortured to death. No Bannocks were present, only Northwestern Shoshones of the Great Shoshone Nation.

Notes

CHAPTER ONE NOTES

1. Russell R. Elliott, *History of Nevada*, p. 26.
2. See Virginia C. Trenholm and Maurine Carley, *The Shoshoni: Sentinels of the Rockies.*
3. See Brigham D. Madsen, *The Bannock of Idaho* and *The Northern Shoshoni.*
4. See Brigham D. Madsen, *The Lemhi: Sacajawea's People.*
5. Madsen, *The Northern Shoshoni*, pp. 30–42.
6. Ake Hultkrantz, *The Shoshones in the Rocky Mountain Area*, p. 24; Brigham D. Madsen, "The Northwestern Shoshoni in Cache Valley," pp. 28–29; see also National Archives (hereafter cited as NA), "Map of 1863," and Julian H. Steward, *Basin-Plateau Aboriginal Groups*, p. 49.
7. Richard Poll, gen. ed., *Utah's History*, pp. 363–64; Helen Z. Papanikolas, ed., *The Peoples of Utah*, pp. 27-60; Andrew Love Neff, *History of Utah, 1847 to 1869*, p. 630; Joel E. Ricks, ed., *The History of a Valley*, pp. 51–52; Hubert Howe Bancroft, *History of Utah*, pp. 630–32.
8. Madsen, *The Northern Shoshoni*, pp. 18–23.
9. Dennis Ray Defa, "A History of the Gosiute Indians to 1900," p. 28.
10. NA, "Western Shoshone Agency." Of the many estimates over the years of all these Shoshoni groups, the U.S. Dept. of the Interior, *Annual Report of the Commissioner of Indian Affairs, 1868*, is fairly accurate. See pp. 148–49.
11. Richard F. Burton, *The City of the Saints,*, p. 532.
12. Walker D. Wyman, ed., *California Emigrant Letters*, pp. 62–63.
13. David Moore, Compiled Writings.
14. Ward G. DeWitt and Florence Stark DeWitt, eds., *Prairie Schooner Lady*, p.127.
15. Osborne Russell, *Journal of a Trapper*, p. 122.
16. Washington Irving, *The Adventures of Captain Bonneville*, p. 279.
17. NA, "Letters Received, 1824-1881. M234. Utah Superintendency, 1849-1880" (hereafter cited as "Letters, Utah"), Roll 899, Lander to Commissioner of Indian Affairs (hereafter cited as "CIA"), Feb. 18, 1860.
18. Wilford Woodruff, Journal, p. 313.
19. Thomas Bullock, Journal, p. 39. For an earlier report of the extent of grass cover in the Utah valleys, see Gerald C. Bagley, "Daniel T. Potts, Chronicles of the Fur Trade, 1822-1828," p. 137.
20. Fred B. Rogers, *Soldiers of the Overland*, p. 41.
21. NA, "Letters, Utah," Roll 899, Lander to CIA, Feb. 18, 1860.

22. Whitney McKinney, *A History of the Shoshone-Paiutes of the Duck Valley Indian Reservation*, p. 7.

23. Defa, "A History of the Gosiute," p. 15.

24. Steward, *Basin-Plateau Aboriginal Groups*, pp. 14, 16, 19–20.

25. Peter Skene Ogden, *Peter Skene Ogden's Snake Country Journals*, pp. 157–58.

26. John Clark Dowdle, Journal, p. 5.

27. NA, "Letters, Utah," Roll 897, Hurt to Young, Aug. 27, 1855.

28. *Sacramento Union*, Apr. 6, 1860.

29. Jacob Hamblin, *A Narrative of His Personal Experiences*, pp. 87–89.

30. George C. Yount, *George C. Yount and His Chronicles of the West*, pp. 88–90.

31. Ogden, *Journals*, pp. 157–58.

32. Earl S. Pomeroy, *The Territories and the United States, 1861-1890*.

33. NA, "Letters Received by the Office of Indian Affairs, 1824-81, Oregon Superintendency" (hereafter cited as "Letters, Oregon"), Microcopy 234, Nesmith to CIA, Salem, Ore., June 16, 1857.

34. See Madsen, *The Northern Shoshoni*, pp. 28–29, for a discussion of these territorial changes.

35. Ibid., pp. 30–31.

36. John Unruh, *The Plains Across*, pp. 179, 185, 189, 194–96, 200.

37. Don Russell, "How Many Indians Were Killed? White Man Versus Red Man: The Facts and the Legend," *The American West* 10, no. 4 (July 1973): 45.

38. Stan Hoig, *The Sand Creek Massacre*, p. 135.

39. Ibid., pp. 45–46.

40. Robert M. Utley, *The Indian Frontier of the American West, 1846-1890*, p. 71.

41. Paul I. Wellman, *Death on Horseback*, pp. 72–74, 90–93, 236–39, 316–19.

42. Oliver Knight, *Following the Indian Wars*, pp. 90–97, 310–15.

43. S. L. A. Marshall, *Crimsoned Prairie*, pp. 34–41, 227–49.

44. Stan Hoig, *The Battle of the Washita*, pp. 126–43, 200–201; Hoig, *The Sand Creek Massacre*, pp. 145–61.

45. Dee Brown, *Bury My Heart at Wounded Knee*, pp. 87–92, 104, 166–70, 177–78, 204–5, 439–45.

46. Robert M. Utley, *Frontiersmen in Blue*, pp. 219–24; Robert M. Utley, *Frontier Regulars*; Robert M. Utley and Wilcomb E. Washburn, *The American Heritage History of the Indian Wars*, pp. 223–24; Utley, *The Indian Frontier*, p. 71.

47. Rogers, *Soldiers of the Overland*.

48. Edward Tullidge, "The Cities of Cache Valley and Their Founders," *Tullidge's Quarterly Magazine* 1, no. 4 (July 1881): 536.

49. *Deseret News*, May 20, 1868.

50. Bancroft, *History of Utah*, pp. 631–32.

51. *New York Times*, Feb. 25, 1863; *New York Tribune*, Feb. 3, 1863; *New York Herald*, Feb. 3, 1863; *Chicago Times*, Jan. 29–Feb. 3, 1863; *Chicago Tribune*, Jan. 29–Feb. 18, 1863.

52. *New York Herald*, Jan. 22, 27, 29, Feb. 1, 3, 4, 11, 12, 1863.

CHAPTER TWO NOTES

1. Harry N. M. Winton, ed., "William T. Newby's Diary of the Emigration of 1843," *Oregon Historical Quarterly* 40 (Sept. 1939): 223, 231, June 17, Aug. 23, 1843.

2. Unruh, *The Plains Across*, chap. 5, "Emigrant-Indian Interaction," pp. 156–200. Unruh gives an excellent and detailed description of Indian assistance and acts of kindness toward the early travelers to the Pacific Coast.

3. George R. Stewart, ed., *The Opening of the California Trail*, pp. 26, 64–65, 98, n. 23.

4. Peter H. Burnett, "Recollections and Opinions of an Old Pioneer," *Quarterly of the Oregon Historical Society* 5 (Mar. 1904): 76–77.

5. John Bidwell, *A Journey to California*, pp. 23–24, 26, 27, Oct. 6, 7, 9, 12, 15, 16, 24, 25, 27, 1841.

6. Fred Lockley, ed., "Recollections of Benjamin Franklin Bonney," *Quarterly of the Oregon Historical Society* 24 (Mar. 1923): 41–43.

7. Ibid., pp. 43–44; Hubert Howe Bancroft, *History of Nevada, Colorado, and Wyoming, 1540–1888*, pp. 60–61.

8. Lansford Hastings, *The Emigrants' Guide to Oregon and California*, p. 150.

9. Chester Ingersoll, *Overland to California in 1847*, pp. 38–39, Sept 10, 1847.

10. Ansel James McCall, *The Great California Trail*, p. 68.

11. Journal History, July 31, 1847.

12. Ibid., Aug. 1, 1847.

13. Brigham Young, Manuscript History, May 30, 1852, p. 53.

14. Brigham Young, "Message to the Legislative Assembly of the Territory of Utah," p. 53.

15. Young, Manuscript History, Feb. 27, 1849, p. 24.

16. Ibid., May 12, 1849, pp. 76–78; June 15, 1849, p. 93; Journal History, May 7, 11, 26, July 15, 1849.

17. Thomas D. Clark, ed., *Off at Sunrise*, p. 70.

18. Herbert Eaton, *The Overland Trail to California in 1852*, p. 212.

19. Isaac S. P. Lord, Diary, 1849–51, May 27, 1849.

20. Sarah Eleanor Bayliss Royce, *A Frontier Lady*, p. 13.

21. Raymond W. Settle, ed., *The March of the Mounted Riflemen*, p. 41.

22. James Mason Hutchings, Diary, 1849, June 9, 1849.

23. Brigham D. Madsen, "The Colony Guard: To California in '49," *Utah Historical Quarterly* 51, no. 1 (Winter 1983): 21–22.

24. Dale L. Morgan, ed., *The Overland Diary of James A. Pritchard from Kentucky to California in 1849*, July 15, 1849.

25. Howard Stansbury, *An expedition to the Valley of the Great Salt Lake of Utah*, p. 97.

26. Robert Glass Cleland and Juanita Brooks, eds., *A Mormon Chronicle*, p. 112.

27. Lucy Foster Sexton, ed., *The Foster Family*, p. 47.

28. William Glover, *The Mormons in California*, p. 25.

29. History of Brigham Young, p. 148.

30. Unruh, *The Plains Across*, p. 182.

31. Alonzo Delano, *Across the Plains and Among the Diggings*, p. 105

32. Merrill J. Mattes and Elsey J. Kirk, eds., "From Ohio to California in 1849: The Gold Rush Journal of Elijah Bryan Farnham." *Indiana Magazine of History* 46 (Dec. 1950): 416.

33. Charles W. Bush, Letter, 80 miles from Sacramento, Jan. 10, 1850.

34. Finley McDiarmid, Letters, July 21, 1850.

35. W. S. McBride, Journal of an Overland Trip from Goshen, Ind. to Salt Lake City, June 22, 1850.

36. Joyce Rockwood Muench, ed., *The Kilgore Journal*, p. 39; Burton J. Williams, ed., "Overland to California in 1850: The Journal of Calvin Taylor," *Utah Historical Quarterly* 38, no. 4 (Fall 1970): 330–31.

37. David M. Kiefer, ed., "Over Barren Plains and Rockbound Mountains: Being the Journal of a Tour by the Overland Route . . . ," *Montana Western History* 22, no. 4 (Oct. 1972): 24.

38. Young, Manuscript History, 1849, p. 154; 1850, pp. 1, 17–18, 21–23; Peter W. Conover, Autobiography.

39. Young, Manuscript History, 1850, p. 17.

40. Ibid., 1849, p. 155.

41. John W. Gunnison, *The Mormons, or Latter-day saints, in the Valley of the Great Salt lake*, p. 147.

42. Brigham D. Madsen, ed., *A Forty-niner in Utah: Letters and Journal of John Hudson*, p. 79.

43. Gunnison, *The Mormons*, p. 146.

44. David Moore, Journal and Life History, pp. 2, 5; "Utah State Militia Correspondence, 1849–63, Wells to Farr, Mar. 6, 1850.

45. Moore, Journal, pp. 8–9.

46. *Portland Oregonian*, May 1, 1852; Moore, Journal, pp. 10–11; Utah State Militia Correspondence, 1849–63, Brown to Fulmer, Sept. 17, 1850.

47. Moore, Journal, p. 10.

48. Utah State Militia Correspondence, 1849–63 General Orders, Daniel H. Wells, Sept. 18, 1850; Wells to McBride, Sept. 17, 1850; Wells to Fulmer, Sept. 17, 1850; three letters, Wells to Eldredge, Sept. 17, 1850.

49. Ibid., Wells to Ward, Sept. 17, 1850; Wells to Eldredge, Sept. 18, 1850.

50. Ibid., Wells to Eldredge, Sept 18, 1850.

51. Moore, Journal, p. 11.

52. Utah State Militia Correspondence, 1849–63, Eldredge to Ferguson, Adj. Gen., Sept. 20, 1850.

53. Ibid., Wells to Robinson, Sept. 19, 1850; Wells to Kimball of the Nauvoo Legion, Sept. 25, 1850.

CHAPTER THREE NOTES

1. Madsen, *The Northern Shoshoni*, p. 28.

2. NA, "Letters, Oregon," Lane to CIA, Oregon City, Oct. 13, 1849.

3. Ibid., Brown to Ewing, Sec. of the Interior, Feb. 13, 1850.

4. Ibid., Dart to CIA, June 6, 1851.

5. Ibid., Dart to Wampole, July 21, 1851.

6. Ibid., Dart to CIA, Sept 4, 1851.

7. Neff, *History of Utah*, p. 168.

8. NA, "Letters, Utah," Roll 897, Proclamation by Governor Brigham Young, July 21, 1851, Young to Rose, July 21, 1851; Journal History, July 21, 1851; Brigham Young, Indian Affairs, Miscellaneous Papers, folder 28.

9. Brigham Young, Indian Affairs Out Correspondence—Commissioners, 1851–1852, June, folder 8, Young to CIA, Aug. 13, 1851.

10. John Lawrence Johnson, Diary, 1851, pp. 65–66.

11. P. V. Crawford, "Journal of a Trip Across the Plains, 1851," *Oregon Historical Society Quarterly* 25, no. 1 (Mar. 1924): 136–37.

12. U.S. Dept. of the Interior, *Annual Report, 1851*, Holeman to CIA, p. 445.

13. Charles Howard Crawford, *Scenes of Earlier Days*, pp. 44–46.

14. T. W. Davenport, "Recollections of an Indian Agent," *Oregon Historical Society Quarterly* 8 (Dec. 1907): 363.

15. Unruh, *The Plains Across*, p. 189.

16. NA, "Letters, Utah," Roll 897, Holeman to CIA, Sept. 21, 1851, Rose to Young, Sept. 21, 1851.

17. Moore, Journal and Life History, p. 4; Utah Territorial Papers, Clark to Canfield, July 8, 1851.

18. NA, "Letters, Utah," Roll 897, Holeman to Young, Nov. 10, 1851.

19. Caroline Richardson, Journal, 1852, p. 37, May 24, 1852.

20. Benjamin G. Ferris, *Utah and the Mormons*, pp. 13-14.

21. NA, "Letters, Utah," Roll 897, Young to CIA, May 25, 1852.

22. *New York Tribune*, Oct. 14, 1852.

23. Frederic Logan Paxson, ed., "T. Turnbull's Travels from the United States across the Plains to California," *Proceedings of the State Historical Society of Wisconsin*, p. 203, July 26, 1852.

24. Young, Indian Affairs, Out Correspondence—Commissioners, June 8, 1852.

25. Abigail J. Duniway, *Captain Gray's Company, or Crossing the Plains*, p. 133.

26. John T. Kerns, "Journal of Crossing the Plains to Oregon in 1852," *Transactions of the Forty-second Annual Reunion of the Oregon Pioneer Association*, p. 173.

27. NA, "Letters, Utah," Roll 897, Young to CIA, May 25, 1852.

28. Duniway, *Captain Gray's Company*, pp. 139-40.

29. NA, "Letters, Utah," Roll 897, Young to CIA, Mar. 30, 1852, Holeman to CIA, Apr. 29, 1852.

30. Ibid., Holeman to CIA, Apr. 29, 1852.

31. Ibid., Young to CIA, May 25, 1852.

32. Ibid., Holeman to CIA, Apr. 29, 1852.

33. Ibid., Holeman to CIA, June 28, 1852.

34. U.S. Dept. of the Interior, *Annual Report, 1852*, Holeman to Young, pp. 149-52.

35. Ibid., p. 153; NA, "Letters, Utah," Roll 897, Young to CIA, Mar. 30, 1852.

36. Ibid.

37. Brigham Young, Indian Affairs—Miscellaneous Licenses, Permits, etc., 1851-53, folder 29, Nov. 1. 1852.

38. NA, "Letters, Utah," Roll 897, Holeman to CIA, Apr. 29, 1852.

39. Ibid., Young to CIA, May 25, 1852. For a detailed analysis of the Young-Holeman feud, see Dale L. Morgan, "The Administration of Indian Affairs in Utah, 1851-1858," *Pacific Historical Review* 17, no. 3 (Nov. 1948): 384-92.

40. NA, "Letters, Utah," Roll 897, Day to CIA, Jan. 2, 1852, Rose to Young, Mar. 31, 1852.

41. Brigham Young, Indian Affairs Correspondence, 1851-53, folder 22, Day to CIA, Jan. 10, 1852.

42. NA, "Letters, Utah," Roll 897, Holeman to Young, Mar. 30, 1852, Rose to Young, Mar. 31, 1852.

43. Young, Indian Affairs, Correspondence, 1851-53, folder 16, Sept. 25, 1852.

44. Journal History, Young to Martin, May 29, 1852.

45. Young, Indian Affairs, Miscellaneous papers, folder 28, May 24, 1852.

46. James Palmer, Reminiscences, p. 118.

47. NA, "Letters, Oregon," Roll 608, Palmer to CIA, 1853.

48. Ibid., Alvord to Townsend, Mar. 31, 1853.

49. Ibid., Palmer to CIA, May 27, 1853.

50. Ibid., Palmer to Garrison, June 22, 1853.

51. Journal History, May 21, 1853.

52. D. B. Ward, *Across the Plains in 1853*, pp. 44-45.

53. Reminiscences of an Old Pioneer, Aug. 1853.

54. Celinda E. Hines, Diary, *Transactions of the Forty-sixth Annual Reunion of the Oregon Pioneer Association*, pp. 103-5, July 18-22.

55. NA, "Letters, Utah," Roll 897, Young to CIA, June 28, 1853.

56. U.S. Dept. of the Interior, *Annual Report, 1853*, Holeman to CIA, Sept. 30, 1853.

57. Ibid.

58. Unruh, *The Plains Across*, p. 196.

59. Brigham Young, Indian Affairs—Holeman, Correspondence, 1851-53, folder 16, Mar. 30, 1853.

60. Young, Indian Affairs, Miscellaneous Papers, folder 28, May 28, 1853.

61. John Henry Evans, *Charles Coulson Rich: Pioneer Builder of the West*, pp. 229-30.

62. Utah State Militia Correspondence, Moore to Wells, Aug. 29, 1853.

63. Ibid.

64. Unruh, *The Plains Across*, p. 120.

CHAPTER FOUR NOTES

1. Young, Indian Affairs, Correspondence, folder 13, Bedell to Young, Apr. 6, 1854.

2. Mary Ann Frost, Father Murdered and Ward Massacre, vol. 1, MS. 407.

3. Ibid.; NA, "Letters, Oregon," Roll 608, Thompson to Palmer, Sept. 3, 1854.

4. In addition to the above reports, other sources consulted were: "Brief History of the Ward Massacre," MS. 471; Gerald Baydo, "Overland from Missouri to Washington Territory in 1854," *Nebraska History* 52, no. 1 (Spring 1971): 81-82; John Rees, Cause of the Ward Indian Massacre, MS. 545; The Ward Massacre as Told by Newton Ward to Rufus Wood, MS. 472; NA, "Letters, Oregon," Roll 608, Thompson to Palmer, Oct. 11, 18, 1854.

5. NA, "Letters, Oregon," Roll 608, Thompson to Palmer, Sept. 6, 1854.

6. Ibid., Palmer to Olney, Sept. 28, 1854.

7. Ibid., Palmer to Thompson, Sept. 28, 1854.

8. Ibid., Thompson to Palmer, Oct. 11, 18, 1854.

9. Morgan, "The Administration of Indian Affairs in Utah, 1851-1858," pp. 392-93.

10. Brigham Young, Indian Affairs, Miscellaneous Papers, folder 28, 1854.

11. Edward Bode, ed., "Charles Kleinsorge: Missouri to California, 1854," *Missouri Historical Review* 76, no. 4 (July 1982): 441.

12. Richard Brautigan, intro., *The Overland Journey of Joseph Francl*, pp. 46-47.

13. Unruh, *The Plains Across*, p. 184.

14. Young, Indian Affairs, Miscellaneous Papers, folder 4, Sept. 2, 22, 1854; Young, Indian Affairs, Out Correspondence—Commissioners, folder 9, Sept. 30, 1854.

15. NA, "Letters, Utah," Roll 897, illegible to CIA, June 17, 1854.

16. Young, Indian Affairs, Indian Correspondence, June 28, Aug. 15, 1854.

17. Ibid., Nov. 6, 1854.

18. Young, Manuscript History, Sept. 4, 1854, p. 83; Young, Indian Affairs, Indian Correspondence, Nov. 21, 1854.

19. Young, "Message to the Legislative Assembly," 53-1 to 5.

20. NA, "Letters, Oregon," Roll 608, Palmer to CIA, Jan. 30, 1855.

21. Ibid., Palmer to Olney, Feb. 19, 1855.

22. Journal History, Apr. 13, 1855.

23. NA, "Letters, Oregon," Roll 608, Olney to Palmer, Aug. 31, 1855.

24. Ibid.

25. Madsen, *The Bannock of Idaho*, pp. 86-90.

26. Morgan, "The Administration of Indian Affairs in Utah, 1851-1858," pp. 394-99.

27. NA, "Letters, Utah," Roll 897, Hurt to CIA, July 14, 1855, Hurt to Young, Aug. 27, 1855; NA, "Treaty Made on August 7, 1855, between Garland Hurt and Sho-sho-shee nation of Indians," Record of Treaties, 1851-1860, vol. M6, pp. 345-46; Journal History, Aug. 27, 1855; *Deseret News*, Sept. 5, 1855; U. S. Dept. of the Interior, *Annual Report, 1855*, pp. 157-201.

28. U.S. Dept. of the Interior, *Annual Report, 1855*, pp. 157-201; *Deseret News*, Sept. 5, 1855.

29. NA, "Letters, Utah," Roll 897, Young to CIA, June 30, 1855; Journal History, June 30, 1855.

30. Utah Territorial Papers, Brigham Young, Proclamation by the Governor, Oct. 12, 1855, MS. 765.

31. U.S. Dept. of the Interior, *Annual Report, 1855*, Hurt to Young, Sept. 30, 1855, pp. 197-98; *Deseret News*, Sept. 5, 1855.

32. Journal History, Aug. 23, 1855.

33. U.S. Dept. of the Interior, *Annual Report, 1855*, Hurt to Young, Sept. 30, 1855, pp. 199-200.

34. Ibid.; *Deseret News*, Sept. 12, 1855.

35. Jeffrey Simmonds, The First Settlements, pp. 4-7.

36. John Clark Dowdle, Journal.

37. Simmonds, The First Settlements, p. 6.

38. Territory of Utah, *Acts and Resolutions Passed by the Legislative Assembly of the Territory of Utah, During the Sixth Annual Session, 1856-57*, p. 4.

39. *Resolutions, Acts and Memorials Passed at the Fifth Annual Session of the Legislative Assembly of the Territory of Utah*, p. 38.

40. Young, Manuscript History, May 30, 1856.

41. NA, "Letters, Oregon," Roll 609, Hedges to CIA, Oct. 10, 1856.

42. NA, "Letters, Utah," Roll 898, Hurt to Young, Sept. 1856.

43. Ibid.

44. Ibid.

45. Ibid., Young to CIA, Aug. 30, 1856.

46. Ibid., Hickman, Bullock, Robinson to Young, Aug. 11, 1856.

47. Brigham Young, Indian Affairs, Indian Correspondence, Aug. 11, 1856.

48. NA, "Letters, Utah," Roll 898, Hurt to Young, Sept. 11, 1856.

49. Simmonds, The First Settlements, pp. 9-10.

50. Kate B. Carter, comp., "Journal of Mary Ann Weston Maughan," *Our Pioneer Heritage*, vol. 2, pp. 384-85.

CHAPTER FIVE NOTES

1. NA, "Letters, Oregon," Roll 610, Nesmith to CIA, June 16, 1857.

2. Ibid., Nesmith to CIA, 1857.

3. Ibid., Dennison to Nesmith, Aug. 1, 1857.

4. Ibid., Nesmith to CIA, Sept. 1, 1857.

5. Ibid., Browne to CIA, Nov. 17, 1857.

6. Madsen, *The Bannock of Idaho*, pp. 92–93.

7. Young, Brigham Young Papers, Bernard to Young, Malad Valley, Apr. 20, 1857; Journal History, Sept. 15, 16, 1857.

8. Neff, *History of Utah*, p. 458.

9. The best description and analysis of Alfred Cumming's tenure as governor of Utah is Charles S. Peterson, "A Historical Analysis of Territorial Government in Utah under Alfred Cumming, 1857-1861." For a short account of the Utah War, see Eugene E. Campbell, "Governmental Beginnings," in *Utah's History*, pp. 165–68. Campbell's summaries of the complex Utah War and the Mountain Meadows Massacre are succinct and descriptive.

10. Utah Territorial Papers, Wells to Alexander, Oct. 15, 1857.

11. Madsen, *The Northern Shoshoni*, p. 34.

12. Brigham Young, Indian Affairs—In-Correspondence, Commissioners, 1854, Aug. 1857, Denver to Young, Nov. 11, 1857.

13. *Sacramento Union*, Aug. 10, 1857.

14. Ibid., Aug. 12, 1857.

15. William Audley Maxwell, *Crossing the Plains, Days of '57*, pp. 62–72; George R. Stewart, *The California Trail*, pp. 314–15.

16. Stewart, *The California Trail*, pp. 315–17; Maxwell, *Crossing the Plains*, pp. 116–59.

17. *Sacramento Union*, Sept. 28, 1857.

18. Ibid., Oct. 12, 1857.

19. Ibid., Oct. 5, 1857.

20. Ibid., Nov. 2, 1857.

21. Ibid., Nov. 11, 1857.

22. NA, "Letters, Utah," Roll 898, Brigham Young to CIA, Sept. 12, 1857.

23. E. Campbell, "Governmental Beginnings." p. 167.

24. See ibid., pp. 170–71, for a short account of the Mountain Meadows Massacre; the standard and most detailed treatment is, of course, the superb book by Juanita Brooks, *The Mountain Meadows Massacre*.

25. *Sacramento Union*, Nov. 2, 1857.

26. Ibid., Oct. 19, 1857.

27. Young, Brigham Young Papers, Hickman to Young, Sept. 1, 1857.

28. Young, Indian Affairs, Indian Correspondence, Young to Washakie, Nov. 2, 1857.

29. Morgan, "The Administration of Indian Affairs in Utah, 1851-1858," pp. 405–7; NA, "Letters, Utah," Roll 898, Forney to CIA, Nov. 30, 1857.

30. Brigham Young and the Saints continued to proselyte among the Indians and were successful in baptizing a number into the Mormon church. One Pied Chieftain from Santa Clara was ordained an Elder by Brigham Young and told "to go & preach the Gospel & Baptise among the House of Israel," Dimick B. Huntington, Journal, Sept. 10, 1857.

31. Ibid., Aug. 10, 1857.

32. NA, "Letters, Utah," Roll 898, Forney to CIA, Dec. 4, 1857.

33. Huntington, Journal, Aug. 11, 1857.

34. Ibid., Aug. 12, 1857.

35. Ibid., Sept. 30, 1857.

36. Simmonds, The First Settlements, p. 16.

37. Young, Brigham Young Papers, Maughan to Young, June 4, 1857.

38. NA, "Letters, Utah," Roll 898, Young to CIA, Sept. 12, 1857.

39. Young, Brigham Young Papers, Maughan to Young, Oct. 27, 1857.

40. *Sacramento Union*, Sept. 4, 1858.

41. NA, "Letters, Oregon," Roll 611, Nesmith to CIA, Apr. 24, Nov. 19, 1858.

42. Young, Brigham Young Papers, Smith to Young, Feb. 28, 1858.

43. U.S. Congress, Senate, *Message of the President of the United States*, serial 975, pp. 74-75; Dowdle, Journal, pp. 34-35.

44. U.S. Congress, Senate, *Message of the President*, serial 975, pp. 77-82.

45. Madsen, *The Bannock of Idaho*, pp. 94-108.

46. Young, Indian Affairs, Indian Correspondence, Brigham Young to Tim-a-poo, 1858.

47. Neff, *History of Utah*, pp. 456-516; E. Campbell, "Governmental Beginnings," pp. 165-70.

48. U.S. Congress, Senate, *Message of the President*, serial 1024, p. 15.

49. Young, Manuscript History, July 6, 1858.

50. U.S. Congress, Senate, *Message of the President*, serial 975, pp. 159-60; *San Francisco Bulletin*, Oct. 28, 29, 1858.

51. Young, Manuscript History, Oct. 31, 1858.

52. *Sacramento Union*, Aug. 17, 1858.

53. Ibid., Oct. 20, 1858; *Alta California*, Sept. 6, Oct. 28, 1858; U.S. Congress, Senate, *Message of the President*, serial 975, pp. 141-59; NA, "Letters, Utah," Roll 898, Forney to CIA, Nov. 5, 1858.

54. NA, "Letters, Utah," Roll 898, Forney to CIA, Nov. 5, 1858; *Sacramento Union*, Nov. 16, 1858.

55. Young, Manuscript History, Oct. 31, 1858.

56. *Sacramento Union*, Mar. 3, 1858.

57. NA, "Letters, Utah," Roll 898, Forney to CIA, May 21, 1858.

58. *Sacramento Union*, July 29, 1858.

59. NA, "Letters, Utah," Roll 898, Forney to CIA, Mar. 11, Apr. 17, 1858; U.S. Congress, Senate, *Message of the President*, serial 975, pp. 74-75, 83.

60. James Bywater, Reminiscences, p. 245.

61. U.S. Congress, Senate, *Message of the President*, serial 975, pp. 81-82.

62. NA, "Letters, Utah," Roll 898, Forney to CIA, Nov. 5. 1858.

63. *Deseret News*, Nov. 17, 1858.

64. Young, Manuscript History, p. 972, Young to Maughan, Sept. 23, 1858.

65. Ricks, ed., *The History of a Valley*, p. 37.

CHAPTER SIX NOTES

1. U.S. Congress, Senate, *Message from the President of the United States*, serial 1024, vol. 2, pp. 116, 120.

2. Journal History, Hartnett to Congress, Jan. 12, 1859.

3. NA, "Letters, Utah," Roll 899, 1-7, Forney to CIA, Feb. 15, 1859.

4. Ibid., Egan to Forney, Feb. 19, 1859.

5. Ibid., Forney to Jarvis, Mar. 5, 1859.

6. Ibid., Lander to Sherman, Mar. 23, 1859.

7. *Sacramento Union*, Mar. 16, 1859.

8. Young, Manuscript History, Apr. 2, 1859, p. 303.

9. Mary Ann West Maughan, Memories of Early Days in Logan and Cache County, p. 36.

10. Ricks, ed., *The History of a Valley*, pp. 37-43. John Fish Wright, Memories

of Early Days in Logan and Cache County; Ella Campbell, Memories of Early Days in Logan and Cache County, p. 42; Isaac Sorensen, History.

11. Simmonds, The First Settlements, pp. 29-45. The author gives a complete picture of the settlement of Cache Valley, and these are his estimates of the percentage of people in each village.

12. Henry Ballard, Memories of Early Days in Logan and Cache County, p. 28.

13. Simmonds, The First Settlements, p. 43.

14. Ibid., pp. 43-44; J. H. Martineau, "The Military History of Cache County," *Tullidge's Quarterly Magazine* 2, no. 1 (Apr. 1882): 122.

15. Matthew P. Fifield, Biography. See also H. Ballard, Memories, p. 25, and Sorensen, History.

16. Maughan to Young, June 3, 1859. Young, Papers.

17. Journal History, Maughan to Young, June 15, 1859.

18. Walter Walters, Family Record, pp. 24-25.

19. U.S. Congress, Senate, *Report of the Secretary of War*, 1860, serial 1024, p. 15.

20. Brigham Young, Manuscript History, July 6, 1858, p. 765.

21. U.S. Congress, Senate, *Message of the President*, serial 1024, pp. 175-76, 182-84, 189-90.

22. NA, "Letters, Utah," Roll 899, Forney to CIA, June 9, 1859.

23. Elijah Nicholas Wilson, *Among the Shoshones*, pp. 116-20.

24. This account of the supposed Almo Massacre has been drawn from the following sources: Charles Shirley Walgamott, Reminiscences, pp. 18-22, and *Six Decades Back*, pp. 121-26; *Idaho Statesman*, Oct. 24, 1937; Stewart, *The California Trail*, pp. 223-24; "Almo Massacre," pp. 1-13; *Wenatchee World*, Oct. 8, 1980; Merrill D. Beal, *A History of Southeastern Idaho*, pp. 237-38; Leslie L. Sudweeks, *Indian Troubles on the Sublette Cut-off*, pp. 2-5.

25. LeRoy R. Hafen and Carl C. Rister, *Western America*, pp. 457-61. For a good description of the mail line route, and the general topography, flora and fauna, and Indian tribes along the line, see James H. Simpson, *Report of Explorations Across the Great Basin in 1859*, pp. 41-150, 459-66.

26. *Alta California*, July 6, 1859.

27. Ibid., Sept. 12, 1859; U.S. Congress, Senate, *Message of the President*, serial 1033, pp. 108-9; *Deseret News*, Aug. 17, 1859; NA, "Letters, Utah," Roll 899, Forney to CIA, Aug. 10, 1859.

28. This story of the Shepherd Massacre is based on government reports and the extensive newspaper coverage it received: NA, "Letters, Utah," Roll 899, Forney to CIA, Aug. 10, 1859, Smith to Forney, Aug. 2, 1859; Journal History, Wright to *Deseret News*, Aug. 1, 1859; *Valley Tan*, Aug. 3, 10, 1859; *Deseret News*, Aug. 3, 17, 1859; *San Francisco Bulletin*, Aug. 24, 30, 1859; *Alta California*, Sept. 12, 1859; *Sacramento Union*, Dec. 2, 1859.

29. NA, "Letters, Utah," Roll 899, Smith to Forney, Aug. 2, 1859, Forney to CIA, Aug. 10, 1859; *Deseret News*, Aug. 3, 17, 1859; U.S. Congress, Senate, *Message of the President*, serial 1033, pp. 18-20.

30. U.S. Congress, Senate, *Message of the President*, serial 1033, pp. 20-21, 37; *Deseret News*, Aug. 3, 1859.

31. U.S. Congress, Senate, *Message of the President*, serial 1033, pp. 22-23.

32. Ibid.; Young, Manuscript History, Aug. 14, 1859, p. 631; *Valley Tan*, Aug. 17, 24, 1859; *San Francisco Bulletin*, Aug. 30, 1859; *Alta California*, Sept. 21, 1859.

33. *Valley Tan*, Aug. 24, 1859.

34. Young, Papers, Maughan to Young, Aug. 22, 25, 1859.

35. Young, Manuscript History, Maughan to Young, Aug. 27, 1859, p. 646.

36. *Deseret News*, Aug. 31, 1859.

37. *Alta California*, Sept. 8, 1859.

38. *Deseret News*, Sept. 21, 1859.

39. The story of the Miltimore Massacre is based on the following sources: Young, Manuscript History, Sept. 12, 1859, pp. 681–85; NA, "Letters, Utah," Roll 899, Eckels to Sec. of the Interior, Sept. 23, 1859, Report of F. W. Lander to CIA, Feb. 18, 1860; *Valley Tan*, Sept. 21, 1859; *Sacramento Union*, Oct. 27, 1859; *San Francisco Bulletin*, Nov. 19, 1859; *Alta California*, Oct. 28, 1859; *Deseret News*, Sept. 21, 1859; U.S. Congress, Senate, *Message of the President*, serial 1033, pp. 28, 33, 111–14, 119–20; Milton S. Harrington, Affidavit of Milton S. Harrington before Court of Claims, 1909.

40. U.S. Congress, Senate, *Message of the President*, serial 1033, pp. 14–15, 32.

41. Ibid.

42. Ibid., pp. 28–29.

43. Ibid., pp. 29–30, 133–34.

44. *Valley Tan*, Sept. 7, 14, 1859; *Alta California*, Oct. 5, 6, 1859; *San Francisco Bulletin*, Oct. 31, 1859.

45. U.S. Congress, Senate, *Message of the President*, serial 1033, p. 34.

46. *Sacramento Union*, Sept. 19, 1859.

47. U.S. Congress, Senate, *Message of the President*, serial 1033, pp. 25–27.

48. Utley, *Frontiersmen in Blue*, pp. 133–35.

49. Ibid., pp. 159–60.

CHAPTER SEVEN NOTES

1. U.S. Congress, Senate, *Message of the President*, serial 1118, pp. 528–34.

2. An abundance of material describes the Otter Massacre, much of it newspaper reports: Miles Cannon, Sinker Creek Tragedy of Early Pioneer Days, pp. 1–13; *New York World*, Dec. 6, 1860; Larry Jones, "Otter Massacre Site"; *Deseret News*, Oct. 31, 1860; NA, "Letters, Utah," Roll 899, Lander to CIA, Oct. 31, 1860; Hubert Howe Bancroft, *History of Oregon*, pp. 469–76; *New York Times*, Oct. 23, 1860; U.S. Congress, House, *Depredations and Massacre by the Snake River Indians*, pp. 1–2, 10–16; U.S. Congress, Senate, *Message from the President*, serial 1079, vol. 2, pp. 143–44; U.S. Congress, House, *Indian Depredations in Oregon and Washington*, pp. 84–90.

3. U.S. Congress, Senate, *Message from the President*, serial 1079, pp. 141–43.

4. John Owen, *The Journals and Letters of Major John Owen, Pioneer of the Northwest, 1850–1871*, Owen to Geary, Flathead Agency, Washington Terr., Feb. 13, 1861. p. 243.

5. Ibid., Owen to Blake, Feb. 18, 1861, pp. 247–48, Owen to Kendall, Sept. 12, 1861, pp. 262–63.

6. NA, "Letters, Utah," Roll 899, Thompson to Floyd, Jan. 23, 1860.

7. Hooper-Young Letters, Young to Hooper, May 31, June 7, 1860.

8. James A. Evans, Journal of Trip to Oregon (1860).

9. *Deseret News*, Oct. 3, 1860.

10. "Almo Massacre."

11. *Sacramento Union*, Oct. 2, 1860.

12. *Deseret News*, Oct. 3, 1860.

13. U.S. Congress, Senate, *Message from the President*, serial 1079, pp. 101, 104.

14. *Sacramento Union*, May 28, 1860.

15. *Territorial Enterprise*, May 5, 1860.

16. Young, Papers, Cook to Young, June 8, 1860; Raymond W. Settle and Mary L. Settle, *Saddles and Spurs*, pp. 146-47.

17. There were many newspaper reports of the battle. Good summaries can be found in, Settle and Settle, *Saddles and Spurs*, p. 149, and Russell R. Elliott, *History of Nevada*, pp. 92-93. See also U.S. Congress, Senate, *Message from the President*, serial 1079, pp. 73-78; *Sacramento Union*, May 9, 11, 14, 15, 23, 24, June 4, 1860.

18. NA, "Letters, Utah," Roll 899, Lander to CIA, Oct. 31, 1860.

19. *Sacramento Union*, May 14, 1860; Elliott, *History of Nevada*, p. 93.

20. For descriptions of Hays's battle see: Elliott, *History of Nevada*, p. 93; U.S. Congress, Senate, *Message from the President*, serial 1079, pp. 89-92, 93-100; *Sacramento Union*, June 1, 5, 8, 9, 12, 1860; *Territorial Enterprise*, June 9, 1860.

21. *Sacramento Union*, June 20, July 6, 9, 1860.

22. Ibid., July 13, 14, 1860.

23. NA, "Letters, Utah," Roll 899, Lander to CIA, Oct. 31, 1860.

24. Hafen and Rister, *Western America*, pp. 461-64; Ralph Moody, *Stagecoach West*, pp. 182-85; Settle and Settle, *Saddles and Spurs*, pp. 29-34, 115.

25. Settle and Settle, *Saddles and Spurs*, pp. 136-43. Names of some of the stations varied from time to time, and probably not all are included in the list cited.

26. Peter Gottfredson, *History of Indian Depredations in Utah*, p. 110.

27. Settle and Settle, *Saddles and Spurs*, pp. 150-51.

28. U.S. Congress, Senate, *Message from the President*, serial 1079, p. 73.

29. Myron Angel, ed., *History of Nevada*, p. 177.

30. Hooper-Young Letters, Young to Hooper, May 24, 1860.

31. Ibid., Young to Hooper, June 7, 1860.

32. U.S. Congress, Senate, *Message from the President*, serial 1079, pp. 83-84, 97.

33. Gottfredson, *Indian Depredations*, p. 110.

34. U.S. Congress, Senate, *Message from the President*, serial 1079, pp. 87-88.

35. *Deseret News*, July 21, 1860.

36. Young, Manuscript History, July 5, 1860, p. 201.

37. Wilson, *Among the Shoshones*, pp. 153-58.

38. *Sacramento Union*, Aug. 21, 1860.

39. *Deseret News*, Aug. 29, 1860.

40. U.S. Congress, Senate, *Message from the President*, serial 1079, pp. 93-94.

41. Ibid.; *Deseret News*, Aug. 29, 1860; *Sacramento Union*, Aug. 21, 1860.

42. *Sacramento Union*, Aug. 21, 1860; U.S. Congress, Senate, *Message from the President*, serial 1079, p. 106.

43. U.S. Congress, Senate, *Message from the President*, serial 1079, p. 106.

44. Settle and Settle, *Saddles and Spurs*, pp. 159-60.

45. Journal History, Memorial to United States Government, Nov. 1, 1860; NA, "Letters, Utah," Roll 899, Stambaugh to Smith, Jan. 25, 1860, Forney to CIA, Feb. 27, 1860; *Sacramento Union*, Aug. 1, 1860.

46. NA, "Letters, Utah," Roll 899, Stambaugh to Smith, Jan. 25, 1860, Forney to CIA, Feb. 27, 1860.

47. Journal History, Memorial to United States Government, Nov. 1, 1860; *Deseret News*, Nov. 14, 1860.

48. Young, Papers, West to Young, Apr. 16, 1860; Hooper-Young Letters, Young to Hooper, Apr. 19, 1860; *Sacramento Union*, May 4, 1860.

49. Ricks, ed., *The History of a Valley*, pp. 43–48.

50. Samuel Handy, History, 1819–1882, p. 17; Official Program, Franklin, Idaho, Semi-Centennial Celebration, p. 19.

51. Simmonds, The First Settlements, 1855–1860, pp. 45–56.

52. Young, Papers, Preston to Young, Mar. 17, 1860, Maughan to Young, Jan. 27, 1860.

53. Robert D. Roberts, Memories of Early Days in Logan and Cache Valley, p. 42.

54. NA,"Letters, Utah," Roll 899, Lander to CIA, Feb. 18, 1860.

55. Angus Taylor Wright, Autobiography, pp. 7, 16; Charles W. Nibley, *Reminiscences of Charles W. Nibley, 1849–1931*, p. 31.

56. Young, Manuscript History, Maughan to Young, May 1, 1860, p. 123.

57. James H. Martineau, "The Military History of Cache County," *Tullidge's Quarterly Magazine* 2, no. 1 (Apr. 1882): 122.

58. Young, Manuscript History, June 4, 1860, p. 162.

59. There are many contemporary accounts of this incident, but the most accurate is probably Peter Maughan's. See Young, Papers, Maughan to Young, July 26, 1860. See also Kate B. Carter, "Excerpts from the Diary of William F. Rigby," *Our Pioneer Heritage*, vol. 4, p. 253; William G. Nelson, A History of His Life, p. 21; Simmonds, The First Settlements, 1855–1860, pp. 1–4; Ricks, *The History of a Valley*, pp. 48–50; *Deseret News*, Aug. 1, 1860; Ralph Smith, Journal of Ralph Smith, 1846–1897, July 24, 1860, p. 7.

60. Young, Papers, Maughan to Young, July 29, 1860.

CHAPTER EIGHT NOTES

1. NA, "Letters, Utah," Roll 900, Chase to Davies, May 5, 1861, Crosby to Davies, May 28, 1861, Davies to CIA, May 29, 1861.

2. Don Richard Mathis, "Camp Floyd in Retrospect," pp. 139–42.

3. NA,"Letters, Utah," Roll 900, Davies to CIA, Jan. 20, 1861.

4. Elliott, *History of Nevada*, pp. 63–68.

5. Gov. James W. Nye, Correspondence [2] (hereafter Nye Correspondence [2]), Robertson to Nye, July 9, 1861, Committee of Safety, Star Canion, to Nye, July 9, 1861.

6. Utah Territorial Papers, John C. Burche to Francis H. Wootten, Aug. 22, 1861, no. 1791.

7. Settle and Settle, *Saddles and Spurs*, pp. 181–89; Roscoe P. Conkling and Margaret B. Conkling, *The Butterfield Overland Mail, 1857–1869*, pp. 336–39; Moody, *Stagecoach West*, pp. 202–12; J. V. Frederick, *Ben Holladay: The Stagecoach King*, pp. 62–64.

8. Utah Territorial Papers, Greene to Superintendent of Indian Affairs, Feb. 19, 1861, no. 1726.

9. Wilson, *Among the Shoshones*, pp. 161–64.

10. U.S. Dept. of the Interior, *Annual Report, 1861*, Martin to CIA, Oct. 1, 1861, pp. 134–38.

11. NA, "Pacific Department, Letters Received, 1861–1865" (hereafter cited as "Pacific Department, Letters"), Baker to Adjutant, Fort Churchill, Oct. 1861, Docket nos. 326, 356, 307, Exh. no. 157.

12. NA, "Letters, Utah," Roll 900, Doty to CIA, Dec. 14, 1861.

13. Ibid., Martin to CIA, Nov. 7, 1861.

14. Ibid., Center to CIA, Nov. 17, 1861.

15. Ibid., Center to Latham, Dec. 19., 1861.

16. Gov. James W. Nye, Correspondence [1] (hereafter Nye Correspondence [1]), Dawson to Nye, Dec. 20, 1861.

17. U.S. Congress, Senate, *Message of the President of the United States*, serial 1122, Dec. 21, 1861, p. 4.

18. Nye Correspondence [1], Wasson to Nye, Dec. 22, 1861.

19. Settle and Settle, *Saddles and Spurs*, p. 160.

20. Neff, *History of Utah*, pp. 388–89.

21. NA, "Letters, Utah," Roll 900, Davies to CIA, Jan. 20, 1861.

22. U.S. Dept. of the Interior, *Annual Report, 1861*, Humphreys to CIA, Sept. 30, 1861, pp. 139–41.

23. NA,"Letters, Utah," Roll 900, Doty to CIA, Oct. 21, 1861.

24. Bancroft, *History of Utah*, pp. 621–22.

25. Alice Elizabeth Smith, *James Duane Doty: Frontier Promoter*, pp. 368–69.

26. NA, "Letters, Utah," Roll 900, Davies to CIA, Jan. 20, 1861.

27. Utah Territorial Papers, Greene to Davies, Feb. 19, 1861, no. 1726.

28. Young, Manuscript History, Mar. 11, 1861, p. 107.

29. *Deseret News*, Mar. 13, 1861.

30. Margaret McNiel Ballard, Memories of Early Days in Logan and Cache County, p. 17.

31. Young, Papers, Thomas to Young, Feb. 28, 1861.

32. Young, Manuscript History, Apr. 1, 1861, p. 122.

33. Young, Papers, Nichols to Young, May 9, 1861, Maughan to Young, June 14, 1861.

34. Young, Papers, Maughan to Young, July 15, 1861; Seth M. Blair, Journal, July 20, 1861.

35. *Deseret News*, Sept. 18, 1861.

36. Young, Papers, Maughan to Young, Sept. 18, 1861.

37. Richard H. Orton, comp., *Records of California Men in the War of the Rebellion, 1861 to 1867*, p. 12.

38. Leland Stanford, Governor's Office, Letterbook 2, Downey to Connor, Sept. 4, 1861, p. 33.

39. There is presently no full-scale biography of Connor. The following accounts examine the events of his early career: Rogers, *Soldiers of the Overland*, pp. 1–4; C. C. Goodwin, *As I Remember Them*, pp. 18–19; Leo P. Kibby, "Patrick Edward Connor: First Gentile of Utah," *Journal of the West* 2, no. 4 (Oct. 1963): 425; Thomas P. Prendergast, *Forgotten Pioneers: Irish Leaders in Early California*, pp. 250–51; "In Memoriam: Patrick Edward Connor," Military Order of the Loyal Legion of the United States; Hubert Howe Bancroft, "Biographical Sketch of General P. E. Connor," p. 1; Hugh Quigley, "The Irish Race in California," pp. 245–46; Kate B. Carter, comp., "Ft. Douglas-Civil War Veterans," *Our Pioneer Heritage*, vol. 6, pp. 113–15; Aurora Hunt, *The Army of the Pacific*, p. 186; Francis B. Heitman, *Historical Register and Dictionary of the United States Army*, vol. 1, pp. 321–22.

40. Rogers, *Soldiers of the Overland*, pp. 5–13; Goodwin, *As I Remember Them*, pp. 266–67; Kibby, "Patrick Edward Connor," pp. 425–26; Prendergast, *Forgotten Pioneers*, pp. 251–54; "In Memoriam"; Bancroft, "Biographical Sketch of General P. E. Connor," pp. 1–4; Quigley, "The Irish Race in California," pp. 245–46; Carter, "Ft. Douglas-Civil War Veterans," p. 115; Hunt, *The Army of the Pacific*, p. 186; Thomas J. Gordon, "Joaquin Murieta: Fact, Fiction and Folklore."

41. Rogers, *Soldiers of the Overland*, pp. 14–15.

42. Hunt, *The Army of the Pacific*, p. 187; Quigley, "The Irish Race in California," n.p.

43. U.S. Congress, House, *The War of the Rebellion*, (hereafter *War of the Rebellion*) pt. 1, serial 3583, Wright to Thomas, Dec. 9, 1861, pp. 753-54.

44. Orton, *Records*, Wright to Thomas, Dec. 9, 1861, pp. 753-54.

45. *War of the Rebellion*, serial 3583, Wright to Thomas, June 28, 1862, pp. 1164-65.

46. Ibid., serial 3583, Drum to Connor, Mar. 28, 1862, p. 960, Wright to Thomas, Apr. 10, 1862, p. 996, Apr. 29, 1862, p. 1039, May 13, 1862, p. 1069, May 30, 1862, pp. 1109-10, June 28, 1862, pp. 1164-65.

47. Nye Correspondence [1], Jacobs to Nye, Jan. 2, 1862.

48. Ibid., Mason to Nye, Mar. 18, 1862.

49. NA, "Letters Received, Nevada Superintendency, 1862" (hereafter "Letters, Nevada"), Burche to Lockhart, May 1, 1862.

50. Nye Correspondence [2], Mc Dermit to Nye, May 15, 1862.

51. NA, "Letters, Nevada," Nye to CIA, Feb. 3, 1862.

52. Nye Correspondence [1], Butterfield to Nye, Jan. 24, 1862.

53. Ibid., Stebbins and all the citizens to Wasson, Jan. 26, 1862.

54. Ibid., Bunker to Nye, Mar. 13, 1862.

55. Ibid., Butterfield to Nye, Feb. 11, 1862.

56. Ibid., Mar. 18, 1862.

57. Ibid., Wasson to Nye, Mar. 19, 1862.

58. NA, "Letters, Utah," Roll 900, Doty to CIA, Aug. 13, 1862; Dale L. Morgan, ed., "Washakie and the Shoshoni," pt. 6, *Annals of Wyoming* 28, no. 1 (Apr. 1956): 84-86.

59. Young, Manuscript History, Apr. 21, 1862, p. 495.

60. Utah Territorial Papers, Bromley to Holladay, Apr. 22, 1862, no. 1890.

61. Ibid., Flowers to Eastern Line, Apr. 22, 1862, Ely to Eastern Line, Apr. 23, 1862; *Sacramento Union*, May 8, 9, 1862.

62. *Sacramento Union*, May 9, 1862.

63. Utah State Militia Correspondence, 1849-63, Downs, Mourley, Goodell, Warner, and others "To all whom it may concern," May 10, 1862, and T. Goodale Statement, May 22, 1862.

64. NA, "Letters, Utah," Roll 900, Doty to CIA, Mar. 24, 1862.

65. Morgan, "Washakie and the Shoshoni," pt. 6, pp. 87-88.

66. Margaret M. Fisher, *Utah and the Civil War*, p. 112, has a very full account of the Burton and Lot Smith expeditions. See also E. B. Long, *The Saints and the Union*, pp. 82-83, *Sacramento Union*, May 9, 1862.

67. Fisher, *Utah and the Civil War*, pp. 113-30; Utah Territorial Papers, Burton to Fuller, May 5, 16, 1862, Utah Archives, nos. 1896, 1901; Long, *The Saints and the Union*, p. 83; *Sacramento Union*, May 9, 31, 1862.

68. Fisher, *Utah and the Civil War*, pp. 21-25; Long, *The Saints and the Union*, pp. 83-86; *War of the Rebellion*, pt. 1, Apr. 24, 1862, pp. 1023-24; Wells to "Dear Bro.," Apr. 28, 1862.

69. Utah State Archives, Militia Correspondence, Holladay to Young, May 2, 1862.

70. Young, Papers, Maughan to Young, Feb. 5, 1862.

71. NA, "Letters, Utah," Roll 900, Doty to CIA, Apr. 15, 1862.

72. Young, Manuscript History, May 19, 1862, pp. 551-52.

73. Blair, Journal, May 20, 1862.

74. Young, Papers, Maughan to Young, May 26, 1862.

75. James Shurlock Cantwell, Diary, May 25, June 21, 1862.

CHAPTER NINE NOTES

1. NA, "Letters Received by the Office of Indian Affairs, 1824-81, Washington Superintendency, 1842-1880," (hereafter "Letters, Washington"), Roll 907, Francis to CIA, May 18, 1861.

2. "Report of the Superintendent of Indian Affairs, 1862," Map of Wash'n Terry.

3. U.S. Dept. of the Interior, *Annual Report, 1862*, Kirkpatrick to CIA, July 22, 1862, pp. 265-68.

4. Ibid., Hole to CIA, Oct. 19, 1862, pp. 398-99, 401.

5. *War of the Rebellion*, Alvord to Pickering, July 28, 1862, pt. 2, pp. 42-43.

6. NA, "Letters, Washington," Roll 907, Hole to CIA, Sept. 4, 1862.

7. Ibid., Hole to CIA, Aug. 13, 1862.

8. *Washington Statesman*, Dec. 6, 1862.

9. Betty M. Madsen and Brigham D. Madsen, *North to Montana*, p. 23.

10. U.S. Congress, House, *Report of the Secretary of the Interior*, pp. 536-37.

11. James S. McClung, *Diary*, p. 2; *War of the Rebellion*, pt. 1, p. 154; U.S. Congress, Senate, "Report of Captain Medorem Crawford," pp. 1-14.

12. E. S. McComas, *A Journal of Travel*, pp. 11-16.

13. There is a plethora of accounts of the three engagements with the best summary being that provided by the Idaho State Historical Society in pamphlet form for distribution to visitors at Massacre Rocks State Park. See also, *Idaho World*, Mar. 31, 1911; *Deseret News*, Nov. 26, 1862; McComas, *A Journal of Travel*, pp. 15-16; *Washington Statesman*, Oct. 4, 1862; Hamilton Scott, "A Trip Across the Plains in 1862," *Power County Press* (American Falls, Idaho), July 7, 1949; Henry M. Judson, Diary of 1862, Omaha to Oregon, pp. 63-66; McClung, *Diary*, p. 4; H. C. Ellis, *The Story of Massacre Rocks*, pp. 1-3; *Aberdeen Times*, Aug. 16, 1962; U.S. Congress, Senate, "Report of Medorem Crawford," letter Oct. 30, 1862, pp. 154-55; *American Falls Press*, Alva Zaring, Diary, and Letter from John C. Hilman, Aug. 11, 1927. Recent information indicates that Chief Pocatello and his Northwestern Shoshoni band were responsible for the attacks at Massacre Rocks, Aug. 9-10, 1862. Interview with Sven Liljeblad, Reno, Nev., June 29, 1984, and Idaho State Historical Society, Reference Series, no. 234.

14. Morgan "Washakie and the Shoshoni," pt. 6, p. 86.

15. McComas, *A Journal of Travel*, pp. 17-20.

16. *Washington Statesman*, Oct. 15, 1862.

17. *Deseret News*, Sept. 17, 18, 1862.

18. NA, "Letters, Utah," Roll 900, Doty to CIA, Sept. 16, 1862.

19. Morgan, "Washakie and the Shoshoni," pt. 6, p. 90.

20. *Deseret News*, Sept. 24, 1862; *Sacramento Union*, Oct. 2, 1862.

21. *Washington Statesman*, Oct. 18, 1862; *War of the Rebellion*, pt. 1, p. 153.

22. NA, "Utah, Letters," Roll 900, Doty to CIA, Aug. 5, 1862. Dale Morgan speculated on the identity of Pash-e-go and War-a-gika in a footnote to his article on "Washakie and the Shoshini," pt. 6, p. 83: "Frederick Lander placed the range of Pash-e-go as the head of John Days River and west of the Blue Mountains—that is, in Oregon and apparently it is he who is referred to here. But there seems to have been a subchief of similar name among the Wyoming Shoshoni, called by Lander Push-e-can or Pur-chi-can, who as Lander said, bore upon his forehead the scar of a blow of the tomahawk given by Washikee in one of their altercations. The diaries of Mat Field in the Missouri Historical Society mentions this latter chief in connection with the celebrated raid by Cheyennes and Arapahoes upon the horses of Shoshoni and moun-

tain men at Fort Bridger in the summer of 1843, and intermittent later mention may be found of him. Some confusion of identity is possible. It seems likely that Doty was again referring to Pash-e-go, and that the name War-a-gika refers rather to the tribe or band, whose name was rendered by Lander as Warraricas, or sun flower seed-eaters. This was the division of the Bannock headed by Pash-e-go."

23. *Sacramento Union*, Aug. 15, 1862.

24. Morgan, "Washakie and the Shoshoni," pt. 6, pp. 90–92; U.S. Congress, House, *Report of the Secretary of the Interior*, Mann to Doty, Sept. 20, 1862, pp. 348–49; U.S. Dept. of the Interior, *Annual Report, 1862*, p. 32.

25. NA, "Letters, Utah," Roll 900, Martin to CIA, July 19, 22, Oct. 9, 10, 15, 28, 1862, Doty to CIA, Aug. 25, 29, 1862.

26. U.S. Congress, House, *Support of Utah and Other Indians*, pp. 1–3.

27. Nye Correspondence [2], Doty to Nye, Nov. 29, 1862.

28. NA, "Letters, Utah," Roll 900, Doty to CIA, July 30, 1862.

29. Ibid., Doty to CIA, Aug. 13, 1862.

30. U.S. Dept. of the Interior, *Annual Report, 1862*, pp. 198–200.

31. Ibid., p. 208.

32. *War of the Rebellion*, pt. 2, pp. 19, 31; Rogers, *Soldiers of the Overland*, p. 8; Hunt, *The Army of the Pacific*, p. 188; Orton, *Records of California Men*, pp. 506–7.

33. *War of the Rebellion*, pt. 2, p. 55.

34. Ibid., p. 61.

35. Ibid., p. 84.

36. Orton, *Records*, pp. 196–303, 523, 593.

37. "California Volunteers and the Civil War," National Guard of California, vol. 16, Second Regiment of Cavalry, p. 3.

38. Orton, *Records*, p. 507.

39. *Deseret News*, Oct. 15, 1862; Fred Albert Shannon, *The Organization and Administration of the Union Army, 1861-1865*, p. 136.

40. Barbara Ferguson, unpublished manuscript, p. 8.

41. Nye Correspondence [2], Wright to Nye, Nov. 13, 1862.

42. *Deseret News*, Oct. 1, 1862; see also *Sacramento Union*, Sept. 22, 1862.

43. *War of the Rebellion*, pt. 2, p. 144; *San Francisco Bulletin*, Oct. 8, 1862.

44. *San Francisco Bulletin*, Oct. 4, 1862.

45. Ibid., Oct. 8, 1862.

46. *War of the Rebellion*, pt. 1, pp. 178–79.

47. Ibid.

48. Ibid., pt. 2, pp. 119–20.

49. See Long, *The Saints and the Union*, pp. 106–12, for a detailed description of Connor's relationship with Mormon authorities and his insistence that the Mormon people were traitorous and subversive.

50. *War of the Rebellion*, pt. 2, p. 195.

51. Young, papers, Maughan to Young, Aug. 7, 1862.

52. *Deseret News*, Aug. 6, 1862.

53. Young, Papers, Jones, Oct. 2, 1862.

54. Cantwell, Diary, p. 87.

55. *Deseret News*, Oct. 8, 1862; Young, Papers, Maughan to Young, Sept. 29, 1862. For a very detailed account of the horse-stealing episode, see Martineau, "The Military History of Cache County," pp. 123–25.

56. Madsen, *The Bannock of Idaho*, p. 125.

57. U.S. Dept. of the Interior, *Annual Report 1861*, p. 133.

58. *War of the Rebellion*, pt. 1, pp. 181–82. For a full account of the release of Reuben Van Orman, see Newell Hart, "Rescue of a Frontier Boy," *Utah Historical Quarterly* 33, no. 1 (Winter 1965): 51–54.

59. Church of Jesus Christ of Latter-day Saints, History Department Journals, vols. 24–27, no. 4, Nov. 25, 1862, p. 307.

60. Willard Duane Cranney, Sr., *His Life and Letters*, p. 23.

61. *War of the Rebellion*, pt. 1, pp. 182–83.

62. Ibid., p. 183; *Deseret News*, Dec. 3, 1862; Martineau, "The Military History of Cache County," p. 125; *Sacramento Union*, Jan. 6, 1863. Private Henry Forbes of Company "M" later wrote the *Jacksonville Sentinel* that the troops had captured thirty-seven warriors, "besides taking seven scalps—I have one." Record this statement as a vainglorious boast of a soldier after the fact. See *Washington Statesman*, Feb. 14, 1863.

63. Morgan, "Washakie and the Shoshoni," Moore to Doty, Nov. 23, 1862, pt. 6, p. 193; *Deseret News*, Dec. 3, 1862; Hart, "Rescue of a Frontier Boy," p. 54.

64. *Sacramento Union*, Dec. 26, 1862.

65. Cranney, *His Life and Letters*, p. 24; Martineau, "The Military History of Cache County," p. 125.

66. *Deseret News*, Dec. 17, 1862.

67. Ibid., Dec. 10, 1862; *Sacramento Union*, Dec. 26, 1862.

68. *Deseret News*, Dec. 17, 1862.

69. *Sacramento Union*, Dec. 26, 1862.

70. Ibid., Jan. 6, 1863.

71. Ibid.

CHAPTER TEN NOTES

1. Hiram S. Tuttle, Diary, Jan. 5, 1863.

2. *Deseret News*, Jan. 7, 1863; *Sacramento Union*, Jan. 26, 1863.

3. *Sacramento Union*, Jan. 14, 1863.

4. *War of the Rebellion*, pt. 1, pp. 256–57; *Deseret News*, Jan. 28, 1863.

5. *Sacramento Union*, Jan. 19, 1863.

6. *Deseret News*, Jan. 14, 1863; *Sacramento Union*, Feb. 26, 1863.

7. *Deseret News*, Jan. 21, 1863.

8. Ibid., Jan. 28, 1863; *Sacramento Union*, Jan. 31, 1863; Henry Ballard, Memories of Early Days in Logan and Cache County, Jan. 7, 1863.

9. Newell Hart, *The Bear River Massacre*, p. 112; Lyman Clarence Pedersen, Jr., "History of Fort Douglas, Utah," p. 55.

10. *Deseret News*, Jan. 28, 1863; *Sacramento Union*, Jan. 31, Feb. 7, 1863. It should be noted that Chief Justice Kinney was in error when he issued warrants for the arrest of Bear Hunter and the other chiefs. He should have applied to the governor of Washington Territory for extradition of the Indian leaders because the Bear River camp was in Washington Territory. See Larry Jones, "Battle of Bear River, Jan. 29, 1863," Reference Series, no. 325.

11. *War of the Rebellion*, pt. 1, p. 187.

12. Ibid., p. 992.

13. *Sacramento Union*, Jan. 31, 1863.

14. *Deseret News*, Feb. 4, 1863.

15. *Journal History*, Smith, Jan. 26, 1863, p. 110.

16. Tuttle, Diary, Jan. 19, 1863.

17. *War of the Rebellion*, pt. 1, p. 185.

18. *Sacramento Union*, Feb. 12, 1863.

19. Tuttle, Diary, Jan. 22-28, 1863.

20. NA, "California. Regt'l Order Book 2d Cavalry Adjutant General's Office," Jan. 24, 1863.

21. Charles E. Middleton, Diary, Jan. 28, 1863, p. 2.

22. Lorenzo H. Handy, Interview.

23. NA, "California. Regt'l Book, 2nd Cav. Regt'l Reports Indian Scouts, etc., April 29/62 to Dec. 15/63, Casualties," p. 15. In "Liberal's" description of the fight (*Sacramento Union*, Feb. 17, 1863), he indicated that the soldiers who examined the field after the encounter found the Indians had been "bountifully supplied with ammunition and fire-arms. . . ." They no doubt had sufficient rifles and good ones at that, but no large supply of ammunition.

24. Orton, *Records*, p. 174.

25. Randy Steffen, *The Frontier, the Mexican War, the Civil War, the Indian Wars, 1851-1880*, pp. 72, 75, 80-81, 85.

26. Orton, *Records*, p. 174.

27. *San Francisco Bulletin*, Feb. 20, 1863.

28. NA, "California. Regt'l Order Book. 2d Cavalry. Adjutant General's Office," Special Orders No. 11.

29. Harold Schindler, *Orrin Porter Rockwell: Man of God, Son of Thunder*, p. 326.

30. *Deseret News*, Jan. 28, 1863.

31. *Sacramento Union*, Feb. 7, 1863.

32. William Hull, "Identifying the Indians of Cache Valley, Utah and Franklin County, Idaho"; *Franklin County Citizen*, Jan. 25, 1928.

33. Journal History, Stalker to Maughan, Jan. 30, 1863; *Alta California*, Feb. 17, 1863.

34. *War of the Rebellion*, pt. 1, p. 185.

35. *Franklin County Citizen*, Feb. 1, 1917; Hart, *The Bear River Massacre*, p. 119.

36. *War of the Rebellion*, pt. 1, p. 185.

37. Hart, *The Bear River Massacre*, p. 254; Moroni Timbimboo, interview by Colin Sweeten, Dec. 9, 1970, Plymouth, Utah.

38. *War of the Rebellion*, pt. 1, p. 186; "Liberal," *Sacramento Union*, Feb. 17, 1863, reported the river at the ford as being seventy yards wide.

39. The best contemporary description of the battle site and the engagement is that of the only correspondent who accompanied the expedition and sent a detailed report to his newspaper, the *San Francisco Bulletin*. The editor of the *Alta California* and *Sacramento Union* had to be content with the second-hand report sent them by a single correspondent for both who signed himself as "Verite" for the *Alta* and "Liberal" for the *Union* and who used the account by the *Bulletin* journalist supplemented by interviews with soldiers and officers after their return to Camp Douglas. The local *Deseret News* reporter followed the same procedure. When the *Bulletin* editor had not received a complete report from his correspondent by February 17, 1863, and noted a two-column account of the battle by the *Alta* man, the editor chastised his reporter for his failure to be present at "the recent fight . . . in Washington Territory . . ." and who "for some unexplained cause, did not witness this engagement, and we are constrained to delicately remind him of the opportunity he missed for immortality, by copying the best points of a two-column description furnished by a city contemporary," i.e., the *Alta California*. This sarcastic comment

was premature; three days later, on February 20, the *Bulletin* editor was able to print the detailed and comprehensive report of his journalist under the title, "Letters From the Plains (From Our Own Correspondent, Accompanying Col. Connor's Command)." The reporter explained, "The agent from the Associated Press at Salt Lake has kept you so well posted in regard to the Battle of Bear River, that I have preferred waiting until authentic details could be gathered from those who participated therein, rather than give you an earlier and less reliable account." Further evidence that he had accompanied the dragoon contingent comes from his report itself. In describing the ride to the north in the bitterly cold weather, he wrote, "those 220 cavalry—and your correspondent (who is an infantry man, and most heartily prays God to bless them for their noble manhood)—rode 68 miles in the teeth of the savage north wind, to Brigham's City in Box Elder county. . . ."

40. NA, "Compiled Records Showing Service of Military Units in Volunteer Union Orgs. California 1st Cav.-2d Inf., Co. M of 2d Cavalry Company Muster Roll Jan. & Feb. 1863, Record of Events"; *New York Times*, Feb. 25, 1863.

41. *Salt Lake Tribune*, Feb. 3, 1930; Robert M. Utley and Wilcomb E. Washburn, *The American Heritage History of the Indian Wars*, p. 223.

42. NA, "Letters, Utah," Roll 901, Doty to CIA, Feb. 16, 1863.

43. Edward J. Barta, "Battle Creek: The Battle of Bear River," pp. 86, 93.

44. Hart, *The Bear River Massacre*, p. 130.

45. There are many accounts of the battle. The most accurate description is that of the only on-the-scene newspaper reporter whose column appeared in the *San Francisco Bulletin* Feb. 20, 1863. Lt. Col. Edward G. Barta's careful analysis of each maneuver and action during the encounter makes fairly clear what otherwise is a not surprisingly confused picture of events in a chaotic battle situation—Barta, "Battle Creek: The Battle of Bear River," pp. 121-30; Colonel Connor's handwritten account, now reposing in the U.S. National Archives, does not differ substantially from his official report as published in *War of the Rebellion*, pt. 1, pp. 184-87, but it is being used here as the most accurate portrayal—NA, "Col. P. Edward Connor to Lt. Col. R. C. Drum, February 6, 1863, Battle at Bear River, W. T., with Indians 29 January 1863" (hereafter "Connor to Drum"), pp. 1-6. The many other accounts in newspapers, letters, diaries, etc., are mostly copycat reproductions of the *San Francisco Bulletin* article and Connor's official report. Where interesting or significant additions to the story are introduced, the proper references will be cited; see also *Deseret News*, Feb. 11, 1863, and *Alta California*, Feb. 17, 1863.

46. Journal History, Stalker to Maughan, Jan. 30, 1863.

47. Hayes Scraps, Indians, Feb. 5, 1863, pp. 214-17; *Sacramento Union*, Feb. 13, 1863.

48. *Sacramento Union*, Feb. 17, 1863; Barta, "Battle Creek: The Battle of Bear River," pp. 126-30.

49. Hart, *The Bear River Massacre*, p. 172.

50. *Union Vedette*, Jan. 29, 1867; see also *Blackfoot Bulletin*, Jan. 19, 1929, in which Abraham C. Anderson claimed that "General Connor ordered his interpreters to hollo to, and inform the Indian squaws and the papooses to get out in the open away from the willows and the battle so they would not get hit."

51. *New York Times*, Feb. 25, 1863.

52. Journal History, Roskelley to Benson and Maughan, Feb. 8, 1863.

53. Journal History, Martineau, Feb. 7, 1863, p. 144.

54. *Franklin County Citizen*, Jan 25, 1928.

55. *Alta California*, Feb. 17, 1863.

56. NA, "Connor to Drum," p. 187.

57. Ibid.

58. Journal History, Stalker to Maughan, Jan. 30, 1863, and Roskelley to Benson and Maughan, Feb. 8, 1863; L. Handy, Interview; Harold Schindler, "Blood for Blood" *True West* (Sept.-Oct. 1965): 61; NA, "California. Regt'l Order Book, 2d Cavalry. Adjutant General's Office," Feb. 17, 1863.

59. NA, "California. Regt'l. Order Book, 2d Cavalry. Adjutant General's Office," Feb. 17, 1863.

60. Timbimboo, Interview, pp. 2-3; Journal History, Roskelley to Benson and Maughan, Feb. 8, 1863.

61. Hart, *The Bear River Massacre*, p. 6.

62. NA, "Connor to Drum," p. 187.

63. NA, "California. Regt'l Order Book, 2d Cavalry. Adjutant General's Office," Feb. 17, 1863.

64. Timbimboo, Interview, p. 2.

65. NA, "Letters, Utah," Roll 901, Doty to CIA, Feb. 16, 1863.

66. *New York Times*, Feb. 25, 1863; *Alta California*, Feb. 17, 1863; *Deseret News*, Feb. 11, 1863; *Union Vedette*, Jan. 29, 1867.

67. Richard J. M. Bee, Autobiographical Sketch of Life, p. 29. See also Joseph Campbell, Memories of Early Days in Logan and Cache County, p. 61, who thought 1,000 Indians had perished in the fight.

68. Dowdle, Journal, p. 38; Wilford Woodruff, Diary, as quoted in Young, Manuscript History, Feb. 3, 1863.

69. H. Ballard, Memories, p. 32.

70. There are several accounts by Nelson or his son Taylor Nelson with some discrepancies, but all agree that seventy-six bodies were counted; *Franklin County Citizen*, Feb. 1, 1917, Jan. 25, 1928; *Preston Citizen*, July 22, 1954; Nelson, History of Life, pp. 21-22.

71. Young, Papers, Roskelley to Benson and Maughan, Feb. 8, 1863.

72. Ibid., Stalker to Maughan, Jan. 30, 1863.

73. Edward W. Tullidge, *History of Salt Lake City*, pp. 289-90.

74. Church of Jesus Christ of Latter-day Saints, History Department Journals, Feb. 7, 1863, p. 348.

75. Young, Papers, Maughan to Young, Feb. 4, 1863.

76. *Union Vedette*, Jan. 29, 1867; *Sacramento Union*, Feb. 17, 1863.

77. Young, Papers, Stalker to Maughan, Jan. 30, 1863, Maughan to Young, Feb. 4, 1863.

78. Tullidge, *History*, p. 290.

79. History of Brigham Young, Feb. 7, 1863.

80. Young, Papers, Roskelley to Benson and Maughan, Feb. 8, 1863.

81. Young, Papers, Maughan to Young, Feb. 13, 1864.

82. Ibid., Maughan to Young, Feb. 4, 1853.

83. Ibid., Roskelley to Benson and Maughan, Feb. 8, 1863.

84. Fifield, Biography.

85. L. Handy, Interview; *Franklin County Citizen*, Jan. 25, 1928; Mary Ann Chadwick Hull, Interview.

86. U.S. Congress, House, *The Expedition of Captain Fisk to the Rocky Mountains*, p. 32; see also Lucy Petty Turner, Interview.

87. *Deseret News*, May 20, 1868.

88. Tullidge, "The Cities of Cache Valley and Their Founders," *Tullidge's Quarterly Magazine* 1, no. 4 (July 1881): 536.

89. Young, Papers, Maughan to Young, Feb. 4, 1863.

90. For a detailed list of the names of the killed and wounded and the types of wounds, see Appendix A, which is an analysis of the record submitted by Surgeon Reid and lists compiled by Orton in *Records*; most of the California newspapers as well as the *Deseret News* (Feb. 11, 1863), printed the names of the deceased and wounded: *Alta California*, Feb. 17, 1863; *Sacramento Union*, Feb. 23, 1863; *Sacramento Bee*, Feb. 3, 6, 1863; *San Francisco Bulletin*, Feb. 2, 3, 20, 1863. For details of movement to Franklin see: Journal History, Stalker to Maughan, Jan. 30, 1863; *Sacramento Union*, Feb. 13, 1863; *Union Vedette*, Jan. 29, 1867; Nelson, History of Life, p. 21.

91. *Franklin County Citizen*, Feb. 1, 1917.

92. *Sacramento Union*, Feb. 12, 1863.

93. NA, "Connor to Drum," p. 187.

94. H. Ballard, Memories p. 32; see Tuttle, Diary, for dates of movement back to Salt Lake City.

95. M. Hull, Interview, and *Franklin County Citizen*, Jan. 4, 1917; Sorensen, History.

96. *Herald Journal*, Mar. 25, 1956.

97. Martineau, "The Military History of Cache County," p. 126.

98. M. Ballard, Memories, p. 17.

99. *Sacramento Union*, Feb. 17, 1863.

100. Journal History, Amasa Lyman, Journal, Feb. 1, 1863.

101. Nelson, History of Life, p. 22.

102. Church of Jesus Christ of Latter-day Saints, History Department Journals, Feb. 4, 1863, p. 345.

103. NA, "California. Regt'l Order Book, 2d Cavalry Adjutant General's Office"; *San Francisco Bulletin*, Feb. 2, 1863; Church of Jesus Christ of Latter-day Saints, History Department Journals, Feb. 5, 1863, p. 346.

104. See Appendix B; Tuttle, Diary, Feb. 5, 6, 8, 9, 1863.

105. Church of Jesus Christ of Latter-day Saints, History Department Journals, Feb. 5, 1863, p. 346.

106. *New York Times*, Feb. 25, 1863.

107. NA, "Pacific Department, Letters," 1863; *Sacramento Union*, Mar. 2, 1863. For those interested in other works on the Bear River encounter not already cited in this volume, see also: Irma Watson Hance and Irene Warr, *Johnston, Connor, and the Mormons: An Outline of Military History in Northern Utah*; Charles G. Hibbard, "Fort Douglas 1862–1916: Pivotal Link on the Western Frontier"; Melvin J. Littig, "The Battle of Bear River"; Pedersen, "History"; Bill Judge, "Battle of Bear River," *True West*, 8, no. 3 (Jan.-Feb. 1961): 16–17, 64; Utley, *Frontiersmen in Blue*; Harmon Zufelt, "The Battle of Bear River," *The Utah Magazine* 9, no. 3 (Dec. 1892): 83–84.

108. *War of the Rebellion*, pt. 2, p. 301.

109. *Deseret News*, Feb. 11, 1863.

110. NA, "Connor to Drum."

111. *War of the Rebellion*, pt. 2, p. 318.

112. Ibid., pt. 1, p. 184.

113. Leland Stanford, Correspondence, Wright to Stanford, Feb. 19, 1863, and Stanford to Connor, Mar. 29, 1863.

114. *War of the Rebellion*, pt. 2, pp. 368–69.

115. *Sacramento Union*, May 16, 1863.

116. Edward Tullidge, "The Battle of Bear River," *Tullidge's Quarterly Magazine* 1, no. 2 (Jan. 1881): 194.

117. H. Ballard, Memories, p. 32.
118. Sorensen, History, p. 53.
119. Young, Papers, Roskelley to Benson and Maughan, Feb. 8, 1863.
120. *New York Times*, Feb. 25, 1863.
121. *Portland Oregonian*, Mar. 9, 1863.
122. Mae T. Parry, "Massacre at Boa Ogoi," has also been published in Hart, *The Bear River Massacre*, pp. 217-28, and in Newell Hart, ed., *The Trail Blazer*, pp. 128-37. In one of the Duke collection of Indian interviews at Marriott Library of the University of Utah, Henry Woonsock recalled "My Grandmother's Tale About the Bear River Battle" which tells the story of the Indian boy whose life was spared by the California Volunteer who finally could not kill the youth. (See Doris Duke, Number 352, of the American Indian History Project, Western History Center, Marriott Library, University of Utah).

CHAPTER ELEVEN NOTES

1. *Washington Statesman*, Feb. 28, 1863.
2. William Lowry Ritchey, A Sketch of the Wanderings of William Lowry Ritchey.
3. *Washington Statesman*, Mar. 28, 1863.
4. Ibid., Mar. 7, 21, 1863.
5. Thomas M. Pomeroy and four others to W. H. Wallace, Aug. 10, 1863; Robert Watson and eight others to W. H. Wallace, Nov. 21, 1863.
6. Mrs. A. A. Cooper, Diary, pp. 16-17, 25-26.
7. NA, "Letters, Oregon," Roll 901, Huntington to CIA, June 1, 1863.
8. *War of the Rebellion*, pt. 1, pp. 215-25; *Washington Statesman*, Sept. 17, 1863.
9. Madsen, *The Northern Shoshoni*, pp. 54-55.
10. NA, "Utah, Letters," Roll 901, Hatch to CIA, Feb. 18, 1863.
11. Ibid., Doty to CIA, Apr. 22, 1863.
12. NA, "Letter Books, Commissioner of Indian Affairs, 1863," Dole to Doty, May 22, 1863, p. 476; *Sacramento Union*, Feb. 17, 1863.
13. *Deseret News*, June 24, 1863.
14. NA, "Pacific Department, Letters," Connor to Drum, Apr. 22, 1863; *War of the Rebellion*, pt. 2, pp. 410-11.
15. *War of the Rebellion*, pt. 2, pp. 226-29; Tuttle, Diary, May 5, 6, 1863; Church of Jesus Christ of Latter-day Saints, History Department Journal, Mar. 25, 1863, p. 27; NA, "Pacific Department, Letters," Connor to Drum, June 29, 1863; *Deseret News*, June 3, 1863. Camp Connor remained a military post until February 1865 when the general removed his troops, explaining that the new town of Soda Springs was now permanently established and could protect itself. See Long, *The Saints and the Union*, p. 255.
16. *War of the Rebellion*, pt. 2, p. 479.
17. NA, "Pacific Department, Letters," Connor to Drum, June 7, 1863.
18. *Sacramento Union*, May 30, 1863.
19. NA, "Letters, Utah," Roll 901, Doty to CIA, June 20, 1863.
20. Ibid., July 1863; Charles J. Kappler, *Indian Affairs: Laws and Treaties*, pp. 848-51.
21. *Deseret News*, Apr. 15, July 8, 1863; *Sacramento Union*, Apr. 28, 1863; *War of the Rebellion*, pt. 1, pp. 198-201.

22. Ibid., pp. 201–3, 205, 206; *Sacramento Union*, Apr. 14, 28, 1863; *Deseret News*, Apr. 15, 1863. For a detailed description of the difficulties between Connor's troops and the Mormons, see Long, *The Saints and the Union*, pp. 174–96, 206–8.

23. NA, "Letters, Utah," Roll 901, Doty to CIA, Apr. 22, 1863.

24. *War of the Rebellion*, pt. 2, pp. 627–28; *Deseret News*, July 1, 1863; Long, *The Saints and the Union*, p. 186.

25. NA, "Letters, Utah," Roll 901, Doty to CIA, July 1863.

26. *Sacramento Union*, Feb. 17, 1863.

27. Church of Jesus Christ of Latter-day Saints, History Department Journals, Mar. 23, 1863, p. 26.

28. NA, "Pacific Department, Letters," Connor to Drum, Mar. 23, 1863; *War of the Rebellion*, pt. 2, pp. 369–70, pt. 1, pp. 369, 379, 420.

29. *Deseret News*, Apr. 1, 1863.

30. Ibid., Apr. 8, 1863.

31. *Sacramento Union*, May 16, 1863.

32. Ibid., June 13, 1863; *Deseret News*, June 17, 1863; Church of Jesus Christ of Latter-day Saints, History Department Journals, June 10, 1863, p. 72.

33. NA, "Pacific Department, Letters," Connor to Drum, June 18, 1863.

34. *War of the Rebellion*, pt. 1, p. 229.

35. *Deseret News*, Aug. 5, 1863.

36. Howard Egan, *Pioneering the West, 1846 to 1878*, pp. 263–64; Tuttle, Diary, July 6, 1863.

37. General Patrick Edward Connor, p. 1, col. 1.

38. *War of the Rebellion*, pt. 2, p. 415, pt. 1, p. 199; NA, "Pacific Department, Letters," Connor to Drum, Apr. 28, June 24, 1863.

39. *Deseret News*, May 13, 1863.

40. Mark Twain to *Alta California*, Aug. 11, 1867, as quoted in General Patrick Edward Connor,

41. *War of the Rebellion*, pt 1, p. 187.

42. Ibid., p. 227; *Deseret News*, Apr. 22, May 13, June 3, 1863; *Sacramento Union*, May 30, 1863.

43. NA, "Letters, Utah," Roll 901, Doty to CIA, July 6, 1863.

44. "Utah Superintendency files, field records, Misc. 1862-3-4," Nichols to Doty, July 11, 1863.

45. *War of the Rebellion*, pt. 2, p. 529.

46. Ibid., p. 530.

47. Journal History, Stalker to Benson and Maughan, Feb. 8, 1863.

48. *Deseret News*, Apr. 1, 1863.

49. Joseph Grafton Hovey, Journal, p. 141; Newell Hart, ed., *The Trail Blazer* pp. 41–42; Cantwell, Diary, May 12, 15, 1863; Utah Territorial Papers, Maughan and Benson to Wells, May 9, 1863.

50. Wright, Memories of Early Days in Logan and Cache County, Feb. 2, 1924.

51. Winslow Farr, Diary, p. 53; Utah Territorial Papers, Maughan and Benson to Wells, May 9, 1863.

52. *Deseret News*, May 13, 20, 1863.

53. Ibid. See also letter NA, "Letters, Utah," Roll 901, CIA, June 24, 1863. John C. Douglass asked for compensation amounting to $2,685 for thirty-five horses stolen from William Nieswanger on June 20 at Bear River.

54. Utah Territorial Papers, Maughan and Benson to Wells, May 9, 1863.

55. Young, Papers, Maughan to Young, May 23, 1863.

56. Kappler, *Indian Affairs*, p. 851.

57. *Deseret News*, Aug. 5, 1863.

58. Kappler, *Indian Affairs*, pp. 848-51; NA, "Letters, Utah," Roll 901, Doty to CIA, July 1863; U.S. Dept. of the Interior, *Annual Report, 1864*, p. 319; *Deseret News*, Aug. 5, 1863.

59. NA, "Letters, Utah," Roll 901, Doty to CIA, Nov. 25, 1863.

60. Young, Papers, Maughan to Young, July 28, 1864.

61. NA, "Letters, Utah," Roll 901, Connor to Irish, Nov. 4, 1864, Irish to CIA, Nov. 9, 1864.

62. Ibid., Irish to CIA, Nov. 22, 1864.

63. Nye Correspondence [2], Doty to Nye, Aug. 3, Sept. 14, 1863.

64. U.S. Dept. of the Interior, *Annual Report, 1863*, pp. 416, 419.

65. Ibid., *Annual Report, 1864*, p. 319; *Deseret News*, Oct. 14, 1863.

66. Kappler, *Indian Affairs*, pp. 851-53.

67. U.S. Dept. of the Interior, *Annual Report, 1864*, pp. 319-20.

68. Kappler, *Indian Affairs*, pp. 859-60.

69. U.S. Dept. of the Interior, *Annual Report, 1864*, p. 320. For a fuller discussion of this treaty and its provisions, see Madsen, *The Northern Shoshoni*, pp. 37-38.

70. Ibid.

71. Ibid., pp. 43-56; NA, "Letters, Utah," Roll 901, Doty to CIA, Nov. 25, 1863.

72. U.S. Dept. of the Interior, *Annual Report, 1863*, p. 37.

73. U.S. Congress, Senate, Nye to Seward, Mar. 25, 1864, serial 1176, p. 3; NA, "Letters, Utah," Roll 901, Doty to CIA, June 13, 1864, Irish to CIA, Aug. 26, Nov. 22, 1864; U.S. Dept. of the Interior, *Annual Report, 1864*, Burche to Nye, Humboldt Agency, Aug. 1, 1864, pp. 144-148; "Annual Message of Governor James Duane Doty to Utah Lesiglature," p. 95.

74. NA, "Pacific Department, Letters," Connor to Drum, Oct. 27, 1863.

75. "Annual Message of the Governor," p. 95.

76. U.S. Dept. of the Interior, *Annual Report, 1864*, p. 16.

77. NA, "Letters, Utah," Roll 901, Irish to CIA, Nov. 9, 1864.

78. Ibid., Dec. 23, 1864.

79. U.S. Dept. of the Interior, *Annual Report, 1864*, p. 139.

80. Ibid., pp. 141-48; NA, "Letters, Utah," Roll 901, Irish to CIA, Aug. 26, 1864.

81. U.S. Dept. of the Interior, *Annual Report, 1863*, pp. 37-38.

82. "Annual Message of the Governor," p. 95; NA, "Letters, Utah," Roll 901, Irish to CIA, Dec. 31, 1864.

83. Ibid.

Bibliography

Abbreviations
C—California State Library, Sacramento
CU-BANC—University of California, Bancroft Library, Berkeley
IdHi—Idaho State Historical Society, Boise
IdPI—Idaho State University, Pocatello
NA—National Archives, Washington, D.C.
ULA—Utah State University Library, Logan
UPB—Brigham Young University Library, Provo
US1C—Church of Jesus Christ of Latter-day Saints, Historian's Office, Salt Lake City

Aberdeen Times (Idaho), Aug. 16, 1962.
"Almo Massacre." Reference Series, no. 232. IdHi, June 1970; rev. Feb. 1971.
Alta California (San Francisco), 1859–64.
Angel, Myron, ed. *History of Nevada*. Oakland, Calif., 1881. Reprint with introduction by David F. Myrick. Berkeley, Calif., 1958.
"Annual Message of James Duane Doty to Utah Legislature, December 7, 1864." Utah State Historical Society, Salt Lake City.
Bagley, Gerald C. "Daniel T. Potts, Chronicles of the Fur Trade, 1822–1828." M.A. thesis, Brigham Young University, Provo, Utah, 1964.
Ballard, Henry. Memories of Early Days in Logan and Cache County. Compiled by Joel E. Ricks. ULA.
Ballard, Margaret McNiel. Memories of Early Days in Logan and Cache County. Compiled by Joel E. Ricks. ULA.
Bancroft, Hubert Howe. "Biographical Sketch of General P. E. Connor." CU-BANC.
———. *History of Nevada, Colorado, and Wyoming, 1540–1888*. San Francisco, 1890.
———. *History of Oregon*, vol. 2. San Francisco, 1888.
———. *History of Utah*. San Francisco, 1890.
Barta, Edward J. "Battle Creek: The Battle of Bear River." M.A. thesis, Idaho State University, Pocatello, 1962.
Baydo, Gerald. "Overland from Missouri to Washington Territory in 1854." *Nebraska History* 52, no. 1 (Spring 1971): 65–87.
Beal, Merrill D. *A History of Southeastern Idaho*. Caldwell, Idaho, 1942.
Bee, Richard J. M. Autobiographical Sketch of Life. UPB.

Bidwell, John. *A Journey to California.* 1842. Reprint San Francisco, 1937.

Blackfoot Bulletin (Idaho), Jan. 19, 1929.

Blair, Seth M. Journal. US1C, MS. 839.

Bode, Edward, ed. "Charles Kleinsorge: Missouri to California, 1854." *Missouri Historical Review* 76, no. 4 (July 1982): 421–46.

Brautigan, Richard, intro. *The Overland Journal of Joseph Francl.* San Francisco, 1968.

"Brief History of the Ward Massacre." IdPI, MS. 471.

Brooks, Juanita. *The Mountain Meadows Massacre.* Norman, Okla., 1970.

Brown, Dee. *Bury My Heart at Wounded Knee: An Indian History of the American West.* New York, 1970.

Bullock, Thomas. Journal. Utah State Historical Society, Salt Lake City.

Burnett, Peter H. "Recollections and Opinions of an Old Pioneer." *Quarterly of the Oregon Historical Society* 5 (Mar. 1904): 64–99.

Burton, Richard F. *The City of the Saints.* Edited by Fawn M. Brodie. New York, 1963.

Bush, Charles W. Letter, 80 miles from Sacramento, Jan. 10, 1850. CU-BANC.

Bywater, James. Reminiscences. US1C, F923, no. 7.

"California Volunteers and the Civil War." National Guard of California, vol. 16. Second Regiment of Cavalry. C, WPA Project no. 665-08-3-128.

Campbell, Ella. Memories of Early Days in Logan and Cache County. Compiled by Joel E. Ricks. ULA.

Campbell, Eugene E. "Governmental Beginnings." Chap. 9 in *Utah's History.* Richard E. Poll, gen. ed. Provo, Utah, 1978.

Campbell, Joseph H. Memories of Early Days in Logan and Cache County. Compiled by Joel E. Ricks. ULA.

Canfield, Gae Whitney. *Sarah Winnemucca of the Northern Paiutes.* Norman, Okla., 1983.

Cannon, Miles. Sinker Creek Tragedy of Early Pioneer Days. IdHi, MS. 979.6.

Cantwell, James Shurlock. Diary. ULA.

Carter, Kate B., comp. "Excerpts from the Diary of William F. Rigby." *Our Pioneer Heritage*, vol. 4. Salt Lake City, 1961.

———. "Ft. Douglas. Civil War Veterans." *Our Pioneer Heritage*, vol. 6. Salt Lake City, 1963.

———. "Journal of Mary Ann Weston Maughan." *Our Pioneer Heritage*, vol. 2. Salt Lake City, 1959.

Chicago Times, Jan. 29–Feb. 18, 1863.

Church of Jesus Christ of Latter-day Saints. History Department Journals. Vols. 24–27. US1C.

Clark, Thomas D., ed. *Off at Sunrise: The Overland Journal of Charles Glass Gray.* San Marino, Calif., 1976.

Cleland, Robert Glass, and Juanita Brooks, eds. *A Mormon Chronicle: The Diaries of John D. Lee, 1848–1876.* San Marino, Calif., 1955. Reprint Salt Lake City, 1983.

Conkling, Roscoe P., and Margaret B. Conkling. *The Butterfield Overland Mail, 1857–1869.* Glendale, Calif., 1947.

Connor, Gen. Patrick Edward. C.

Conover, Peter W. Autobiography. Utah State Historical Society, Salt Lake City.

Cooper, Mrs. A. A. Diary. University of Oregon Library, Eugene, C784.

Cranney, Willard Duane, Sr. *His Life and Letters.* Delta, Utah, 1957.

Crawford, Charles Howard. *Scenes of Earlier Days.* 1898. Reprint Chicago, 1962.

Crawford, P. V. "Journal of a Trip Across the Plains, 1851." *Oregon Historical Society Quarterly* 25, no. 1 (Mar. 1924): 136–69.

Davenport, T. W. "Recollections of an Indian Agent." *Oregon Historical Society Quarterly* 8 (Dec. 1907): 353–74.

Defa, Dennis Ray. "A History of the Gosiute Indians to 1900." M.A. thesis, University of Utah, 1979.

Delano, Alonzo. *Across the Plains and Among the Diggings.* New York, 1936.

Deseret News (Salt Lake City), 1850–64.

DeWitt, Ward G., and Florence Stark, eds. *Prairie Schooner Lady.* Los Angeles, 1959.

Dowdle, John Clark. Journal. Joel E. Ricks Collection of Transcriptions, vol. 8. ULA.

Duniway, Abigail J. *Captain Gray's Company, or Crossing the Plains.* Portland, Ore., 1859.

Eaton, Herbert. *The Overland Trail to California in 1862.* New York, 1974.

Egan, Howard. *Pioneering in the West, 1846–1878.* Richmond, Utah, 1917.

Elliott, Russell R. *History of Nevada.* Lincoln, Nebr., 1973.

Ellis, H. C. The Story of Massacre Rocks. Idaho State Library, Boise.

Evans, James A. Journal of Trip to Oregon (1860). State Historical Society of Iowa, Iowa City, 1927.

Evans, John Henry. *Charles Coulson Rich: Pioneer Builder of the West.* New York, 1936.

Farr, Winslow. Diary. UPB.

Ferguson, Barbara. Unpublished manuscript. Nevada Historical Society, Reno.

Ferris, Benjamin G. *Utah and the Mormons.* New York, 1854.

Fifield, Matthew P. Biography. ULA, MS. 546.

Fisher, Margaret M. *Utah and the Civil War.* Salt Lake City, 1929.

Franklin County Citizen (Idaho), Feb. 1, 1917; Jan. 4, 25, 1928.

Frederick, J. V. *Ben Holladay: The Stagecoach King.* Glendale, Calif., 1940.

Frost, Mary Ann. Father Murdered and Ward Massacre. IdPI, MS. 407.

Generous, Tom. "Over the River Jordan—California Volunteers in Utah During the Civil War." *California History* 63, no. 3 (Summer 1984): 201–11.

Glover, William. *The Mormons in California.* Los Angeles, 1954.

Goltra, Mrs. E. J. Journal. Oregon Historical Society, Portland, MS. 1508.

Goodwin, C. C. *As I Remember Them.* Salt Lake City, 1913.

Gordon, Thomas J. "Joaquin Murieta: Fact, Fiction and Folklore," M.A. thesis, Utah State University, 1983.

Gottfredson, Peter. *History of Indian Depredations in Utah.* Salt Lake City, 1910.

Gunnison, John W. *The Mormons, or Latter-day Saints, in the Valley of the Great Salt Lake.* Philadelphia, 1852.

Hafen, LeRoy R., and Carl C. Rister. *Western America.* New York, 1950.

Hamblin, Jacob. *A Narrative of His Personal Experiences as Frontiersman, Missionary to the Indians and Explorer.* Salt Lake City, 1881.

Hance, Irma Watson, and Irene Warr. *Johnston, Connor, and the Mormons: An Outline of Military History in Northern Utah.* Salt Lake City, 1962.

Handy, Lorenzo H. Interview. IdPI, MS. 83.

Handy, Samuel. History, 1819–1882. ULA, MS. 92.

Harrington, Milton S. Affidavit of Milton S. Harrington before Court of Claims, 1909. IdPI, MS. 445.

Hart, Newell. *The Bear River Massacre.* Preston, Idaho, 1982.

————. "Rescue of a Frontier Boy." *Utah State Historical Quarterly* 33, no. 1 (Winter 1965): 51–54.

————, ed. *The Trail Blazer.* Preston, Idaho, 1976.

Hastings, Lansford. *The Emigrants' Guide to Oregon and California.* Edited by Charles Henry Carey. Princeton, 1932.

Hayes Scraps, Indians, vol. 5. CU-BANC.

Heitman, Francis B. *Historical Register and Dictionary of the United States Army.* Washington, D.C., 1903.

Herald Journal (Preston, Idaho), Mar. 25, 1956.

Hibbard, Charles G. "Fort Douglas, 1862-1916: Pivotal Link on the Western Frontier." Ph.D. diss., University of Utah, 1980.

Hines, Celinda E. "Diary." *Transactions of the Forty-sixth Annual Reunion of the Oregon Pioneer Association*, Portland, June 20, 1918 (Portland, 1921): 103-5.

History Department Journals. US1C.

History of Brigham Young. US1C.

Hoig, Stan. *The Battle of the Washita: The Sheridan-Custer Indian Campaign of 1867-69.* New York, 1976.

———. *The Sand Creek Massacre*, Norman, Okla., 1961.

Hooper-Young Letters. Marriott Library, University of Utah, Salt Lake City.

Hovey, Joseph Grafton. Journal. US1C.

Hull, Mary Ann Chadwick. Interview. IdPI, MS. 83.

Hull, William. "Identifying the Indians of Cache Valley, Utah and Franklin County, Idaho." Indian Claims Commission, Shoshone Indians, et al. v. United States. Docket Nos. 326, 366, 367, Exhibit no. 170. Daughters of Utah Pioneers, Salt Lake City.

Hultkrantz, Ake. *The Shoshones in the Rocky Mountain Area.* New York, 1974.

Hunt, Aurora. *The Army of the Pacific.* Glendale, Calif., 1951.

Huntington, Dimick B. Journal. US1C.

Hutchings, James Mason. Diary, 1849. Microfilm of MS. CU-BANC.

Idaho Statesman (Boise), Oct. 24, 1937.

Idaho World (Idaho City), Mar. 31, 1911.

Ingersoll, Chester. *Overland to California in 1847; Letters Written en route to California, West from Independence, Missouri, to the Editor of the* Joliet Signal. Edited by Douglas C. McMurtrie. Chicago, 1937.

"In Memoriam. Patrick Edward Connor." Military Order of the Loyal Legion of the United States, Memorial Pamphlets, vol. 2. C.

Irving, Washington. *The Adventures of Captain Bonneville.* New York, 1885.

Johnson, John Lawrence. Diary, 1851. Beinecke Rare Book and Manuscript Library, Yale University, New Haven.

Jones, Larry. "Battle of Bear River, Jan. 29, 1863." Reference Series, no. 325. IdHi, n.d.

———. "Otter Massacre Site." Reference Series, no. 233. IdHi, n.d.

Journal History of the Church of Jesus Christ of Latter-day Saints. US1C.

Judge, Bill. "Battle of Bear River." *True West* 8, no. 3 (Jan.-Feb. 1961): 16-17, 64.

Judson, Henry M. Diary of 1862, Omaha to Oregon. Nebraska State Historical Society, Lincoln, no. 358, MS. 953.

Kappler, Charles J. *Indian Affairs: Laws and Treaties*, vol. 2. Washington, D.C., 1904.

Kerns, John T. "Journal of Crossing the Plains to Oregon in 1852." *Transactions of the Forty-second Annual Reunion of the Oregon Pioneer Association*, Portland, June 25, 1914 (Portland, 1917): 148-93.

Kibby, Leo P. "Patrick Edward Connor: First Gentile of Utah." *Journal of the West* 2, no. 4 (Oct. 1963): 425-34

Kiefer, David M., ed. "Over Barren Plains and Rock-bound Mountains: Being the Journal of a Tour by the Overland Route. . . ." *Montana Western History* 22, no. 4 (Oct. 1972): 16-29.

Knight, Oliver. *Following the Indian Wars.* Norman, Okla., 1960.

Liljeblad, Sven. Interview. June 29, 1984, Reno, Nev.

Littig, Melvin J. "The Battle of Bear River." Paper presented to Fort Douglas Museum of Military History, Fort Douglas, Utah, 1977.

Lockley, Fred, ed. "Recollections of Benjamin Franklin Bonney." *Quarterly of the Oregon Historical Society* 24 (Mar. 1923): 36–55.

Long, E. B. *The Saints and the Union.* Urbana, Ill., 1981.

Lord, Isaac S. P. Diary, 1849–51. MS. and clippings from the Elgin, Ill. *Western Christian.* Henry E. Huntington Library, San Marino, Calif.

Lyman, Amasa. Journal. US1C.

McBride, W. S. Journal of an Overland Trip from Goshen, Ind. to Salt Lake City. Henry E. Huntington Library, San Marino, Calif.

McCall, Ansel James. *The Great California Trail.* Bath, N.Y., 1882.

McClung, James. S. Diary. IdHi.

McComas, E. S. *A Journal of Travel.* Portland, Oreg., 1954.

McDiarmid, Finley. Letters. CU-BANC.

McKinney, Whitney. *A History of the Shoshone-Paiutes of the Duck Valley Indian Reservation.* Salt Lake City, 1983.

Madsen, Betty M. and Brigham D. Madsen. *North to Montana: Jehus, Bullwhackers and Muleskinners on the Montana Trail.* Salt Lake City, 1980.

Madsen, Brigham D. *The Bannock of Idaho.* Caldwell, Idaho, 1958.

————. "The Colony Guard: To California in '49." *Utah Historical Quarterly* 51, no. 1 (Winter 1983): 5–29.

————. *The Lemhi: Sacajawea's People.* Caldwell, Idaho, 1979.

————. *The Northern Shoshoni.* Caldwell, Idaho, 1980.

————. "The Northwestern Shoshoni in Cache Valley." In *Cache Valley: Essays on Her Past and People,* pp. 28–44, edited by Douglas D. Alder. Logan, Utah, 1976.

————, ed. *A Forty-niner in Utah: Letters and Journal of John Hudson.* Salt Lake City, 1981.

Marshall, S. L. A. *Crimsoned Prairies.* New York, 1972.

Martineau, James H. "The Military History of Cache County." *Tullidge's Quarterly Magazine* 2, no. 1 (Apr. 1882): 122–28.

Mathis, Don Richard. "Camp Floyd in Retrospect." M.A. thesis, Brigham Young University, 1959.

Mattes, Merrill J., and Elsey J. Kirk, eds. "From Ohio to California in 1849: The Gold Rush Journal of Elijah Bryan Farnham." *Indiana Magazine of History* 46 (Sept. and Dec. 1950): 318, 403–20.

Maughan, Mary Ann Weston. Memories of Early Days in Logan and Cache County. Compiled by Joel E. Ricks. ULA.

Maxwell, William Audley. *Crossing the Plains, Days of '57.* San Francisco, 1915.

Middleton, Charles E. Diary. US1C.

Moody, Ralph. *Stagecoach West.* New York, 1967.

Moore, David. Compiled Writings. UPB, MSD 1892.

————. Journal and Life History. UPB.

Morgan, Dale L. "The Administration of Indian Affairs in Utah, 1851–1858." *Pacific Historical Review* 17, no. 3. (Nov. 1948): 383–409.

————, ed. *The Overland Diary of James A. Pritchard from Kentucky to California in 1849.* Denver, 1959.

————, ed. "Washakie and the Shoshoni," part 6, *Annals of Wyoming* 28, no. 1 (Apr. 1956): 80–93.

_____ , ed. Washakie and the Shoshoni," part 7, *Annals of Wyoming* 28, no. 2 (Oct. 1956): 193–207.

Muench, Joyce Rockwood, ed. *The Kilgore Journal.* New York, 1949.

National Archives. "California. Regt'l Order Book, 2d Cavalry. Adjutant General's Office." Camp Douglas, Utah. RG 393. Old Military Records Division.

_____. "California. Regt'l Order Book, 2nd Cav. Regtl Reports Indian Scouts, etc., April 29/62 to Dec. 15/63, Casualties." RG 393. Old Military Records Division.

_____. "Col. P. Edward Connor to Lt. Col. R. C. Drum, February 6, 1863, Battle at Bear River, W.T., with Indians 29 January 1863." Records of the Adjutant General's Office, 1780s–1917. RG 94. Old Military Records Division.

_____. "Compiled Records Showing Service of Military Units in Volunteer Union Orgs. California 1st Cav-2d Inf., Co. M of 2d Cavalry Company Muster Roll Jan. & Feb. 1863, Record of Events." Microcopy no. M594, Roll no. 2. Old Military Records Division.

_____. "Letter Books, Commissioner of Indian Affairs, 1863." Vol. 70. Bureau of Indian Affairs.

_____. "Letters Received, 1824–1881. M234. Utah Superintendency, 1849–1880." U.S. Department of the Interior. Records of the Bureau of Indian Affairs. RG 75. Microfilm Rolls 897–901.

_____. "Letters Received by the Office of Indian Affairs, 1824–81, Oregon Superintendency 1842–1880." U.S. Department of the Interior. Records of the Bureau of Indian Affairs. RG 75. Microcopy Rolls 607–11.

_____. "Letters Received by the Office of Indian Affairs, 1824–81, Washington Superintendency, 1842–1880." U.S. Department of the Interior. Bureau of Indian Affairs. RG 75. Microcopy Roll 907.

_____. "Letters Received, Nevada Superintendency, 1862." Bureau of Indian Affairs. N. 104.

_____. "Map of 1863," James Duane Doty. Map Division.

_____. "Pacific Department, Letters Received, 1861–1865," U.S. Army Continental Commands, 1821–1920. RG 393. Military Records Division.

_____. "Report of Superintendent of Indian Affairs, 1862. Map of Wash'n Terry."

_____. "Treaty Made on August 7, 1855, between Garland Hurt and Sho-sho-nee nation of Indians." Record of Treaties, 1851–1860, vol. M6, unprinted record. Office of Indian Affairs.

_____. "Utah Superintendency files, field records, Misc. 1862-3-4." Unprinted record. Bureau of Indian Affairs.

_____. "Western Shoshone Agency. Statistical Reports, 1870, 1873." RG 75, Box 391. San Bruno, Calif.

Neff, Andrew Love. *History of Utah, 1847 to 1869.* Salt Lake City, 1940.

Nelson, William G. A History of His Life. ULA.

New York Herald, Jan. 22, 27, 29, Feb. 1, 3, 4, 11, 12, 1863.

New York Times, Oct. 23, 1860; Feb. 25, 1863.

New York Tribune, Oct. 14, 1852; Feb. 3, 1863.

New York World, Dec. 6, 1860.

Nibley, Charles W. *Reminiscences of Charles W. Nibley, 1849-1931.* Salt Lake City, 1934.

Nye, Governor James W. Correspondence [1]. Nevada State Archives, Carson City.

_____. Correspondence [2]. Nevada State Historical Society, Reno.

Official Program. Franklin, Idaho, Semi-Centennial Celebration, June 14 and 15, 1910. Franklin, Idaho, Museum.

Ogden, Peter Skene. *Peter Skene Ogden's Snake Country Journals, 1827-1828 and 1828-1829*. Edited by Glyndwyr Williams. London, 1971.

Orton, Richard H., comp. *Records of California Men in the War of Rebellion, 1861 to 1867*. Sacramento, 1890.

Owen, John. *The Journals and Letters of Major John Owen, Pioneer of the Northwest, 1850-1871*. Vol. 2. Edited by Seymour Dunbar. New York, 1927.

Palmer, James. Reminiscences. US1C.

Papanikolas, Helen Z. *The Peoples of Utah*. Salt Lake City, 1976.

Paullin, Charles O. *Atlas of the Historical Geography of the United States*. Plate 64. Baltimore, 1934.

Paxson, Frederic Logan, ed. "T. Turnbull's Travels from the United States across the Plains to California," *Proceedings of the State Historical Society of Wisconsin at Its Sixty-first Annual Meeting, 1913* (Madison, 1914): 151-225.

Pedersen, Lyman Clarence, Jr. "History of Fort Douglas, Utah." Ph.D. diss. Brigham Young University, Provo, Utah, 1967.

Peterson, Charles S. "A Historical Analysis of Territorial Government in Utah under Alfred Cumming, 1857-1861." M.A. thesis, Brigham Young University, Provo, Utah, 1958.

Poll, Richard D., gen. ed. *Utah's History*. Provo, Utah, 1978.

Pomeroy, Earl S. *The Territories and the United States, 1861-1890*. Seattle, Wash., 1969.

Pomeroy, Thomas M., and four others to W. H. Wallace, Aug. 10, 1863. IdPI, MS. 554.

Portland Oregonian, May 1, 1852; Mar. 9, 1863.

Prendergast, Thomas P. *Forgotten Pioneers: Irish Leaders in Early California*. San Francisco, 1942.

Preston Citizen (Preston, Idaho), July 22, 1954.

Quigley, Hugh. "The Irish Race in California." Quoted in *Biographical Dictionary*. San Francisco, 1878. C.

Rees, John. Cause of the Ward Indian Massacre. IdPI, MS. 545.

Reminiscences of an Old Pioneer. IdPI, MS. 436.

Resolutions, Acts and Memorials Passed at the Fifth Annual Session of the Legislative Assembly of the Territory of Utah; convened at Fillmore City, December 11, 1855. Vol. 2, 1856. Marriott Library, University of Utah, Salt Lake City.

Richardson, Caroline. Journal, 1852. CU-BANC.

Ricks, Joel E., ed. *The History of a Valley: Cache Valley, Utah-Idaho*. Logan, Utah, 1956.

Ritchey, William Lowry. A Sketch of the Wanderings of William Lowry Ritchey. IdPI, MS. 432.

Roberts, Robert D. Memories of Early Days in Logan and Cache Valley. Compiled by Joel E. Ricks. ULA.

Rogers, Fred B. *Soldiers of the Overland*. San Francisco, 1938.

Royce, Sarah Eleanor Bayliss. *A Frontier Lady: Recollections of the Gold Rush and Early California*. Edited by Ralph Henry Gabriel. New Haven, 1932.

Russell, Don. "How Many Indians Were Killed? White Man Versus Red Man: The Facts and the Legend." *The American West* 10, no. 4 (July 1973): 42-47, 61-63.

Russell, Osborne. *Journal of a Trapper*. Boise, Idaho, 1921.

Sacramento Union, 1856-64.

Salt Lake Tribune, Feb. 3, 1930.

San Francisco Bulletin, 1859-64.

Schindler, Harold. "Blood for Blood." *True West* (Sept.-Oct. 1965): 47-48, 60, 62.

_____. *Orrin Porter Rockwell: Man of God, Son of Thunder*. Salt Lake City, 1983.

Scott, Hamilton. "A Trip Across the Plains in 1862." *Power County Press* (American Falls, Idaho), July 7, 1949.

Settle, Raymond W., and Mary L. Settle. *Saddles and Spurs*. Harrisburg, Pa., 1955.

Settle, Raymond W., ed. *The March of the Mounted Riflemen*. Glendale, Calif., 1940.

Sexton, Lucy Foster, ed. *The Foster Family: California Pioneers*. Santa Barbara, 1925.

Shannon, Fred Albert. *The Organization and Administration of the Union Army, 1861-1865*. Cleveland, 1928.

Simmonds, Jeffrey. The First Settlements, 1855-1860, unpublished ms. ULA.

Simpson, James H. *Report of Exploration Across the Great Basin in 1859*. 1876. Reprint Reno, Nev., 1983.

Smith, Alice Elizabeth. *James Duane Doty: Frontier Promoter*. Madison, Wis., 1954.

Smith, Ralph. Journal of Ralph Smith, 1846-1897. US1C.

Sorensen, Issac. History. ULA, MS. 920.

Stanford, Leland. Correspondence, 1863. C.

_____. Governor's Office, Letterbook 2. 1860-1-2. C.

Stansbury, Howard. *An Expedition to the Valley of the Great Salt Lake*. Philadelphia, 1852.

Steffen, Randy. *The Frontier, the Mexican War, the Indian Wars, 1851-1880*. Norman, Okla., 1978.

Steward, Julian H. *Basin-Plateau Aboriginal Groups*. Smithsonian Institution, Bureau of American Ethnology, Bulletin 120, Washington, D.C., 1938.

Stewart, George R. *The California Trail*. New York, 1962.

_____., ed. *The Opening of the California Trail*. Berkeley, 1953.

Sudweeks, Leslie L. "Indian Troubles on the Sublette Cut-off." IdPI.

Territorial Enterprise (Nevada), May 5, June 9, 1860.

Territory of Utah. *Acts and Resolutions Passed by the Legislative Assembly of the Territory of Utah, During the Sixth Annual Session, 1856-57*. Great Salt Lake City, 1857.

Timbimboo, Moroni. Interview by Colin Sweeten, Dec. 9, 1970, Plymouth, Utah. Charles Redd Center. UPB.

Trenholm, Virginia C., and Maurine Carley. *The Shoshoni: Sentinels of the Rockies*. Norman, Okla., 1964.

Turner, Lucy Petty. Interview. IdPI.

Tullidge, Edward. "The Battle of Bear River." *Tullidge's Quarterly Magazine* 1, no. 2 (Jan. 1881): 189-98.

_____. "The Cities of Cache Valley and Their Founders." *Tullidge's Quarterly Magazine* 1, no. 4 (July 1881): 529-75.

_____. *History of Salt Lake City*. Salt Lake City, 1886.

Tuttle, Hiram S. Diary. C.

Union Vedette (Salt Lake City), Jan. 29, 1867.

Unruh, John D. *The Plains Across: The Overland Emigrants and the Trans-Mississippi West, 1840-60*. Urbana, Ill., 1979.

U.S. Congress. House. *Depredations and Massacre by the Snake River Indians*. 36th Cong., 2d sess., 1861. Ex. Doc. 46. Serial 1099.

_____. *Indian Depredations in Oregon and Washington*. 36th Cong., 2d sess., 1861. Ex. Doc. 29. Serial 1097.

_____. *Report of the Secretary of the Interior*. 37th Cong., 3d sess., 1862. Ex. Doc. 1. Serial 1157.

_____. *Report of the Secretary of War*. 35th Cong., 2d sess., 1858-59. Ex. Doc. vol. 2, no. 2, pt. 2. Serial 998.

_____. *Support of Utah and Other Indians.* 37th Cong., 3d sess., 1863. Ex. Doc. 30. Serial 1161.

_____. *The Expedition of Captain Fisk to the Rocky Mountains.* 38th Cong., 1st sess., 1864. Ex. Doc. 45. Serial 1189.

_____. *The War of the Rebellion.* 55th Cong., 1st sess., no. 59, series I, vol. L, pts. 1 and 2, 1897. Serial 3583, 3584.

U.S. Congress. Senate. Gov. Nye to Mr. Seward, Mar. 25, 1864. 38th Cong., 1st sess., 1864. Ex. Doc. 41. Serial 1176.

_____. *Message of the President of the United States.* 35th Cong., 2d sess., 1858. Ex. Doc. 1. Serial 975.

_____. *Message of the President.* 36th Cong., 1st sess., 1860. Ex. Doc. 2. Serial 1024.

_____. *Message of the President of the United States.* 36th Cong., 1st sess., 1860. Ex. Doc. 42. Serial 1033.

_____. *Message from the President of the United States.* 36th Cong., 2d sess., 1860. Ex. Doc. 1. Serial 1079.

_____. *Message of the President of the United States.* 37th Cong., 2d sess., 1861. Ex. Doc. 1. Serial 1118.

_____. *Message of the President of the United States.* 37th Cong., 2d sess., Dec. 21, 1861. Serial 1122.

_____. *Report of Captain Medorem Crawford.* 37th Cong., 3d sess., 1862. Ex. Doc. 17. Serial 1149.

U.S. Department of the Interior. *Annual Reports of the Commissioner of Indian Affairs.* In *Annual Report of the Secretary of the Interior.* Washington, D.C., 1849–1864.

Utah State Militia Correspondence, 1849–63. Utah State Archives, Salt Lake City.

Utah Territorial Papers. Utah State Archives, Salt Lake City.

Utley, Robert M. *Frontiersmen in Blue: The United States Army and the Indian, 1848–1865.* New York, 1967.

_____. *Frontier Regulars: The United States Army and the Indian, 1866–1891.* New York, 1973.

_____. *The Indian Frontier of the American West, 1846–1890.* Albuquerque, 1984.

_____., and Wilcomb E. Washburn. *The American Heritage History of the Indian Wars.* New York, 1977.

Valley Tan (Salt Lake City), Aug. 3, 10, 17, 24, Sept. 7, 14, 21, 1859.

Walgamott, Charles Shirley. *Reminiscences.* Vol. 2. Twin Falls, Idaho, 1926.

_____. *Six Decades Back.* Caldwell, Idaho, 1936.

Walters, Walter. Family Record. ULA, MS. 7.

Ward, D. B. *Across the Plains in 1853.* Seattle, n.d.

The Ward Massacre as Told by Newton Ward to Rufus Wood. IdPI, MS. 472.

Washington Statesman (Walla Walla), Oct. 4, 15, 18, Dec. 6, 1862; Feb. 14, 28, Mar. 7, 21, 28, Sept. 17, 1863.

Watson, Robert, and eight others to W. H. Wallace, Nov. 21, 1863. IdPI, MS. 249.

Wellman, Paul I. *Death on Horseback.* Philadelphia, 1947.

Wells, Daniel H. to Col. David Moore, Apr. 4, 1863. US1C, Msd. 6304, fd. 2.

Wenatchee World (Washington), Oct. 8, 1980.

Williams, Burton J., ed. "Overland to California in 1850: The Journal of Calvin Taylor." *Utah Historical Quarterly* 38, no. 4 (Fall 1970): 312–49.

Wilson, Elijah Nicholas. *Among the Shoshones.* Salt Lake City, 1969.

Winton, Harry N. M., ed. "William T. Newby's Diary of the Emigration of 1843," *Oregon Historical Quarterly* 40 (Sept. 1939): 219–42.

Woodruff, Wilford. Journal. UPB.

Wright, Angus Taylor. Autobiography. ULA.

Wright, John Fish. Memories of Early Days in Logan and Cache County. Compiled by Joel E. Ricks. ULA.

Wyman, Walker D., ed. *California Emigrant Letters*. New York, 1952.

Young, Brigham. History of Brigham Young. US1C.

————. Brigham Young, Indian Affairs, Correspondence, 1851–53, folders 16, 22. US1C.

————. Brigham Young, Indian Affairs—In-Correspondence, Commissioners, 1854, Aug. 1857. US1C.

————. Brigham Young, Indian Affairs, Indian Correspondence. US1C.

————. Brigham Young, Indian Affairs—J. H. Holeman, Correspondence, 1851–53, folder 16. US1C.

————. Brigham Young, Indian Affairs—Miscellaneous Licenses, Permits, etc., 1851–53, folders 29–30. US1C.

————. Brigham Young, Indian Affairs, Miscellaneous Papers, folders, 4, 28. US1C.

————. Brigham Young, Indian Affairs, Out Correspondence—Commissioners, 1851–52, folders 8–9. US1C.

————. Brigham Young Papers, 1801–1877. US1C.

————. Manuscript History. US1C.

————. "Message to the Legislative Assembly of the Territory of Utah, December 11, 1854." Utah State Historical Society, Salt Lake City.

————. "Message to the Legislative Assembly of the Territory of Utah, December 11, 1855." Utah State Historical Society, Salt Lake City.

Yount, George C. *George C. Yount and His Chronicles of the West*. Edited by Charles L. Camp. Denver, 1966.

Zufelt, Harmon. "The Battle of Bear River." *The Utah Magazine* 9, no. 3 (Dec. 1892): 83–84.

Index